Introduction

Why am I writing a book on the Virgin Mary? I'm an angelologist; I talk to angels! My relationship with the Virgin started off, embarrassingly, in the most benign and superficial of ways. I asked Mary to go shopping with me and from that one simple request, came a slow and joyful journey of finding her in daily life.

This book is a collection of small vignettes, not only about shopping, (even though I have sprinkled in our shopping experiences) but also about my growing relationship, knowledge, and understanding of Mary – sometimes silly, other times serious. After I wrote that first short story about my shopping experience with the Virgin Mary, amazingly, odd coincidences kept happening and I enjoyed them so much, I wrote them down. When I understood she wanted these anecdotes to be collected in a book, I asked for her support and she said, "Yes, dear, I will help."

I have attempted to be as accurate as possible with the information within these pages, but sometimes the sources themselves differed. So I ask for your flexibility and forgiveness if details are in error.

Being Protestant, I had no early religious education about Mary, only that she is the mother of Jesus and I remember seeing her in plastic, ceramic, or wood Christmas scenes standing over the manger looking, well . . . motherly. Maybe being untrained in this way has kept me ignorant of her ways and how to formally talk to her, but it could have been a blessing in my case, because I had no preconceived ideas about her. It doesn't seem to matter I didn't know how to properly say the rosary or she needed to be venerated instead of just asking her to jump in the car and go to the mall with me.

Even though I have a Master of Divinity from a non-Catholic seminary and a Ph.D. in religion/metaphysics, this is not a theological tome. My training and professional work as a clairvoyant and teacher of intuitive studies has helped me listen to Mary's gentle, but persistent voice. But no one needs to have special skills because, as I found out, anyone, *anyone* can talk, listen, and be with the Virgin Mary.

No story seemed too silly and all seemed important to Mary. When I would get stuck in the writing process, I would ask for help and she always gave added inspiration, a new insight, a funny news clipping, or filled in the details by guiding me to a resource of some kind. I could not have done this without her.

I have learned much over these last 15 years since our first shopping excursion. The most important is that the holy is available to us everywhere: in large cathedrals, on majestic mountains, and in our own backyards. They are here, not just for the pious or religiously good either, but for each and every one of us . . . if we but ask.

We often think great beings of light only appear and communicate in momentous ways or exclusively offer assistance with world upheavals, emergencies, and grand disasters, but actually, they are always available for us in our everyday lives. By first asking the Virgin to go shopping with me, I learned even beings as great as the Virgin Mary actually *like* to be consulted on the most humble, mundane, and fun requests.

So Mary, with deep gratitude and reverence, I offer this book you have inspired and helped co-create. I greatly appreciate your aid and being allowed to be in your presence during its immaculate inception and production.

I pray that this work will be of the highest and best good for those who read it. May the Divine bless its pages and you, dear reader. So here's to you Mary! Hope you like it.

Kermie

Shopping with the Virgin Mary

Kermie Wohlenhaus, Ph.D. has also authored:
How to Talk and Actually Listen to Your Guardian Angel
(available in Spanish, French, German and Dutch)

Dr. Wohlenhaus has annotated foundation texts for the field of
Angelology
Angels in Sacred Texts series which includes:
The Complete Reference to Angels in The Bible
A Quick Reference Guide to Angels in The Bible
The Complete Reference to Angels in The Book of Mormon
The Complete Reference to Angels in The Koran (Qur'an)

Shopping with the Virgin Mary

Kermie Wohlenhaus

Kermie & the Angels Press   Tucson, Arizona

This edition was prepared for publication by
Ghost River Images
5350 East Fourth Street
Tucson, Arizona 85711
www.ghostriverimages.com

Front Cover Design by Glenna Shepherd
Author photo by Britta Van Vranken

ISBN 978-0-9907327-1-6

Library of Congress Control Number: 2016903018

Printed in the United States of America
First Printing: March, 2016

Contents

Introduction

Shopping with the Virgin Mary

Many years ago, when I was teaching spiritual healing, I found myself experiencing leg cramps and foot discomfort. I was advised by a channeler to wear shoes with leather soles so the excess energy could pass through my body, out my feet, and into the Earth. Apparently, petroleum products and synthetic soles block this movement of energy, grid locking in my legs. I was working mostly barefoot or with cotton socks in warm weather, but in the winter I would wear shoes for warmth, thus the leg cramps.

Where in the world was I going to find shoes with leather soles in this American plastic and "leather uppers, balance man-made" footwear world of ours? "You will be led – if you ask for help and guidance," was the clear message I heard in response to my question to the Universe. So I asked . . .

I was quite surprised when the image of the Virgin Mary came instantly into my mind. I had already been communicating with spirit guides and angels by this time, so asking for assistance from other dimensional beings was not new to me, but I was startled and honored to have Mary appear. She made perfect sense. Here was a gentle, feminine being of light who might be willing to assist me on a mission of finding footwear to enable me to continue my healing work without pain.

In a silent prayer I invited Mary to come shopping with me as I began my search for leather-soled shoes. She immediately responded, smiling with great love saying, "Yes dear, I would love to go shopping with you." Usually called upon to heal the sick, feed the hungry, or grant world peace, Mary seemed tickled to be requested to go on a lighter mission. I inquired if it was sacrilegious to ask her to go shopping and she said, "I am rarely asked to go shopping with someone; it would be delightful."

So off we went and I could feel a difference immediately. Her presence made itself known as a soft, quiet leading. Whenever I invite her along on a shopping errand, or in any endeavor for that matter, everything seems to flow more smoothly. If I stay open to her inner guidance, she always directs me well.

Of course, I know that everyone has shopping experiences where they find *just* the right thing, but continually and consistently, when I go shopping with Mary, I find the very last item left on the rack which happens to be in my size and color or what I am looking for is on sale for *One Day Only*. I have even had complete strangers standing in the check-out line unexpectedly hand me extra coupons they no longer needed. What I experience, when I take Mary along, is that life becomes richer, easier, and more productive.

One day, as I was driving, I felt Mary's gentle, but consistent nudge to go into a store tucked away in a strip mall that I don't usually frequent. Salespeople in this store work on commission and the first person to assist me was an older individual. However, a younger saleswoman would come over periodically and give me fashion tips for each item I tried on. The older woman began to act a bit testy with this interaction. I asked Mary what to do, since this was not our normal, friendly shopping experience. She simply said, "Just let it be; this is an important contact for you."

The young woman explained to the older saleswoman that she wasn't busy and just wanted to help her with the sale and she wasn't expecting any portion of the commission. The older woman immediately relaxed and seemed to appreciate the help in finding me *even more* clothing knowing she would benefit financially.

I mentioned to the younger woman that I had a local cable TV show, taught, and spoke publically. She seemed to know exactly what I needed and found many important items to add to my career wardrobe. I bought some amazing clothes that day. At the end of the sale, I tried to tip the young woman for sharing her fashion wisdom, knowing she wasn't getting a commission for her invaluable help. But she refused to take my money.

I told her I occasionally used the services of a personal shopper and asked if she might be willing to do that. She told me she had just graduated as a stylist and would love to work with me. Her name was Maria (!) and we exchanged cards. My style has certainly come up a notch since Mary brought Maria into my life.

Mary has led me to great finds when it comes to jewelry, houses, plants, cars, plumbing supplies, skincare products, housewares, and much, much more. She is a great bargain hunter and connoisseur of quality too. When I am in doubt about an item, I ask for Mary's advice and the message is direct and honest: "too loose," "too tight," "wrong color," "not quite right," "that part won't fit," "this car has hidden defects," or . . . "Yes, it is perfect in every way!" She is always right!

Over the years Mary has used shopping to teach me important life lessons.

- If you seek, travel, look, sort, hunt, ask, negotiate, and persist, *you shall find.*

- Don't settle for anything you don't absolutely love; you will never be happy with it.

- Always buy items with the best quality you can afford. Quality does not always mean high prices and fine shops; treasures can be found in the most unlikely places.

- Go to the back of the store and work your way forward. Lower-priced items seem to be in the furthest corners – without the flashy displays. Look at life and people from behind the scenes for a truer perspective; it isn't always the ones in the limelight that have the most to offer.

- Be kind to all you meet. Service providers have a very specialized and demanding mission in life.

- Gratitude and patience enhance the shopping experience, as in all of life.

- But the most important lesson for me has been that the Virgin Mary is not only available in times of great catastrophe, she is on hand for assistance in everyday living as well.

You may be asking if I ever found leather soled shoes as I first requested. Well, yes, I did. On the edge of town, I just "happened" upon a Cole Haan outlet store and in the clearance back room were tall shelves filled with beautiful, leathered soled shoes for a fraction of the retail price. Thank you, Mary!

Over the years, my relationship with Mary has been joyful and has deepened beyond my wildest dreams. It all started when I took a chance and asked her to go shopping.

Glow-in-the-Dark Virgin Mary

I have a plastic, glow-in-the-dark statue of the Virgin Mary on my altar. She glows as I turn out the lights to go to bed at night; there for me as I fall asleep, emanating a faint, phosphorescent, lime-green light. She loves me, I know, because of her constant presence in my room.

Sometimes I move my Virgin Mary glow-in-the-dark statue around the house, just to see Mary in a variety of backgrounds and to give *her* a different perspective. Somehow I can sense when it is time to change her location, but no matter where I move her, she is always consistent with an illumined, prayerful presence.

Mary seems to like to be in the pot of pink violets best; standing in the blossoms quietly glowing them to sleep. The violets seem to grow better when she is among them. Mary, surrounded by their pink softness during the day, is a beautiful sight.

The violets sit on a table by the window and Mary captures the daylight, sending it forth into the night. Curiously, the violets tend to grow towards her instead of the light from the window.

I understand why.

The Virgin on the Window

On Drew Street in Clearwater, Florida is a new Virgin Mary shrine. Someone noticed that the large, tinted window on the side of a bank had stained in the shape of the Virgin Mary. It caused quite a stir. The bank had to eventually relocate because no one could get into the bank parking lot anymore due to the crowds of people coming to look at the vision of Mary on the window.

Overflow parking to handle all the devotee's cars was at the Stop and Save Super Store lot across the street. Because the lot was in the center of the block, the police had to come to direct traffic. It seems that there was too much foot traffic from visitors crossing the street who didn't want to wait at the corner stop light and the police didn't want any pilgrims hit in their haste to see the Virgin.

Finally, transportation officials put a traffic light right in the middle of the block. Mothers pushing strollers, elderly with walkers, relatives with pictures of out-of-town family members, all cross the street safely now, to the base of the window, praying for healing or comfort.

After a while, a Catholic church set up folding tables in the bank parking lot where young girls handed out plastic rosaries and instructions on how to say the prayers properly. I met Emily who attended the rosary table. She offered free holy beads and instruction sheets. Somehow, she knew my friend and I were not Catholic, so she gave us a free video about Mary's rosary, sensing we would need *extra* explanation.

Now, years later, there is ample parking at the site. The vacant lot behind the building is paved. Half-burnt candles are lined up several layers deep around the perimeter of the property and the Virgin's image. A high, 8-foot fence has been erected to keep people from climbing the retaining wall of the old bank to kiss the window. Pictures of loved ones are weathered and worn, hung by bobby pins, bubble gum, or folded between the wires of the fence, hoping Mary will pray for them.

White plastic lawn chairs are now arranged in rows around the Virgin window and even kneeling benches have been set up. At dusk, when the candles are lit, you can still see Mary gleaming in the twilight; it can cause even the strongest unbeliever to think maybe, just maybe, Mary is there.

There used to be a gas station on the corner that sold post-card sized pictures of the window. I would buy 20 at a time. I gave them to sick relatives, friends on their birthdays, and used them as bookmarks. I have only one of those post cards left now. The gas station is gone. I guess the post-card trade wasn't as profitable as gas. Customers would come to get a closer look at the window, jump out of their cars, take a picture, and then leave . . . without buying gas.

I liked having Mother Mary so close to my home. When I needed a lift or to feel her presence, I would go to the Drew Street shrine to pray and talk with her. Even if the image on this window is just a stain from the landscape watering system, or from the Florida sun bleaching out the window tinting, it is now a shrine – a sacred place. It hardly matters, for either way it makes us stop – even if only for a moment and ponder the mysteries of the spiritual realm. We join anonymous others to remember her again in the midst of our daily lives on this busy street. But we will always wonder if Mary did, indeed, touch this window, impressing her image upon it, giving all a message of hope and love.

The Blessed Virgin Sighting at the Mother Cabrini Shrine

One Easter morning several years ago, a woman was on top of the hill at the Mother Cabrini Shrine in the foothills outside of Denver, Colorado. Standing at the foot of the giant Jesus statue, looking out over the city, she glanced over to her right, beyond the outstretched arms of Jesus and saw a vision of Mary, mother of Jesus, hovering above a bush. She fell to her knees immediately, pointing to the bush, shouting over and over again that she was seeing the Virgin Mary!

Like a foothills brush fire, word spread quickly about the sighting of Our Blessed Mother at the Mother Cabrini Shrine. Within days, a Denver TV station set up cameras for a live shot on location for the local evening news. Hundreds and thousands of believers swamped to see the bush where Mother Mary had appeared.

I went to see that Virgin Mary bush about a year later. It was very scraggly, with hardly any leaves left on it. Apparently, seekers had been picking leaves to have a piece of this sacred shrub for their own. Crutches and canes were strewn on the ground in front of the bush and pictures of babies and children were poked on its bare branches. The Mother Cabrini nuns had put up a sign asking people not to pick the leaves so others could see a bush and not just a stalk of twigs growing out of the ground. Most people ignored the sign and picked the leaves anyway. They knew a blessed-bush leaf was more important than obeying a nun's sign.

All who go on this Mary pilgrimage have a long and arduous climb up the 373 steps to the top of the hill just to get a glimpse of this small, blessed bramble. The climb is at altitude and there are no railings; it is not for the feeble-hearted. It may take the devoted quite a while to get to the site, longer if they stop at the Stations of the Cross, rest, or have a cane in one hand and a grandchild pulling the other. But there is a satisfaction in making that kind of effort to give homage to the Blessed Mother, a sense of accomplishment by making the sacred ascent. It doesn't matter if the faint hope that Mary will appear again, is not realized. You came, said your prayers and had the experience. She might come back one day and maybe you will be one of the lucky ones to experience an actual vision or sighting.

I have visited this site myself, and have returned on subsequent Easters to see if she would reappear. Climbing those many steps up that steep hill along with the other faithful, finally arriving at the base of the Christ statute, and sneaking past the hedge to see the sacred Blessed Virgin Mary bush, it was well worth the trip. Even without a vision of Mary, the effort was a way of honoring what once was.

At the bottom of the slope are water fountains and shrines to a handful of saints. A gift shop sells Holy water bottles and candles to light for the venerated in the shade of the trees and cool waters after such a trek.

Finally, full of the holy and having said all the prayers, it is time to go. You sleep well that night, tired from the climb, the mountain air, the nearness to the peace and presence of Mary, Jesus, and the saints. And as you drift off, a comfort comes to you knowing you have a small leaf from the sacred Virgin Mary bush safely tucked under your pillow.

Let It Be

I used to drive an old car with a tape cassette player in it. The sound was great, and I played my favorite old tapes while driving, enjoying the classics as I cruised through traffic. One day, I was cleaning out a closet and I ran across a shoe box *full* of long-forgotten cassette tapes. After sorting through them, I pulled out certain cartridges to play. One of the tapes was *Let It Be* by the Beatles. Wow, how long has it been since I heard that?

The next day, while driving to work, I put *Let It Be* in my tape deck and fast-forwarded to the title song. I zoned out as it played "Mother Mary calls to me, speaking words of wisdom, Let it be . . ."* It ended with those last four piano notes descending the scale, "dum, dumm, dummm, dummmmm" . . . . aaaahhhhhhhhh. Heaven.

Wanting to experience that again, I tried to rewind the tape. No rewind. Ok, fast forward. No fast-forward either. Finally, I ejected the tape to see what was wrong. There was no familiar chocolate-brown plastic tape threaded over the little fuzzy square; it had broken! No more Mother Mary telling me to let it be. My *Let It Be* was let it be over. Unwilling to believe this was a mere coincidence, I asked, "What does that mean, Mary?" No answer. So I put the cassette on the floor to be thrown away, saddened to find this old friend and then to lose it again so quickly.

Later that week as I was driving to work, I checked the messages on my cell phone while stopped at a red light. One voice mail was from my best friend, Diane. When the message played, it was silent except for some rustling. I couldn't make out any words. Finally, I heard a beep signaling the end of the message and giving me my three options: to erase, save, or call back. I erased, thinking it was a pocket call and there was nothing to save.

That afternoon I received another message from Diane saying she hoped I had received her voice mail from the night before. She proceeded to tell me she had been at the Paul McCartney concert and he was singing *Let It Be*. It was so overpowering, she thought of me immediately and called from the concert. She explained how she had called, held the phone up in the air hoping to capture Paul's singing about Mother Mary. What a coincidence. (?) Unfortunately the phone did not pick up the music, but it was another *Let It Be* moment . . . lost.

A few days after that, an acquaintance of mine told me a random story. She said she was having dreadful, re-occurring nightmares. Nothing worked to stop these nightly horrors. Finally, in her desperation and as a last resort, before she went to bed, she asked the Virgin Mary to help her. My friend, not being a religious person at all, never expected this to work, but was willing to try anything due to her desperation.

To her surprise, that next morning she realized that she had slept very well all through the night and had no nightmares! She also said as she woke up, a tune was playing in her mind. Once she was awake enough to recognize it, she said it was the Beatle's song *Let It Be*. She recognized the lyrics of the song "Mother Mary calls to me . . ." and was so comforted by it, stating she was sure it was a message from Mary and she was there protecting her through the night!

That was the third *Let It Be* experience – I needed to listen. I became silent and asked again what Mary wanted to tell me. Instantly it came to me. I had finished writing my first book *How to Talk and Actually Listen to Your Guardian Angel* but was afraid to send it off to an agent. I had an agent in mind and knew this was Mary affirming my thoughts to take some action and she was with me. I sat down at the computer, printed out sample chapters, a cover letter, and sent them to the foreign rights agent. Amazingly, the agent accepted them and agreed to work with me! Later, the agent asked that I send the manuscript with cover letter to a publisher who was interested in my book. As I sealed the package, I felt a very strong and loving presence behind me. Not wanting to dwell on a possible false hope, I said, "Thank You" and gave a short blessing over the package and decided to . . . let it be.

Years later now looking back, that book was indeed pickup up by a publisher. Over the years, four more foreign publishers have contracted to publish the book in their country and language making it not only available in English but also in Spanish, French, German, and Dutch. It is all because I listened to Mary's persistence in getting my attention, putting it into action, and then . . . letting it be.

  * *Let It Be* lyrics and music by Paul McCartney, on *Let It Be* album by The Beatles 1970.

Informational Mary

The other day I stopped by a library I normally don't frequent. I was driving down an unfamiliar street going home when I noticed the "Library" sign. Having time to spare, I stopped to see if they had any Virgin Mary books I hadn't read yet.

Seated at the information desk were a man and woman with white plastic nametags with their job description: "Information" printed boldly under their names. They were both in front of computers, looking intently at the screens. I could tell they were looking for important information, trying to satisfy their unending desire to extract from the pulsing screen as much knowledge as humanly possible.

The woman looked up and asked if she could be of assistance. I said, "Yes, I am looking for your religious section, books on Mary, Mother of Jesus."

"Oh," she said, pointing to the bookshelves along the far wall, "Mary is Catholic and is in our Catholic section."

I was incensed, "Mary is *not* Catholic!"

By this time the informational man looked up from his screen and was wondering if I knew something they didn't know, more information to be had. Curiosity got the best of him and he asked, "Are you looking for the books on the *Virgin* Mary?"

"Yes!" I said boldly.

"What do you mean, she's not Catholic then?"

"Mary is *Jewish*!" I proudly stated.

"Ohhhhhhh," both nodded and exclaimed in unison, as if prompted by a movie script, acknowledging the long-forgotten knowledge of Mary's true identity and faith – a *Jewish* woman. New awareness crashed forth through layers of Catholic devotion to the Virgin. Mary is for everyone: Jews, Catholics, spiritual seekers, feminists, all races, creeds, sexual orientations, religions, and the non-religious. Everyone! HURRAH!!

Even though there were no new Virgin Mary books to be found, I left the library with a sense of accomplishment that day, knowing I had imparted an important historical fact to two knowledge-seekers whose business it is to pass on such sacred information. Life is good with Mary.

Our Lady of Guadalupe – The Background Story

On Saturday, December 9, 1531 a 57-year-old rural native peasant named Juan Diego was on his way to mass in town when he saw the Virgin Mary on a hill. The hill was called Tepeyac and it was near what is now Mexico City, Mexico.

Mary spoke to Juan Diego that day and asked for a chapel be built on the very spot where she appeared. She told him to inform the bishop of her request. Juan went and asked to see Bishop Zumarraga, but since Juan Diego did not have an appointment, he was kept waiting for several hours. Finally, Juan was called in to see the bishop and told the story of what he had seen and heard on the hill. The bishop was quite skeptical about building anything based on this one strange encounter reported by a mere peasant.

Juan Diego returned to the Virgin and told her what had happened. He begged her to send someone else, telling her he was too insignificant to be heard. But she replied she had chosen *him* for this mission and asked him to return to the bishop again the next day to repeat her request.

The next day, the bishop kept Juan Diego waiting, again, but finally they did meet. This time the bishop asked Juan for proof that this encounter was true. Juan Diego went back to the site and told the Virgin the bishop requested proof of her presence. Mary asked Juan to return the next morning. She would give him a sign to convince the bishop.

Unfortunately, Juan's uncle was very ill and Juan missed the appointment with the Virgin the following day because he was caring for his dying uncle. The day after, Juan's uncle asked him to summon the nearby priest to give him his last rites since he knew he was close to death. Juan was so ashamed he hadn't met the Virgin the day before, he crossed to the other side of Tepeyac to avoid an encounter with her. But Mary wouldn't have any of that nonsense and appeared to him – blocking his path.

Juan was afraid the Virgin would be angry with him, but she reassured him and said his uncle had already recovered from his illness and Juan no longer needed to summon the priest. Mary then asked Juan to go pick flowers from the top of the Tepeyac to give to the bishop. Juan climbed the summit and was amazed there were roses growing in the middle of winter. He wrapped the roses in his cape (tilma) and ran back to the Virgin. She arranged the flowers and tied the corners of the cape so the flowers wouldn't fall out. She then promised Juan the bishop would believe him this time.

Juan returned to Bishop Zumarraga and wouldn't let anyone see what he had in his tilma until the bishop was present. The bishop saw him sooner this time and allowed others in the room. Juan again explained that Mary wanted a chapel built on the hill and untied the cape, letting the roses fall onto the floor. The bishop and the others fell to their knees in awe, for inside the cape was a picture of Mary, just as Juan had described her. She was right, the bishop and those present believed him.

The bishop asked Juan to take him to the spot where the Virgin had appeared and, within 13 days, a simple chapel was built. The day after Christmas, the cape was carried there with great fanfare. Juan was allowed to build a hut next to the chapel where he lived the rest of his life. He would greet seekers and tell them the story of his vision of the Virgin and the image on the tilma.

Juan's uncle had another story to add. He told Juan while he was near death that day, a young woman, surrounded in light, appeared to him and told him she had sent his nephew to the bishop with a picture of herself. Just before she vanished, she told the uncle to call her and her image, Santa Maria de Guadalupe, after the famous Guadalupe Shrine for Mary in Spain. Then she healed the uncle completely and faded away.

The Tilma Moved to Mexico City

The cape or tilma of Juan Diego is 64 x 41 inches and continues to create miracles to this day. That little chapel at Tepeyac was too small for all the people who came to see it and to hear the story, so Church authorities decided to move the tilma to a larger location within the city limits of Mexico City. The new basilica was named La Villa and it housed the tilma for many years. But again, as the years went on, this basilica was unable to handle the growing crowds and it was not kept in good repair, becoming old and dilapidated. La Villa was finally closed to the public in 1974 after a new Super-Dome-sized Basilica called de Santa Maria de Guadalupe was constructed next to it. This structure continues to house Juan Diego's tilma to this day.

The current basilica has four conveyor belt walkways for visitors to step onto and then move slowly by the high, plexi-glass covered, golden-framed tilma. Three walkways move left to right and the one furthest away moves right to left. Hundreds and thousands of people travel to the Basilica de Santa Maria de Guadalupe each year to see this amazing cape of Juan Diego's, gliding back and forth under the powerful tilma hanging above on the golden wall.

Experts have tried to figure out how this painting was made and why the tilma, which is made of an inferior peasant fabric, has not disintegrated, but has retained its original quality these several centuries. During one examination, researchers photographed the tilma and, upon enlarging the photos, they found an amazing discovery. An image emerged in Mary's right eye, which many believe is the face of Juan Diego. As we develop advanced technology, our analysis of the tilma may bring further surprises and wonders from this celestial art of Mary.

My friend Mary (!) told me she grew up attending parochial schools and was very conceited. She felt sorry for the other kids because she was named after Mary, the Mother of God, and they were not. She was kind though, and did not tell them to their faces, nor did she rub it in that she was blessed with Mary's name. She's kind like that to this day. She just knows she is better than those around her.

Mary once told me she had gone to the Basilica de Santa Maria de Guadalupe in Mexico City when she was 17, as part of a high school field trip. Of course, she had heard the story of Juan Diego meeting the Virgin on a hill, so when she and the other school mates came to the basilica to see the tilma, she was disappointed it was in a major Mexican city and not in a quaint chapel on a lovely Mexican hillside. I was very excited to hear her story about seeing the tilma, but she said she didn't remember much about it other than it was over Christmas break and she had a vague memory of the throngs of people coming into the basilica. My friend and her classmates were smashed and smushed in and had to move wherever the masses pushed them, which was onto the conveyer belt to see the Virgin on the cape.

When asked about any feelings she had from the tilma, she said the sea of people coming at her frightened her so much and this was all she could recall from the trip. She did say she felt safer once she was single file on the conveyor belt, though.

I nodded, knowing Mary devotees are passionate about Mary and would touch, kiss, and stay for days, if given the slightest chance. Apparently, conveyer belts had to be installed to keep the devoted moving along.

I hope to go there someday and envision myself flowing with the river of the masses towards those conveyer belts. I can almost feel being swept by the movement of them, the walkways, and the spirit of the profound moment as we all pass by the image of Our Lady of Guadalupe. The artistry created by Mary herself onto a physical object has lasted the test of time and eternity in our hearts and minds.

Brujeria

There is a blend of Aztec goddess and Christian practices centered on the worship of Our Lady of Guadalupe called *brujeria*. The original Our Lady of Guadalupe chapel on Tepeyac is close to another sacred site, the Temple, in Tepeyax, where native Mexican Indians would travel to worship the Goddess Tonantzin, the mother of the gods. Juan Diego's encounter with Mary is considered, by some, as a way of evangelizing the native Mexican Indians into Catholicism and pacifying the Indians by using the symbol and location of the Goddess.

Our Lady of Guadalupe has not only brought together two aspects of Mexico's past, but continues to be the shining star of her future. It is said that "Mexico was born at Tepeyac," because Our Lady of Guadalupe has been used as a national symbol of Mexico. Our Lady has helped to gain national independence and she is a source of Mexican national identity, a means of continuity between the Indian past and the Spanish invasion and domination. This simple, yet miraculous tilma image has revolutionized a nation, brought people hope, courage, and victory in many a difficult situation. Viva Mexico and Viva Our Lady of Guadalupe, the Mother-Goddess of Mexico and the world.

Mary in the Bathtub

I have a postcard of a Virgin Mary statue standing in a half-buried, bathtub shrine in a front yard; in the background is a storm-shattered home. All is a wreck except for Mary. I always look for a message, and this one is very clear: *Don't leave Mary standing in a bathtub in the front yard. Take her into the house where she can do some good.* Bring her as close as you can. Put her in the car, the driver's seat would be a good place, unless you are the passenger, and then move her over to *your* lap. Get little Marys and keep them in your pocket. Proximity is safety. This is a powerful message, not to be missed.

I read an article in the paper about another house that had a Virgin Mary bathtub shrine. This time it was in the back yard and a big fire broke out in the basement. All was burnt to the ground. The picture in the paper showed the Virgin, clean and unscathed, but the home was leveled. If only they had seen the postcard of the storm-shattered house. Why didn't someone tell them about the power of Mary and to take her inside?

This is a warning for all to hear: Mary in the yard will only protect the yard! Take her indoors NOW, before it is too late. Or, if you want Mary in the yard, then get an additional Mary, or a few of them, and put her in the house, over the fireplace, in the kid's rooms, by the dog's bowl. Put a Virgin Mary magnet on the refrigerator door and one on the stackables. Put them somewhere or everywhere, but put them *in* the house.

Consider yourself warned.

Saint Mary

Mary is a saint according to the Roman Catholic Church. The word saint is not placed at the end of the name like Esquire, Junior, or the 3rd (III), but in front like Mrs., Mr., Ms., or Dr.; thus she is called *Saint* Mary.

The word saint comes from the Latin word *sanctus*, meaning *holy*. The very first saints in the world were Jesus's family, the *holy* family: Mary, Joseph, and Mary's mother Anne. Then Jesus's apostles and early Christian martyrs were next to be sainted. All saints are given a feast day commemorating the anniversary of their death. That day is considered to be most important because it was the day they were taken into heaven. All saints, so far, are no longer in physical incarnation but are in heaven.

In 1170, the Pope decreed only the Popes could approve new saints. Before that time, the people would call whomever they thought was worthy a saint. Apparently, someone had to take control, so the Catholic Church developed a process called "canonization" that would deem a person worthy of this esteemed title.

Popes also have the power to title, sanctify, and canonize many holy beings. For example, one pope sainted the archangels. So archangel Michael is also called Saint Michael in some circles. But usually, saints were human beings; otherwise plants, animals, and minerals could also be considered for canonization for the worthy acts they have done. It would be too much, I suppose, to saint a dog that may have saved many lives during a disaster, or a plant which held a cure for cancer, or a mineral used in life-saving technology. But it is a thought.

The job description of a saint is two-fold. First, they exemplify a holy life while on earth. They, like us, have all the fears, temptations, and weaknesses, but they have overcome these with great strength and bravery. Some were even killed for their holy beliefs. They are held up as spiritual role models for us who are still among the living.

Their second role is they act as go-betweens for us and God. They are our lobbyists, supporters and take prayers and concerns to the Divine, acting as representatives on our behalf. Saints are very busy in heaven. Each saint is given a certain focus which is his or her specialty. For example, Saint Jude is good for finding strength in desperate and lost causes; Saint Anthony is helpful finding lost articles, missing persons, and stolen items; Saint Joseph sells houses.

Mary fits well into the Saint category. She no longer walks the planet in a physical body. Mary's life on earth was exemplary and she is considered by the Pope to be the best role model possible for women throughout time, past, present, *and* future. She also acts as an excellent go-between, taking our requests, prayers, and concerns not only to God, but also to her son, Jesus. Her role is much larger than most Saints, because she was given the responsibility to look after the entire human race. Quite an honor and quite a responsibility she has, helping all of us as we run amuck here on earth.

Later, the Catholic Church gave her all the angels to look after too. Whew, she must be an excellent multi-tasker. While I have never heard if Mary has assistants to help her with all she has to do, but there always seems to be a plethora of angels around her in her many portraits.

I am glad I ask Mary to go shopping once in a while, to get her out, to try on a new outfit or two. If you have a wish to give Mary a break, take her on your next vacation or day at the amusement park. Guaranteed: You will have an amazing trip with Saint Mary at the helm.

Garage Sales with the Virgin Mary

Being a writer, a clairvoyant, and an angelologist, my economic status has many hills and valleys, as you can imagine. As you know by now, I love to shop with Mary. Sometimes, retail shopping just isn't an option, so I go to where the real bargains are – Garage Sales.

Friday night I set the alarm, go to bed early, and wake up at dawn Saturday morning, eager to drive around neighborhoods. I seek those hand-lettered, colorful signs made out of cardboard, paper, or even store-bought plastic. They can be tacked on telephone poles, taped to a sturdy box, or on a stick with two magic words: "Garage Sale" with an arrow showing the way. Mary loves a good treasure hunt and these can be some of the best. We look for corresponding signs on corners pointing the way up and down residential streets until we reach our final shopping destination.

Mary seems to like the cozy, outdoor, friendly atmosphere of families and friends coming together to sell used and odd items to people who are thrilled to find the copious supply of affordable items strewn about in driveways, garages, and yards.

The cost is minimal. I usually take a baggie full of coins from my spare change jar. The weight of such abundance in my jacket pocket gives me the feeling that I am carrying great bags of wealth. I jingle as I jump out of the car and race to find undiscovered riches before the next car pulls up depositing other early shoppers trying to find a good deal.

Mary and I both like the party feel of a garage sale. We also discover how people live in different sections of town, as we are able to look at their houses, yards, neighbors, families, meet the new baby and listen to the stories. We meet the town's folk in an atmosphere of beneficial exchange of goods and money, where everyone is a winner. Old golf clubs, knick-knacks, half melted candles, unused birthday and holiday presents are traded for cash, which is so much easier to store.

The garage sale negotiation system is a friendly way of bartering, swapping, trading, and closing the deal. It is quite complex: "Will you take $3 for this?" or "How much for all this stuff?" Mary loves a good garage sale transaction. We go often. Even when my financial ebb is in its flowing stage, a garage sale serves the purpose of helping the individual householder instead of a massive corporation. Somehow it makes good political and non-consumerism sense to me and Mary. We love to recycle.

One particular garage sale took place on an immense driveway, surrounded by a large manicured yard, at the edge of a sprawling stone mansion. When the house is so nice, the sale can often produce some interesting items, but sometimes at higher prices. It is tough to sell overpriced junk in a garage sale, even in the best neighborhoods.

I usually do not see any Virgin Mary pictures or icons for sale at garage sales, but this time, there she was – whole stacks of Mary, Mother of God prints. Madonna with child, Virgin with the Angel Gabriel, a pregnant Mary on a donkey, works of art from grand masters of different eras all thrown in a box together! I bought all they had; the price was amazingly low too. Some were framed and others not. I didn't care. I wanted the Mary art to have an appreciative home and not be out in the cold, piled under stained placemats, frayed pillowcases, and lovingly used Christmas tree ornaments.

I went home and put mats, frames, and glass together for the framing of my Mary treasures. She looked beautiful in her new surroundings. That day was a day to remember as I found so much Mary art at the mansion garage sale.

Mary, Patron Saint of the Americas

Not only is the Virgin Mary considered a saint, but in 1999, Pope John Paul II proclaimed Our Lady of Guadalupe the "Patron Saint of the Americas." But isn't "Patron" a male distinction? Wouldn't it be gender correct to call her the "Matron Saint of the Americas?" Our Lady may have just gone through a sex reassignment in 1999, according to this papal proclamation. Eons later this title of "Patron Saint" will still be used, but the people may be confused as to Mary's true gender.

We are in an English language, sexual equality revolution. We are no longer calling men and women with a single word that is specifically masculine "he," especially when it comes to spiritual language, for it has excluded women for far too long. When men were the only ones who could vote, own property (including women), and run the world, in other words, the "patriarchy," the language reflected this by using male words for everyone.

The patriarchy kept telling women they were included even though it was written – "all *men* were created equal." The lack of women's opportunities made us realize it really was *men* who were treated equal and not women. Women were still oppressed by uneven pay scales, family roles, and academic barriers. As women and supportive men have fought for women's equal rights, our English language has begun to change to mirror and affirm our just culture and beliefs.

This broadened, linguistic verbiage is called "inclusive" language as opposed to "exclusive" language. Inclusive language includes; exclusive language excludes. For example, "Peace on Earth, goodwill to *men,*" is exclusive and "Peace on Earth, goodwill to *all,*" inclusive. The word "*man*kind" can be expanded to "*human*kind." God does not have to be described by gender using the pronouns He *or* She but can be the Source of All, The Divine, The Almighty, Creator, or may the *Force* be with you.

Some progressive churches and temples are making great strides to inclusify their spiritual language, in bulletins, scriptures, and lyrics of songs, so the Divine is accessible to *all* people. We can applaud them as they bravely stretch the human understanding of the realm of spirit, including *all* humans and not just men deemed sacred by a bearded God touching a male Adam with a very manly finger.

We understand that the traditional Catholic Church is still a bit slow in this updating of patriarchal language. We also know that the Catholic

Church still has men in key ministry positions from Priest to Pope. Women continue to be excluded from ordination into the Priesthood as Bishops and Cardinals. But that may be changing soon.

Even though there is much room for improvement, we are forever in the Catholic Church's debt for bringing us, keeping alive, and enhancing the passion of our Blessed Mother. No matter if we are conservative, traditional, moderate, liberal, or progressive, we know the Virgin Mary is the matron and mother of us *all*.

Mary in Paris

On a winter visit to Paris one year, a group of friends and I went to the Sac De Cur Roman Catholic Church which sits on a hill overlooking the city. It is a breathtaking view and the wind was freezing cold as it whipped up that hillside. The icy temperatures sent us scurrying inside the church after taking quick pictures of Paris from the top of the many steps.

As we entered the vestibule, I told my friend, "I will be at the Virgin Mary statue if you want to find me. Tell the others." Then I quickly searched out the Mary, Mother of God statue all Catholic churches have. Breathless and joyful in my victory of finding her, I placed my hands in a prayerful position right over what appeared like over a hundred candles which were lit for her attentions and graces.

Ahhh, I warmed nicely as I said my prayers and thanked the Virgin for a safe trip. The candles were giving off so much heat and light, they resembled the warmth of a fireplace in that frigid gothic cathedral. I stayed there until my companions located me in that massive structure. They saw what I was doing and they joined me in prayerful position. They looked at me quizzically and in admiration of my spiritual fervor to stay in prayer for so long to our Holy Mother.

Finally, I turned to their inquiring minds and whispered, "I picked the Virgin Mary statue, not only because I love her, but I knew she always has the most candles lit around her. I was freezing!" My friends nodded knowingly as they warmed on the sea of flickering candles.

So if you find yourself frigid from the weather, stop in at your nearest cathedral and find the Virgin Mary statue, light another candle, say a prayer, and warm yourself in the glow of her presence and the many petitions of light.

Black Madonna

The oldest art images of Mary and Jesus portray them as having dark brown or black skin. There are at least 500 original statues and paintings of these ebony Mary images in Europe alone and they are commonly called the *Black Madonnas*.

The legend is that Luke, the author of his namesake gospel, was the first to paint the image of the Virgin Mary and Christ child. It is said he used a wooden tabletop built by the carpenter, Jesus. Mary apparently had taken the table with her when she went to live with John after Jesus' death. While there, Mary sat for Luke as he painted Mary and the baby Jesus upon it. The table depicts Mary and child as having dark skin. Art critics say that the Virgin Mary is the subject of more art works than any other woman in history, beginning with this first table top Black Madonna.

Mary told Luke stories about the life of Jesus while posing for this portrait and Luke wrote her stories down later, creating his gospel. The book Luke wrote in the Bible is considered by many scholars to be the Gospel of Mary since it has stories only Mary would know and are found in no other gospel.

Empress Helena, an avid collector of Christian relics, found the tabletop painting in Jerusalem in the 4th century. She gave it to her son, Emperor Constantine in Constantinople, who built a church around it. It has quite a history of miracles associated with it. One of the first miracles was fending off the attacks of the Saracens by parading the tabletop through the streets of Constantinople.

Somehow, 500 years later the tabletop painting ended up in Poland and, in the 14th century, became the property of the Polish prince Ladislaus. In 1382 the Tatars attacked the prince's castle, and during the attack, an arrow came through the window and struck the table, stabbing the Virgin in the throat. The prince fled with the tabletop to Czestochowa and it was installed in a small church for the night. But the next morning as he was setting off in a carriage with the painting, the horse refused to move and the prince realized it was a sign from God that the tabletop was to remain in Czestochowa. The prince built a Pauline monastery and a larger church to ensure the painting's safety at that very spot.

Then in 1430, Hussites overran the monastery and attempted to steal the portrait. During the raid, one of the attackers struck the painting twice with his sword, but before any major damage was done, the assailant fell, writing in pain, and died. Those gashes on the Virgin and child's painting are still present.

The monks of the monastery were not through defending Mary, for in 1566 the forces of Charles X of Sweden attacked the monastery for 40 days, but the monks successfully protected her. After that battle, the painting became a symbol of Czestochowa, called the Lady of Czestochowa, and Mary was crowned the Queen of Poland. She has continued to defend the country ever since. Even when Russian troops gathered in 1920 across the river, they withdrew after an image of the Virgin appeared in the clouds over the city.

Another Black Madonna is in The Holy House of Loreto in Le Puy, France. Le Puy is considered the 1st place the Virgin Mary appeared after her Assumption into heaven. They have a Black Madonna that was so threatening to the leaders of the French Revolution they took it to Paris and tried to destroy it, but the residents created a replica and honored it with as much reverence as the first. So they left the original alone.

The Church of the Nativity in Bethlehem, the birthplace of Jesus, has a painting of a black Mary and Jesus over the portal. Since both Mary and Jesus came from the Middle East, it is probable both Mary and Jesus had dark brown skin.

When the first, lighter-skinned Our Lady of the Hermits was shown to the people, they were outraged, for their Mary was dark, not light skinned. That seemed to break the proverbial ice, though, for now Mary appears in the race of the people she loves, whether she is black, white, Asian, brown, Native American, or Martian, she is considered the mother of all - in whatever skin tone she may take on or we may give her.

Tattoo Mary

I was attending a music festival in Florida one hot summer day, when I spotted a very large tattoo of the Lady of Guadalupe – on a man's bare back. It was in full color. He was obviously devout . . . or a prisoner. It is known that Hispanic prisoners will tattoo the Virgin of Guadalupe on their backs so they will not get stabbed by other prisoners when their backs are turned. Mary protects them, as evidenced by this man being very much alive and healthy.

I wasn't brave enough to walk up to him and ask about his relationship with the Virgin, but I wanted to. I knew it would be a good story and I hoped it was a spiritual experience for him to have this sacred art inked permanently on his skin.

It was quite striking, as you can imagine. She was over two feet tall from his buttocks to hairy neck – almost like a large, fleshy poster. As he tanned in the sun, she got a darker coating as well; by sundown she had turned into a natural, dark, Black Madonna.

I wondered how his wife felt having Mary in bed between them as he lay on his side with his back to her. That must be powerful for his wife, sleeping so intimately with the Mother of God; always present while you sleep and still praying as you awake.

I have seen the Lady of Guadeloupe painted, carved, and stenciled on many objects throughout the years: on black velvet, walnut shells, wall paper, ceiling fans, ice, tee-shirts, belt buckles, tree stumps, and toilet seat covers – to name just a few; all there for protection and comfort. But I have never seen a more striking image than that of the Beloved Virgin, Our Lady of the Tattoo, on this man's back, at the Clearwater Blues Festival.

Should I Call You Something Different than *Virgin*?

It must be hard to always be known to the world by your non-sexual, never "known" status of The *Virgin* Mary or The Blessed *Virgin*. There are so many other names we call Mary – Queen of Heaven, Blessed Mother, Our Lady – but few really have the zip the word *Virgin* has.

It all began when she was described as a *virgin* in the Bible, first chapter of Luke in the Annunciation story, when she was visited by the Angel Gabriel. This innocent and chaste description just stuck forever – similar to a bad nickname given to someone in elementary school – like, Bucky or Stinky.

Luke 1:26-27 "Now in the sixth month the angel Gabriel was sent by God to a city of Galilee named Nazareth, to a *virgin* betrothed to a man whose name was Joseph, of the house of David. The *virgin's* name was Mary."

There you have it, for all time, she will then and forever be known as the *Virgin* Mary instead of Mary, the woman betrothed to Joseph, and mother of Jesus. No, she is identified from all the other Marys by her lack of sexual experience.

So one day I asked Mary what she would like to be called *if* she had a choice. She said, "Call me anything dear. I like the innocence that the word 'virgin' portrays, but as a grown woman, you can just call me Mary. Mary of Nazareth was what I was referred to in times past."

I once asked her about her experience of having an angel come and talk to her about her future and the baby. She said, "I was a bit scared, but being open to God and being a very spiritual girl, I was also thrilled to be chosen to be Jesus' mother. I knew there would be heartache at some point, but was honored by God's grace and mission. Like most new mothers, I was worried I wouldn't be a good mother, not knowing much about it, even though I came from a large, extended family. Having your own child is different and then to know that he was destined for greatness was a very large responsibility for us (Joseph and me). But we were open to being led and secretly honored by the sacredness of our mission."

"He (Joseph) was very open to the Divine mission once the angel came to him too. We often spoke about it. It was also good to have other family members (referring to her cousin Elizabeth and Zachariah) who were supportive and had had similar angelic visitations. So the family supported us, but we knew we had to keep this secret for a while."

She continued, "It was hard to let Jesus go and begin his work. He was such a loving and caring child. He had his own mind and wouldn't be swayed by anyone or anything. That was only in his favor with what he was led to do. He was very strong in spirit, as you know. He still is. I am glad that so many people come to me and him asking for help. We try to help each and every one. We are all children of God and are never alone."

I am always amazed when I speak to Mary, as she is such a grand woman, both gentle and strong in nature, centered in God, steady, and consistent. She has grown in her responsibilities and grandeur from being the young Virgin Mary to being Mary, Holy Mother.

Precious Marie

While living in Eureka Springs, Arkansas many years ago, I became friends with the owner of the only metaphysical bookstore in town. Her name was Jan. She was a bit of a psychic which was handy when I didn't know what to buy someone for his/her birthday. I would just ask Jan what to purchase for the occasion. She would close her eyes for a moment and pick out something from her stocked shelves. The recipients of these gifts would always be pleased, I have to tell you. It seemed to work out every time.

One day Jan told me that she had a cat for me. It was a cat that had come to live with her and her menagerie of pets; she knew it was going to be my cat. I love cats, but didn't want an animal at that time in my life. So I told Jan I didn't want a cat, she must be mistaken, thank you very much.

She said it was my cat alright; she knew it the day it wandered into her house and stayed. She nodded understandingly, though, and said it could stay as long it is wanted, until I was ready for it. "Yeah sure," I said, "I don't want a cat. Love them, but don't want to own one." She said, "OK, when you are ready, it will be there."

Jan never said another word about that cat and I never thought about it again until one night, months later, when I was attending an event in town and Jan was there. After the event she asked for a ride home. She lived in the mountains close to me and I was happy to give her a lift, besides, I had heard about her beautiful log house in the woods and wanted to see it for myself. As we drove up, I couldn't believe how large and majestic it was nestled among the Arkansas woods. It had a great feel to it too. As we approached, she asked if I wanted a tour of the house and I was excited to see the inside as well.

We went in and left the door ajar for her many pets to come inside and eat dinner. She turned on lights, set the mail down on a large, oval oak table and we proceeded to tour the house. As we came down the stairs, a gray and orange kitty with silky fur wandered in the door. I took one look at her and immediately fell in love. I just had to hold her and what a lover she was – fur so soft. She purred as I held her in my arms, rubbing under her chin. I looked up at Jan with tears in my eyes and said, "I am sorry but I have to have this cat. I am so in love with it."

Jan smiled knowingly and reminded me that, indeed, it was the cat she had told me about a couple of months ago. I had forgotten completely and couldn't believe I could actually take this cat home and love it as my own. Jan was generous and gave me a litter box, litter, a cat bowl, and enough food to tide us over for a few days. I put the cat and her possessions in the car and off we went home, in total astonishment and love.

I called this kitty *Precious Marie*. *Precious* because she was and it was a good southern name, as she was born in the south, and *Marie* for Mother Mary. I asked Mary to protect her since I wasn't the best animal owner – I had very little experience with feline roommates.

Mother Mary did protect her until her transition. I love you Precious Marie and I envision you in the arms of Mary until I can be with you again. She is the only cat I have ever owned . . . before or since.

Mary Books

I began collecting Virgin Mary books many years ago, don't know why, just did. I would buy them whenever and wherever I found them: retail outlets, garage sales, at used bookstores, or spiritual gift shops. During the writing of this book, I have delved deeper into some of my earlier gathered books about Mary, just feeling drawn to one and then another. Now, after all these years, I know why I have them. She has been sending information to me to be kept until the time was right. I am glad the time is now, as each one holds a new insight, inspiration, or story about Mary.

I especially like to read books about her at night before going to bed. The day is done and my brain can rest; the next thing to do is read about Mary and drift off to sleep. It is comforting to slumber with Mary in my thoughts.

She would wake me up many mornings whispering another story in my ear. So I would say my prayers, thank her, go turn on the computer, and write the next story. I know to write it down as soon as possible, otherwise, it will be in my head all day, over and over again until it is typed and filed. I have learned to just give in, turn on, and write. It is a delightful process. As I am writing, it flows like warm butter onto the screen. She guides me if I forget a detail or need to edit a part for clarity. Once the story is written, I can relax, knowing it is safely in its place.

I still continue to find new Mary books in my path. One book I checked out at the library had a large photo of the Virgin Mary in the form of Our Lady of Guadalupe, made out of clouds in the sky. In 2002, the photographer, Eric Giebler, was flying in an airplane when "Guadalupe in the Clouds" appeared; he took out his camera and snapped the picture. What an amazing find it was when I turned the page to a blue and white, fluffy, Our Lady of Guadalupe centerfold. For days, weeks, and months I would lay the book open on my dining room table visible every time I passed by. I kept renewing the book until the allowable time to have a book was exhausted. Then I would turn it back in and check it out again quickly. That went on for four more renewals. They didn't seem to mind since no one had put it on hold.

The book with the photo of Mary in the clouds is *Guadalupe Body and Soul* by Marie-Pierre Colle. It also has an excellent rendition of the story of Juan Diego meeting the Lady of Guadalupe. All my Mary publications are unique – they include history, channelings, apparitions, theology, personal accounts, and even coloring books. I am honored to have this book among the many about her.

Mary's House that the Unsinkable Molly Brown Built

In 1880, the Immaculate Conception Cathedral Association was formed to initiate planning and building a large cathedral in Denver, Colorado. J.J. Brown, the husband of Margaret Brown, known as "Molly" Brown, was one of the four leading Catholic businessmen of the association. The project was fraught with problems from the beginning. The main architect, Coquard, became ill and the design had to be finished by another architect. Also, most of the money raised was lost in bad investments by the association. That didn't stop the unsinkable Molly Brown as she continued to raise funds and, finally, in 1912 it was completed.

Molly and J.J. Brown rented the 6th pew, in the newly built Immaculate Conception Cathedral, for a reported 25 cents for an adult and 10 cents for a child. Each Sunday, Molly would sashay down the center aisle carrying a massive walking staff draped in flowers and ribbons and sit in her pew. The church is known as "Mary's house that Molly built."

The Veil of Mary

The Chartes Cathedral, in Chartres, France houses a miraculous silk veil belonging to Mary of Nazareth. It is called the *Sancta Camisia*. This is said to be the Virgin Mary's veil, possibly worn at the Annunciation when the angel came to her, and/or worn at the birth to Jesus. No matter when she wore it, it still touched the skin of our Virgin Mary. In recent years, and by the use of modern technologies, the veil was tested and the results placed the fabric as originating in Palestine around the 1st century.

Apparently, the Byzantine Empress Irene of Constantinople gifted it to Charlemagne, whose grandson offered it to the Cathedral in Chartres in the 9th century. The veil survived a devastating fire in 1145 which was proof to many of its imperishability. Because of this miracle, the cathedral was rebuilt in the 12th century to better house this great, sacred relic. It is said if an ordinary garment touches the veil, it will have miracle producing powers as well. It is popular practice to gift a blessed shirt to soldiers and pregnant women.

The Veil of Mary, Sancta Camisia, is now encased in a golden reliquary with two gold angels on either side. The Veil is made of raw silk and is .46 meters in width and approximately 5.35 meters long, which is 1.5 feet by 17.5 feet. A woman's veil of this size and quality has many uses. It could have been worn by Mary for warmth, as a covering from the hot sun, as fashion, and over the head in reverence, creating sacred space during worship.

The veil was, no doubt, a beloved piece of clothing donned by Mary and utilized in many situations. Because it was Mary's, it is one of the most sacred relics of our times. I would imagine that she blessed and protected it with her love and gratitude for its service when she was living. I have to wonder, though, if she might have purchased it, since she is such an amazing shopper (and we know she went to Jerusalem many times) or was it a gift from someone special. Either way it is a must see for all Marians.

Mary, Queen of the Angels

One of the many titles for the Virgin Mary is "Queen of the Angels." I am not sure how she received such a lofty distinction, but I always want to be open to the truth of that. Did she get a promotion on the spiritual plane and the Divine deemed her Queen in the angelic realm?

As I research the origin of our human understanding of this title, I always wonder who received this vital information to share with humankind. In meditation, did a monk or priestess receive the celestial bulletin that Mary was now crowned? I tend to believe it is a Roman Catholic distinction given to her by a human source to continue to define her role in the celestial domain. It is uncertain when this distinction first appeared in our liturgy or doctrine. There seems to be no official church document stating that *now* Mary, mother of Jesus, is the Queen of the Angels. It just seems to be known that she rules parts of the heavens.

So, as Queen of the Angels, I suppose, there is great responsibility. So I asked her one day, "Mary, what is it like being Queen of the Angels?" She chuckled, "Child," she said, "Angels don't need me to be their Queen, they have God." End of story, she had nothing more to say about it. There was nothing more to say. If you have God, there is no need for a heavenly royal family.

I like Mary's humility; she chuckled at the thought of being considered as the Angelic Queen. Funny concept for her, but I could tell she was flattered by the reference and title, even though it wasn't actually true. She understood what we were saying about her. We believe her to be the feminine matriarch of the heavenly hosts, the highest Divine angels.

In paintings and sometimes in apparitions we see that she is surrounded by the angels, singing and praising. We can assume she knows angels in ways that are beyond our understanding.

So even in our ignorance Mary, we crown you Queen of the Angels. May your reign be majestic, of truth, and of the highest light possible. Long live the Queen!

Madonna

Mother Mary is often called *Madonna* or *The Madonna.* I always assumed Madonna meant "mother" or "mother with child" because, when Mary is referred to as *The Madonna,* it is usually referring to Mary as a mother or is the name of a painting which shows Mary with her baby Jesus.

One day I decided to look up the word Madonna in my big, fat dictionary and was amazed to learn "Madonna" is an Italian word meaning "My Lady." How elegant is that? One of the other definitions for Madonna is "the Virgin Mary." Since the dictionary is considered the official keeper of known words in our language, I like knowing the Virgin Mary is sanctioned as a definition for Madonna, My Lady.

There was a pop star in recent times named Madonna as well. She was not what most would consider equated with the Virgin Mary or even a lady for that matter, because of some of the edgy videos and music she recorded. Nevertheless, some of her lyrics are about being like a virgin, and she was singing under a cross in one of her music videos.

The pop Madonna was very public about her life as she matured into womanhood. She showed us her struggles with body, physical matters, mind and spirit, her joys of feelings, sensations, and appetites. She broke boundaries in who she loved, in her singing, dancing, and visual images in books, films, CDs, and videos.

This Madonna matured, had children, and studied the Jewish Kabbalah. Fascinating isn't it? She was not born Jewish, but she followed the religion of her namesake, Mary of Nazareth, *The* Madonna. She did become gentler, even spiritual in a later chapter of her life, allowing the feminine energy to rise up in her. She talked about her spiritual walk and Divine love, just as she did when she burned with her earlier physical passions.

At one time, Madonna, pop star, offended the Rabbis with her music and lyrics about a famous 16th century Jewish mystic named Yitzhak Luria in a song called "Isaac." Some Jewish authorities called for her to be banished from community and prophesized she would have Divine retribution for what she has done, spilling sacred secrets to the masses.

So again, Madonna lived up to her name sakes legacy, for Mary Madonna, mother of Jesus, also had the authorities upset at her and her son. Wasn't she the one who birthed this teacher, healer, mystic, lover of God, and rebel? Didn't she steal him away out of the country and protect him at an early age; didn't she travel with an unruly band of disciples and followers; wasn't he upsetting the rabbis and temple authorities in his day; and wasn't Madonna at the cross as he was put to death for his defiance?

Yes, she was the Lady, The Madonna, My Lady, with all her bravery, grace, and love. Be aware when you are named or take on the name of Madonna, My Lady isn't only about gentleness, feminine charm, and elegance, but also about power, love, and courage under fire. God Bless The Madonna!

The Grotto

In Portland, Oregon there is a 62-acre, "internationally renowned, Catholic sanctuary," named *The Grotto*. The Grotto has beautiful gardens, steep hills, sculptured saints sprinkled in the hillside, statues of angels, three chapels, and two large gift shops.

This site is also called "The National Sanctuary of Our Sorrowful Mother." Poor, sad, sorrowful Mary and this Grotto is all about Mary's deep grief when her son was tortured and hung on a cross to die.

The actual grotto portion of the sprawling sanctuary – called "Our Lady's Grotto" – a cavern carved out of the stone hillside with a replica of Michelangelo's "Pieta" – the sculpture of Mary holding her dead son Jesus on her lap. The Pieta is sitting on a large, rock pedestal high up within the 50 foot cavern, flanked by two torch-holding, gold angels.

The death and sorrow theme is set early when you visit this sanctuary. Just after passing the larger of the two gift shops, a short path winds through the trees and opens upon this powerful death scene. The end of Jesus' life is the beginning of the Grotto experience. The Pieta dramatically shows the tragedy of Jesus' death first, so you can carry the sadness with you while traversing the many walkways throughout the gardens.

One bumpy, paved path is called the *Via Matris,* which means "The Way of the Sorrowful Mother." It is self-explanatory. There are 34 wooden carved statues in glass enclosures portraying seven important scenes of Jesus' life, ending with a particularly mournful scene of Jesus dying at the cross and the laying of the body in the tomb. Mary is faithfully in each of the sorrowful scenes.

Another dark spot of The Grotto is the "Stations of the Cross" trail which depicts in bronze the 14 highlighted moments of Jesus' journey to death. This is also called *The Way of the Cross, Via Dolorosa* or *Way of Sorrows* - shortened to *The Way*. Each station has it own prayer and supplication for the one who wishes to relive the tragedy on *The Way* to the top. You would think it would be hard to be happy in such a place, but most people there are smiling, in awe of the beauty and serenity.

The larger chapel on the grounds is called the "Chapel of Mary, Mother of the Human Race," which is quite an auspicious title. Again, the Stations of the Cross and the life of Jesus are portrayed in art throughout the chapel. Mary's statue sits in an alcove in front, next to the sacristy. She has a hint of a smile on her face and her hands are outstretched, offering blessings to all who visit.

The other chapel is high atop the cliff with windows looking out over Portland and one can see Washington state across the Columbia River. On the outside of the top portion of this small/cozy meditation room/chapel is a large cross that lights up at night from the cliff. Inside is a lifelike, polyester-resin, and fiberglass depiction of Mary holding a blonde, blue eyed Jesus encased in a plexi-glass, round column. They both look happy at this point in their lives together.

The statue seems so alive, you almost want to open the door of the clear, round casing to let them breathe a bit. Although the figures are remarkably humanlike, this should not be confused with realistic, as Mary is very fair-skinned and she holds her blonde-haired, blue-eyed boy child. Since they were Semitic, rather than Scandinavian, it is highly unlikely either Mary or Jesus looked anything like this, but, of course, each culture has its own depiction of the Virgin and her son.

Nuns of the "Order of Servants of Mary" attend to the priests and mass at The Grotto. They wear majestic, black robes with oversized rosaries draped at their sides. The habits are starched and white as snow. The sisters have an air of power, structure, sacredness, responsibility, and duty. They are well dressed in their black armor of God – looking scholarly, devoted, and mysterious.

Even though Mary's son died, we know that isn't the whole story. There was tremendous joy on that next Sunday morning. So when you go to the Grotto, you may see the sorrowful Mother, but she isn't sad any more and most of her visitors aren't either.

As I was coming off the upper garden elevator one day, two visiting nuns in full nunnery outfits were waiting downstairs to get on. It did my heart good to see them paying homage to their savior's mother. As I passed them though, I noticed that they both carried neon-green plastic shopping bags that had the words "Maui" on the side. So a visit with Mary at her grotto was on their itinerary, along with a trip to the Hawaiian Islands. They didn't look sad either, in fact they were smiling as they said hello and giggling as they entered the elevator.

The Grotto is a destination spot to relive what seems to be finality, but is really the dawn of a new beginning and one better than we could ever imagine. It is ok to be happy at the Grotto, but it is also a place to cry if you wish.

Hurricane Mary Grotto

Key West, Florida has an outdoor Grotto devoted to Our Blessed Mother within the St. Mary Star of the Sea Roman Catholic Church grounds. In 1919, a category 4 hurricane hit Key West and over 600 people lost their lives. Because of this, an outdoor Grotto was built in 1922 by a Canadian nun, Sister M. Louis Gabriel, in honor of Mary and charging her to protect the town from further hurricane devastation. So far, Mary has done a fabulous job. No hurricanes have made a direct hit on Key West since the Hurricane Grotto was built and dedicated.

At the dedication of the Grotto, Sister Gabriel proclaimed, "For as long as this grotto stands, this island will never suffer the full force of a hurricane." Those Key Westers may be laid back, but they know the power of Mary.

If a hurricane is so strong that it flattens the stone grotto, all bets are off for the rest of the town. It is the loophole Sister Gabriel forgot to mention, but implied in her dedication, "For as long as this grotto *stands*, this island will never suffer the full force of a hurricane." In other words, as long as there isn't a hurricane strong enough to topple the Grotto, all will be well.

When a hurricane is taking aim at their beloved island, many townspeople make a pilgrimage to this Grotto, pray, light candles, and feel protected by the power of the Virgin. On TV recently, a Weather Channel reporter asked a resident if she was preparing to evacuate as a powerful hurricane was barreling toward them. "No," she said, "We have the Grotto, nothing will harm us." She was going about her daily business with the calm certainty that those pesky, tropical cyclones don't stand a chance against Our Blessed Mother in the Key West Grotto.

This is the power Mary still has even in the face of Doppler radar, the Saffir-Simpson Hurricane Wind Scale, and sophisticated storm warning systems.

And so far . . . it's working.

Miryam

I went shopping with Mary at a used bookstore one day and I asked her if she had any books about herself for me to see or buy. My eyes immediately landed on a daily meditation book, 365 meditations for every day of the week – from Mary. I was thrilled to see a book of Mary sayings for life. But as I thumbed through the pages, looking for Mary's wisdom, I noticed it wasn't actually Maryisms. The book had the few common scriptures from the New Testament about Mary, but mostly the author wrote her own thoughts and prayers . . . *to* Mary. Oh well, even though there were no direct quotes, each page ended with a supplication to our Blessed Mother, asking for help in an important aspect of life – world hunger, peace, healing, comfort for the lovesick, on and on.

I put the book back on the shelf, disappointed. When I asked why I was led to that particular book, she said at some point in time I would be writing a meditation book about her that I *will* like. I look forward to the day.

So I continued to glance through the stacks and another book caught my eye, about Miryam of Nazareth. *Miryam* is the Hebrew name for Mary, which means "rebellion." Mary the revolutionary, huh, hadn't heard about a book focused on the rebellious side of Mary before. But as I looked within its pages, again, it was full of prayers praising, pleading, and pledging to Mary – opps . . . Miryam. Even though I returned the book to its place, my interest peaked with this new thought of Mary as a radical.

She was certainly revolutionary in behavior - being pregnant before wedlock, conceiving by the spirit of God, escaping government persecution of her family by sneaking to a foreign land in the middle of the night, on the run, hiding out, marrying an older man, mothering a known spiritual agitator, advocating for the poor, lepers, beggars, harlots, and then finally, remaining a virgin all her married life. How much more radical could that be, Miryam, (rebel) of Nazareth?

Our Lady of Lourdes

On February 11, 1858, near Lourdes, France, a fourteen year old girl named Bernadette Soubirous went with her sister and a friend to collect firewood. Bernadette's family was so improvised that they lived in an abandoned prison cell which was thought to be too foul to even house prisoners. The three girls went to the outskirts of town near the Gave River in an area called Massabielle so as not to be accused of stealing the firewood from private property.

Bernadette had asthma so did not cross the river when the other two girls waded across to the other side where the wood was more plentiful. Since Bernadette wasn't having any luck finding wood, she decided to take off her stockings to go to the other side of the river anyway. At that moment she heard "the sound of wind" – as if a storm was blowing up behind her. She stood up and she noticed the trees were not moving from this "wind," so she looked around to find the source of the sound.

She later tells the story saying, "I looked across the millstream to a niche above a cave in the rock of Massabielle. A rosebush on the edge of the niche was swaying in the wind. It was all that moved. All else was still. A golden cloud came out of the cave and flooded the niche with radiance. Then a lady, young and beautiful, exceedingly beautiful, the like I had never seen, stood on the edge of the niche. She smiled and smiled at me, beckoning me to come closer as though she were my mother, and she gave me to understand in my soul that I was not mistaken. The lady was dressed in white, with a white veil on her head and a blue sash at her waist. A rosary of white beads on a gold chain was on her right arm. On that cold winter's day, her feet were bare, but on each foot was a golden rose radiant with the warmth of summer."

Bernadette went to grab her own rosary and started to make the sign of the cross for spiritual protection, when at the same time, the beautiful lady made the sign of the cross too. Bernadette then began to say the rosary and as she did, the lady did the same. When Bernadette finished, the lady disappeared after giving her a slight bow.

That next Sunday, after Mass, Bernadette went back to the site with a group of friends. Again the lady appeared to Bernadette and Bernadette sprinkled her with holy water from the church and said if she wasn't from God to go away, but if she was from God, please stay. The lady smiled and took on more holy water.

Bernadette was the only child in the group who saw or heard this vision in the rosebush, but the children were amazed at the physical transformation of Bernadette as she spoke to the lady. She had no asthma and appeared to be in holy rapture. When a stone was thrown and hit Bernadette, she didn't even wince. The kids were afraid Bernadette was losing it, so they ran to town to get help. They had to carry Bernadette home; she was so enraptured. Later, when Bernadette resumed her normal state, she said the lady stayed with her until she was carried into the house. Even though Bernadette was divinely happy and in bliss, her parents were angry at her for causing such pandemonium. The children who were with Bernadette at the niche urged her parents to believe her.

On February 18th, seven days after the first appearance, Bernadette again visited the spot where she had met the lady. Two influential women from town accompanied her this time and insisted she write down everything the lady said. Bernadette began to say the rosary and again the lady appeared. The lady laughed when Bernadette asked for her name and what she wanted, so she could write it down as instructed. The lady asked her, "Would you have the grace to come here for fifteen days?" Bernadette was a good girl and said she would ask her parents if she could do that. Then the lady said, "Go and tell the priests a chapel must be built here." With that, she smiled and left.

It was hot news in the town of Lourdes. Bernadette's parents agreed to let her meet with the lady and Bernadette's visits attracted larger and larger crowds. The town authorities were urged by some of the skeptical town's people to take action, so the local police brought her in for questioning. But when Bernadette did not admit it was a hoax, they started to threaten her family. The Church was embarrassed as well and said she was a superstitious girl and they were not about to give this child's story any confirmation. At the time there was no mention of the lady's identity. Bernadette only referred to her as an "indescribable being."

On February 25th, the 9th visitation, Bernadette was told by the lady to drink at the spring and to wash in it. Bernadette went to the Gave River to comply, but the lady called her back. The lady pointed to a rock. Bernadette later wrote, "I found some moisture there, but it was mud. Three times I threw it away even though the lady said to drink it. Then I washed in it only to have my face smeared with mud." The crowd began to sneer at Bernadette; she indeed was crazy and causing a scene. Bernadette's own aunt came to Bernadette and slapped her face and said, "Stop this nonsense!" and sent her home. But that afternoon, the muddy area turned into a flowing spring. Those who were scoffing at her that morning were now drinking from the spring that afternoon.

Many other visitations occurred between the lady and Bernadette. The lady talked about prayers which Bernadette kept secret, about penitence and conversion of sinners and the like. The crowds grew and again the police took Bernadette in for questioning. But she never fluctuated from her original story. The crowds would push towards the rosebush and Bernadette was afraid the lady would be crushed, but the lady just loved them and smiled.

Finally, on the 13th meeting, the lady again urged Bernadette to tell the priest to have a procession to this place and to build a chapel there. The priest, a Father Peyramale, being very doubtful, gave Bernadette a test. He said that he needed to know the name of the lady and for the lady to make the rosebush bloom. Even though people were experiencing miracle cures at the spring and rosebush, he was still unconvinced and needed proof. After hearing of the coming test, great anticipation grew amongst the masses. The news spread even further throughout the region.

Finally, the visitation occurred and approximately 8,000 people were present. Bernadette visited with the lady for 45 minutes and when she was through, she blew out her candle and went home. No blooming bush, no knowing of her name. The crowd was greatly disappointed.

Bernadette later wrote, "The people pestered me, the police watched me, and the public prosecutor almost crushed me." The town officials also harassed her family and continued to threaten her with jail if she ever returned to the grotto again. She wrote, "They forgot I was living in an unused police lockup with the entire family in one room." Jail would be better than home for Bernadette, no threat there.

On March 24th, in the middle of the night, Bernadette had the familiar urge to return to the grotto. At 5 in the morning, she did return and the lady was waiting for her. Bernadette asked her several times for her name and each time the lady refused. "Finally," Bernadette wrote, "the lady extended her hands toward the ground, swept them upwards to join them on her heart, raised her eyes, but not her head to heaven, leaned tenderly towards me and said, 'I am the Immaculate Conception.' She smiled at me. She disappeared. I was alone."

Bernadette did not know what that meant but she repeated the words over and over again so she could remember them when she told the priest.

Father Peyramale was astonished. The Church doctrine of the conception of Mary being without sin was only defined as church doctrine in 1854, four years earlier, and the expression was not common to the average person, much less a poor girl from Lourdes.

This name was the pivotal point which turned the priest into one of her biggest supporters. It was a good thing because she now had an even bigger onslaught of examinations, not only from local authorities, but regional and national officials, medical personnel, and church hierarchy as well. Even though she was extensively threatened and examined, she never deviated from her original story. She would say to them, "I did not ask you to believe, I only told you what I had seen." Finally, three separate Paris doctors announced, after extensive tests, that Bernadette was sound in mind and body.

Even though things were going well for Bernadette at that point, the local authorities closed the grotto and had guards posted to arrest anyone who visited it. They tried to commit Bernadette to an insane asylum anyway, but Father Peyramale stood by her and protected her saying, "I know my duty as pastor of my parish and protector of my flock. Your own doctors find no abnormality in Bernadette. You will have to fell me to the ground, pass over my dead body, and trample it underfoot, before you touch a hair of the child's head."

On July 16th, Bernadette saw the lady again, for the last time. The grotto was closed, so Bernadette knelt in a meadow on the other side of the river. "I began my rosary and my lady stood in the grotto smiling at me. It was the Feast of Our Lady of Mount Carmel. She looked more beautiful than I had ever seen her. This would be the last time I would see her on this earth . . . She left heaven in my heart and it has been there ever since."

The church called a commission to look into all the miraculous healings at the spring. Finally, public pressure forced the reopening of the grotto and a large basilica was built on the site – called Our Lady of Lourdes. Bernadette joined the Sister of Nevers convent in town, but continued to have problems and was even ordered by the other Superiors never to mention her apparition again. Bernadette died at the age of 35, never partaking of the healing waters of the grotto she shared with the lady. He body was exhumed in 1908, some 30 years later, and it was found to be uncorrupted. She was recognized as a saint by the Catholic Church in 1933.

Our Lady of Lourdes is depicted in white with a blue sash, holding a rosary. God bless the steadfastness and innocence of Bernadette, the healing waters, and appearance of Mary in Lourdes, France.

The Eureka Springs Mary Vortex

I was the pastor of Metropolitan Community Church of the Living Spring in Eureka Springs, Arkansas many years ago. Eureka Springs has healing waters just like in Lourdes, France. But the Eureka Springs waters are now polluted and are no longer safe for drinking or bathing. The springs are fenced off so you can't even touch the water for fear of disease. So what does that mean? I shutter to think. The city tacked up a large sign on the fence with an ominous warning about the flowing water of the Eureka Springs.

Even though the springs were toxic, I would baptize congregants on the banks without using the defiled water. I would use the water from the nearby drinking fountain next to a bench, outside of the protected area. As I blessed it, I would ask that the city water from the public fountain have the original healing essence of the springs. The baptisms were beautiful and many tears were shed at these sacred rituals.

Eureka Springs is located on what is called a female vortex. Vortexes are high-energy fields on the earth. When certain energy lines converge or connect, it can make a vortex. There are male and female vortexes on this planet. Sedona, Arizona has a couple of each. I had always wanted to live on a true female vortex. One woman in Eureka Springs told me that this particular female vortex was of Mary, Mother of God, and it was actually centered in the courtyard of a church in town. I was thrilled to have this information, so I immediately went to the church courtyard and stood open to receive the energy of Mary's vortex. It was lovely. The feeling was sweet, subtle, soft, soothing, and powerful – all at the same time.

Living on a female vortex has its challenges, but the townspeople knew where they lived was special. It was hard to conduct business since the energy was so passive, cooperative, healing, and laid back. Businesses would open when the owners arrived, time was not adhered to as in other towns; people just knew things would happen at the right moment and place. Many a city folk would visit and be frustrated with Eureka Spring's timelessness and lessons were learned about letting life happen. These urban warriors also learned that if something wasn't *on time* it always happened at the *right time*. Those who moved there from big cities would have to throw away their written schedules and just go with the flow. It was easier to go with it than fight it, and they would eventually give in and relax into this healing energy.

I was in need of a massage and energy healing when I first arrived in Eureka Springs. One day, as I was driving the curvy road by the church, I noticed a small, quaint building with a sign indicating that it was a massage therapy center. I had driven by before, but never noticed it. This time I stopped.

Upon opening the door, a woman came out to meet me. She was pleasant and asked if she could be of service. I told her I did energy work, meditation, and connected with the Divine during massage and asked if she had any therapists who could handle that. She felt it was an honorable request and said she was a simple massage therapist, but there were others who were trained in Reiki, polarity, and such who were probably better trained for energy healing. I asked, "Do you pray and meditate every day?" She was surprised by my question but answered, "Why, yes I do." I nodded in affirmation and said, "I want you. You have an active connection with the Divine. I don't need someone who is more trained with technique; I need someone who can stand in Divine energy with me." We began and continued to work together while I lived there, and it was an amazing journey for us both. We blended Mary, Divine, and human energy as it flowed into our bodies and spirits in that little healing space near the Mary vortex in Eureka Springs.

Mary Has a Son

The Gospel of Luke begins with a story about the angel of the Lord, Gabriel, visiting and proclaiming to the priest Zacharias that he and his wife, Elizabeth, would be having a child named John. Zacharias asked how this would be since he and his wife were so advanced in years. Because of his question and unbelief, the angel immediately struck him mute. Zacharias was to remain speechless until after the child was born.

Zechariah's wife did, indeed, become pregnant as the angel had said. While Elizabeth was in her sixth month, this same angel, Gabriel, visited Mary of Nazareth, a relative of Elizabeth, and proclaimed that she too was to have a baby boy. Since Mary was a virgin and had no intentions of sleeping with anyone anytime soon, she asked the angel how this was going to happen. The angel explained, "The Holy Spirit will come upon you and the power of the Highest will overshadow you therefore, also, that Holy One who is to be born will be called the Son of God." Gabriel ends by saying important words, "For with God nothing is impossible."* Mary says, "Let it be to me according to your word," and the angel departs.

Mary was not struck mute for her question as Zacharias was and we are not told why her question did not warrant the same consequence. But one possible explanation is this difference proves she was indeed blessed among women, and men, for that matter.

After the angel's joyful news, Mary quickly traveled from Nazareth to visit Elizabeth at her home in the hill country of Judah. When they first saw each other, Elizabeth's baby leapt inside her and Elizabeth was filled with the Holy Spirit. Mary stayed with Elizabeth for three months until the birth of Elizabeth's baby, John.

Zacharias was still unable to talk until eight days after the baby's birth, at the circumcision ceremony. Elizabeth, Zacharias' relatives, and friends gathered for this Jewish ritual and the naming of the child. All the relatives wanted to name the baby after the father, Zacharias, but Elizabeth answered saying adamantly, "His name shall be John."

The guests were not satisfied with that name at all and said there was no relative named John in the family; it would be unheard of to name him "John." If they had said that to angel Gabriel, I suspect, they all would have been struck deaf *and* mute. But, nevertheless, they then turned to the father, Zacharias, knowing he would agree with *them* and asked what the baby's name would be? Zacharias asked for a writing tablet and wrote,

"His name is John." They were all shocked. Then, to the surprise of everyone, Zacharias' "mouth opened and his tongue loosed, as he spoke, praising God."

After all this excitement, our pregnant Mary returned home to Nazareth to ready herself to have her baby. But just before Jesus' birth, a decree was sent forth by Caesar Augustus stating all Jews had to register in the home town of their lineage. Joseph, Mary's fiancé at the time, and Mary were forced to travel to Bethlehem since Joseph was of the lineage of David and Bethlehem was the city of David. It was very crowded in Bethlehem with all the ancestors of David registering and the only accommodation available for this couple was the stable of an inn. That night Mary gave birth to baby Jesus, wrapped him, and made a bed for him in a feeding trough for the animals.

Now, outside of town there was much commotion when an angel of the Lord came to a group of shepherds who were watching their flocks of sheep. The angel told them not to be afraid and bid them "glad tidings." Then the heavens opened and a "multitude of Heavenly Hosts" came singing and praising God. The angel told the shepherds the Son of God was in a manger in town, wrapped in swaddling clothes. After this message was delivered, the angels disappeared and the shepherds said to each other, "Let's go at once to see this child that God has told us about!" They ran to town to see this amazing infant and told whoever would listen what they had heard and seen; the people were astonished. But Mary kept those words the shepherd told her and pondered them in her heart – as we do as well. That night, our Virgin Mary became Mary, mother of Jesus.

*excerpts in quotes are from Luke 1:1-80 and Luke 2:1-20

Author Note: I thought this chapter would be so easy to write. It is in the Bible and familiar to most of the Christian world. I wanted to include this story just in case someone had *not* heard or read it. It was essential to include this story in a book on Mary, I thought. But writing this little chapter has taken me weeks. Not because I am a slow writer, which I am, but because there were so many insights and profound moments which happened to me while writing this.

Apparently, Mary wanted me to ponder it too; to read and reread it again and again. I rewrote it numerous times, condensing it as concisely and accurately as possible. But every time I would come to a different line, my fingers just quit writing. I went with it, took a break, and savored the words.

This short narrative has taken me aback and awakened something, sleeping deep inside. There were times I even cried as I rewrote it . . . again. Small miracles and unexpected events happened in my life: money came when I had none, health issues were resolved, time to write came unexpectedly, and weather suitable to garden broke during my breaks so I could be in nature and bask in her presence before I returned to my writing room. It surprised me and I hope you will feel this birth power of love as well. Maybe there is a different chapter that will capture your soul and awaken it to wisdom, love, and might. Surprisingly, this simple, familiar story was one of the many for me.

The Magnificat – Song of Mary

At the moment our pregnant Mary meets and greets her six month pregnant relative, Elizabeth, Elizabeth's baby leaps in her womb and she says this to Mary in a loud voice:

Luke 1:42b-45 (inclusive version)
"Blessed are you among women, and blessed is the fruit of your womb! But why is this granted to me, that the mother of my Lord should come to me? For indeed, as soon as the voice of your greeting sounded in my ears, the babe leaped in my womb, for joy. Blessed is she who believed, for there will be a fulfillment of those things which were told her from the Lord."

Mary then begins to speak or to sing what is commonly called *The Magnificat*, *Song of Mary* or *Canticle of Mary* in response:

Luke 1: 46-55 (inclusive version)
"My soul magnifies the Almighty, and my spirit has rejoiced in God my Savior.
For God has regarded the lowly state of the Divine's maidservant;
For behold, from now on all generations will call me blessed.
For God who is mighty has done great things for me and holy is God's name.
And the Divine's mercy is on those who fear God from generation to generation.
The Creator has shown strength with a strong arm; scattering the proud in the imagination of their hearts.
The Divine has put down the mighty from their thrones, and exalted the lowly.
The Almighty has filled the hungry with good things, and the rich was sent away empty.
The Holy One has helped the servant Israel, in remembrance of Holy mercy, and then spoke to our fathers, to Abraham and to The Holy seed forever."

Traditionally, this text has been used in many Christian worship services including, but not limited to, Vespers and Evening Prayers. One is also able to buy a Magnificat prayer card which has a picture of a pregnant Mary on the front and the Song on the back for around 70 cents or a pack of 25 for $15. It is a powerful song of praise. Miracles have happened when people study and recite this Magnificat.

I recently ordered a Catholic devotional called *The Magnificat*®. Usually each printing has a different, classical painting of Mary is featured on the front cover. Inside the back cover is the *Canticle of Mary*. This magazine/devotional is so sweet to hold and I particularly like the way its soft, thin pages feel in my hand. The language is traditional Catholic, no inclusive language here, but it is chucked full of prayers, verses, writings, and a daily mass.

One day I was sitting on the banks by the Oak Creek, on a vortex, in Sedona reading the mass from *The Magnificat*® with an ex-Catholic priest. He had left the Catholic Church because of some of its political stands on human rights. The ex-priest told me about how the mass was recited: first him, then me, then us. It was something we both will always remember, as we sat by the flowing river, nestled in between red, towering, vortex, rocks. Mary directed me to tell him that when someone is ordained, he or she is ordained for life and God would help him find a way to serve in harmony with him. He has since become an Episcopalian priest and works as a hospice chaplain. He is happier in this new denomination, but he continues to revere the depth of mass and the writings of the Catholic Church, as do I, even though we had to change it into inclusive language that day.

This Song of Mary, The Magnificat, pulls us all together in the worship and adoration of the Divine. This Canticle is the most we have of Mary's words from her Earthly walk. It is fitting that it is Mary's song of praise to God.

Mary, Queen of the Roses

Mary is associated with roses; often, whenever Mary appears in an apparition, people also report smelling a strong fragrance of roses. For example:

- Queen of Heaven Cemetery in Hillside, Illinois has a cross where Mary, Archangel Michael, and three additional angels have appeared. At each appearance, it was reported that a strong scent of roses was in the air when the heavenly beings arrived.

- In 1983, on a farm in Conyers, Georgia, Nancy Fowler reported sightings of Mary; she also reported smelling roses during her contact with the Virgin.

One of the ways we pray to Mary is by using the Rosary, the "garland of roses." The statue of Our Lady of Guadalupe has a variety of roses depicting the roses she asked Juan Diego to pick that winter morning as a sign for the Bishop. Legend has it that the White Roses in Paradise blushed pink when Mary kissed them and the Golden Rose symbolizes the glory of the Virgin Mary. Mary is often referred to as the "Mystical Rose" or the "Thornless Rose."

At Mary Help of Mothers Shrine in Flushing, New York many miracles have happened with rose petals. Laminated rose petals, blessed by Jesus and Mary, can be purchased from this shrine for 20 cents. I ordered two by mail. When they arrived, I opened the package eagerly and out fell my plastic laminated rose petals, beautifully preserved with the words, "The Lourdes of America" printed on each card. On the back is the story of Mary appearing to Veronica Lueken during Rosary Vigils at Bayside, New York between the years of 1970-1995. Mary must have had a lot to tell Veronica in those 25 years.

Photos of Veronica talking to the air are on the shrine's web site and are available for viewing. The card also stated that Mary will remain on the sacred grounds forever and, "The Power from Heaven shall be known through the Roses." I also ordered rose petals on cards covered with plastic wrap. Those specific rose petals are for cures and conversions. I have five altogether. Each rose petal is a different color and size, very well preserved and cared for. I am honored to own them.

Coincidentally, I am writing this portion of the book on Mary in Portland, Oregon which is called, "The City of Roses." Roses grow very well in the Portland climate. I began growing roses when I moved into my new home here. There was no fence between the renter's townhouse next door and my yard. The neighbor children used my front yard as their playground. I told them they would have to stop playing in my yard. Apparently the last occupants of the house had allowed them to have free reign of their property.

I did not want to erect a fence between the yards to set the boundary; it seemed too drastic, so I bought several rose bushes from my local discount store and planted them in a row between the yards. They were on sale for $1.50 a piece. It worked – no children crossing that thorny fence since and beautiful roses bloom for both the neighbors and me to enjoy all summer long.

I asked Mary to bless my boundary, rose garden. Those roses grew fast and strong. I picked them for my writing room and for the house. Funny, I never knew I could grow such beautiful roses.

On a hill in town, is a world famous rose garden that overlooks the city and the Columbia River. It is said to be the largest and most complete rose garden in the world. When in full bloom, it is a beautiful sight to behold – sitting on a bench looking over the roses and seeing a snow covered Mt. Hood in the background.

Every year in June, Portland has a Rose Festival. Seems to always rain at the Rose Festival, but rain isn't unusual for Oregon. Apparently the roses like it. The Rose Festival crowns one beautiful woman, "The Rose Queen." Throughout the years we have had only two Marys crowned as Rose Queen; one in 1959 and the other in 1972. Mary, we crown you Rose Queen for eternity.

Mari-el

A woman came to Eureka Springs, Arkansas, to give a Mary presentation on Friday night and a day workshop on Saturday. Friday night was free. We all crowded into the small church on the hill to hear about healing with the power of the Virgin Mary. She called the healing technique "Mari-el." The presenter explained how she was going to teach us to call in Mary and heal people. The workshop would take all day Saturday and would cost quite a bit of money, but we would all be powerful healers afterwards. The technique was a secret and could only be passed on orally, thus the high price.

Toward the end of the Friday presentation, she said, "I know there is someone who is supposed to be here, but isn't. They are being called to the workshop." We all fell for that one; we called our friends and significant others who weren't at the presentation telling them Mary wanted them to come to the workshop and to pay lots of money to learn to heal with her energy.

So, on Saturday morning, all bright and early, we showed up at the retreat center where the workshop was being held. It was chilly and dewy. We were all cuddled in with our coffee and notebooks, ready to have the secret of Mary's healing power revealed to us. The teacher came and was pleased by the crowd of wannabe Mari-el healers. She took our money, gratefully, and we began with meditation and a prayer.

The teacher talked about how Mary heals with roses. The facilitator opened our charkas, waving a stemmed rose up and down our bodies and calling on the name of Mary. Then we were to use the vision of roses and call on Mary to heal each other. That was it. We spent the whole morning doing just that.

In the afternoon she told us she just found out there was a self-sustaining farm nearby (which we all knew about and bought veggies from) and she wanted us all to go there. So we all followed her to our local, organic, off-the-grid compound. We were not impressed to have spent so much money to heal with Mary's roses for four hours and then see a sight we were familiar with. So much for the secret healing power of Mary – she could have told us that in 10 minutes on Friday night. Our loved ones, who we coerced into going to the workshop, were very disappointed and said they would never go to another workshop again in their entire lives.

One woman did get healed that morning, though. An attendee who was working on a healing with roses said she saw a light form, but it didn't go to the intended person, instead, it shot from her to a woman across the room. Mary just directed it to the one with the most need, we concluded. No one else had a healing that day, even though we were doing exactly what the teacher had taught. But we knew that Mary was there. We did all smell the roses.

So if you need a healing from Mary, just ask her and visualize roses being sent from Mary to the intended. It may hit someone across town – but a healing will take place. And that isn't a secret and it is my offering to you for free.

RoseMary, the Herb

Rosemary is a fragrant, evergreen herb used in food, healing oil, and as a flower essence. As we know, Mary loves her roses and this herb has the energetic combination of the two: Rose and Mother Mary. Legend is that the flowers of the rosemary plant were originally white, but turned blue when the Virgin cast her cloak over them – forever blue.

Curiously, at the beginning of the growing season I bought a small rosemary shrub at the Portland Nursery and planted it outside my writing room, with no particular thought about it. I just knew it belonged there. But upon writing this and looking out to the back yard, I notice, *for the first time*, the importance of having this, now, large rosemary shrub growing beneath my writing room window!

Subtle, healing rosemary seems to pop into our environment and awareness without much conscious thought. I go to Sedona quite often. Each morning I sit on a rock eating my breakfast among the enormous red rock formations. One day I looked down at the plants around me and there were four blooming rosemary bushes all within 10 feet! Its quiet presence, with its aromatic fragrance, is surprisingly stealth in our lives. Just like Mary herself, always present – but many times, going virtually unnoticed.

One day I asked my friend Rosemary if she knew the origin of her name. She said she didn't know why her parents named her that. She said she never gave it much thought. Interesting, I would think an adult woman may have asked about the lineage of her name. So we can only guess. Maybe her parents just named her after the herb in their backyard garden.

I told her she had a very powerful name and it was possible she was named after the Virgin Mary and her beloved roses. She nodded, thoughtfully, and I noticed she took in a deep breath, as if to breathe in the essence of the three – the roses, the Virgin Mary, and the herb. She thanked me for this important insight into her name and walked away as if pondering the new perspective.

I also met a woman named Mary Rose. It seemed obvious to me she came from a Catholic family and was named after the Virgin, but I wanted to find out for sure.

"I love your name," I told her when we met, and indeed, when I inquired, she told me she was named by her mother after the Virgin Mary and her cherished roses. She also told me she was a "recovering"

Catholic and even though she no longer practiced that religion, she loved the significance of her name.

So when rosemary shows up in your life, either the herb or a person, pay attention to the significance of the appearance. Mary is sure to be around there somewhere.

Going in for Black Pants & Coming Out with a Red Sweater

Shopping with Mary has also taught me that sometimes I go out looking for black pants and find an adorable, on clearance, red sweater, instead. I take advantage of the find and purchase the red sweater, knowing it was probably the red sweater I was supposed to get in the first place and the need for black pants was the lure that got me into the store.

Invariably, I find if I go ahead and purchase the serendipitous item, I will find a time in the near future that it is the perfect garment to wear for a certain occasion. I am proud of myself for taking the risk, even though I didn't think it exactly the purchase I was intending at the time. But it was there, perfect fit and color, just not the focus of my shopping search on that particular day.

On the way home from work the very next day, I stopped at a store which I normally don't go to. I was guided to turn into the parking lot and walk in. Viola! – black pants on sale – perfect fit.

So, if you are looking for something in life: black pants, love, house, apartment, job, car – go look and see what happens. You may run into an unexpected red sweater, potential friend, a free trip, or a great lawn service lead. Celebrate the red sweater, the unexpected gift in whatever package it comes. Just trust that the odd item or connection is just what you need to have at the time, and you will get the black pants later.

The Rosary

In most of Mary's visitations, she requests we increase our praying of the Rosary. She seems very insistent about this. Many report Mary is holding a rosary in her hand, just to emphasize this point.

There are many theories about the origin of the "rosary." Some say St. Dominic was the first to use it, but the use of the rosary actually predated his time. In the 9th century, before St. Dominic, Irish monks were reciting a set group of prayers to Mary which caught on with the laity. Many people at the time were illiterate so they needed to memorize their devotions and sought something to help keep track of their recitations. Knotted rope was first used by the monks; this later evolved into beads on a string. When the Irish monks traveled to Europe, they brought their devotions and their string of beads with them, but it was in the 13th century when St. Dominic, after a visitation from Mary, began calling the set prayers and beads "The Rosary."

The word "Rosary" comes from the Latin meaning "a garland of roses." It is said every bead and prayer is a rose offered to Mary, Mother of All. We give a rose with a prayer to console Mary's great heart.

Gifted craftsmen, named "Paternosters" (named after the "Our Fathers"), began creating these garlands of roses on stringed beads. It is a great honor to be a Paternoster and to be in the guild of such sacred masters of the rosary.

The Rosary honors the Virgin Mary and is Divine in intent. The actual prayers have gone through a few changes throughout the years, but have settled into our current form now for quite some time. These supplications to Mary are universally consistent.

The specific prayers when reciting the Rosary are: Apostles' Creed, The Lord's Prayer, The Hail Mary, and The Glory or The Glory Be.

Author Note: I have inclusified some of the prayers, which is to say I did not make pronouns gender specific. My hope is not to offend anyone, but to allow the modern non-Catholic masses better access to these prayers. The process is still the same, if not greatly simplified for this chapter. Please refer to the many glorious references of the rosary for the true and expanded Catholic version of this most sacred Marian ritual. Some wording differs, depending on the source.

A Rosary begins:

First you hold the cross at the end of the rosary and make a sign of the cross on yourself and pray the Apostles Creed:

"I believe in God, the Divine almighty, Creator of heaven and earth. I believe in Jesus Christ, God's only Son, our Lord. He was conceived by the power of the Holy Spirit and born of the Virgin Mary. He suffered under Pontius Pilate, was crucified, died, and was buried. He descended into Hell. On the third day he arose again. He ascended into heaven, and is seated on the right hand of God Almighty. From there He will come to judge the living and the dead. I believe in the Holy Spirit, the holy Catholic Church, the communion of saints, the forgiveness of sins, the resurrection of the body and life everlasting. Amen."

On the first bead you pray the Lord's Prayer:

"Our Creator, who art in heaven, hallowed by thy name, thy kingdom come, thy will be done on Earth as it is in heaven. Give us this day our daily bread and forgive us our trespasses, as we forgive those who trespass against us. Lead us not into temptation but deliver us from evil. (Optional: For thine is the kingdom and power for ever and ever.) Amen.

The second, third and fourth bead you pray three Hail Marys:

"Hail Mary, full of grace! The Lord is with thee. Blessed are you among women and blessed is the fruit of your womb, Jesus. Holy Mary, Mother of God, pray for us sinners now and at the hour of our death. Amen." (See two alternative versions to follow)

The first part of the Hail Mary is in reference to the words from the Angel Gabriel proclaiming to Mary the news of the spiritual conception of Jesus. Taken from the Luke 1:28 a and b passage, Hail Mary, full of grace, the Lord is with thee.

Then the fifth bead you pray The Glory:

"Glory to the Creator, and to the Son, and to the Holy Spirit. As it was in the beginning, is now and will be forever, (Optional: or ever shall be) world without end. Amen."

You then name the first Mystery (mysteries given below) and pray the Lord's Prayer again, all on that same 5th bead.

Pray 10 more Hail Marys as you start around the loop of beads, one Hail Mary for every bead. There will be a break in the beads that cues you to pray The Glory, name the 2nd Mystery and pray the Lord's Prayer.

You will repeat 10 Hail Marys, Glory, Mystery and the Lord's Prayer until you reach the end of your rope (?). When you finish, you end with one more Glory and the finale of Hail Holy Queen:

"Hail holy Queen, Mother of mercy, our life, our sweetness, and our hope! To you do we cry, poor banished children of Eve. To you we send up our sighs, mourning and weeping in this vale (or valley) of tears. Turn then, most gracious advocate, your eyes of mercy toward us, and after this our exile, show unto us the blessed fruit of thy womb, Jesus. O clement, O loving, O sweet Virgin Mary."

The Mysteries are in 4 categories: Five Joyful Mysteries, Five Luminous Mysteries, Five Sorrowful Mysteries and Five Glorious Mysteries.

The Five Joyful Mysteries include the Annunciation, the Visitation, the Nativity, the Presentation of Jesus in the Temple, and the finding of the child Jesus in the Temple.

The Five Luminous Mysteries are The Baptism of Jesus, Jesus Changes the Water into Wine at the Wedding Feast, Jesus Preaches the Kingdom of God, The Transfiguration, Jesus Gives the Eucharist.

The Five Sorrowful Mysteries includes the Agony in the Garden, the Scourging, the Crowning of the Thorns, Jesus Carrying the Cross, and the Crucifixion.

The final Five are the Glorious Mysteries including the Resurrection, the Ascension, the Descent of the Holy Spirit, the Assumption of Mary into Heaven, and her Coronation Crowning her Queen of Heaven and Earth. These last two mysteries are not stated in the Bible, but included by Catholic consensus this is scriptural and within the Catholic tradition; they are accepted as truth.

A rosary can be broken up throughout the day to bring us back to blessed thinking.

Elizabeth Clair Prophet, a metaphysical teacher and leader, talked to Mary often and received this new rosary from her in 1972. It is called the "Scriptural Rosary of the New Age" or "New Age Hail Mary" for short:

Hail Mary, full of Grace,
The Lord is with thee,
Blessed art thou among women
And blessed is the fruit of thy womb, Jesus
Holy Mary, Mother of God,
Pray for us, sons and daughters of God,
Now and at the hour of our victory
Over sin, disease and death.

My own inclusive version is:

Hail Mary, Full of Grace,
The Divine is with you,
Blessed are you among women
And blessed is the fruit of your womb, Jesus
Holy Mary, Mother of God,
Pray for us now and forever.
Amen.

Various Rosaries

The types of rosaries are as diverse as the people who use them. Believers can make their own rosary or purchase one that will fit their individual needs. Here is a sample of the variety of rosaries available:

- Pop bead or gumball rosaries for the younger set. The gumballs can be bitten off after each prayer. It makes a very large wad of gum at the end, but each prayer has its own chewy reward
- Flashing light, glow-in-the-dark, or luminous rosaries for late night devotions
- Rosary bracelets, rings, earrings, key chains, used as jewelry or accessories
- Rosaries with birthstones, various gems, and metals that match your outfit
- One decade rosaries, two decade rosaries or the traditional five decade rosaries
- Rosaries for teachers, nuns, priests, mothers, fathers, friends, newborns, boys, girls, brides, grooms, and for the whole family
- Chaplets and rosaries of individual saints, angels, and the Holy Family
- Rosary accessories, cases, pouches, and boxes
- Kits for making, cleansing, and repairing rosaries
- Personalized rosaries – antique, modern, and in between
- Rosaries for occasions: weddings, 1st communion, Easter, Christmas, and Advent
- Rosaries for the counting "on the bead" group and for the "between the bead" group
- Ladder rosaries
- Rosaries that are free and others for as much as you want to spend $,$$$,$$$
- They can be engraved, imprinted, and/or monogrammed
- Blessed rosaries for the living and on the site of the dead
- Mary apparition-blessed rosaries
- Holy rosary parts – blessed beads, blessed crucifixes, holy metal
- Designer rosaries
- Rosaries with a variety of crucifixes of different faith traditions
- Rosaries made of flowers, wood, and stones
- Black matte rosaries for our men and women in the armed forces - so it will not reflect light and alert the enemy where they are while they

say their devotions
- Digital rosaries - just push a button and it is said for you in either female or male voices
- Repeat after me rosaries that will get you started and stopped at the right time

So many to choose from!

Don't miss the Don Brown Rosary Collection which is reported to be *the* largest rosary collection with nearly 4,000 rosaries at the Spiritual Quest Gallery in Stevenson, Washington. Don Brown did not travel much, but these rosaries were sent to him from those who heard he was a collector. The Kennedy's sent him one (we are not told which Kennedy, but maybe it was Rose), one was blessed by Padre Pio, some blessed by the various Popes, and even Father Flannigan of Boys Town sent a blessed olivewood rosary.

My favorite of the collection is the "Rosary of Roses" which is made of tiny, handmade, red rose blossoms. Red roses for Our Blue Lady.

Rosary Online

For those who wish to have a high tech alternative to their regular rosary practice, there are websites. Just Google "Online Rosary" and you will see a variety of options to suit your unique situation.

One website has a checklist to click when finished with the different aspects of the rosary: the Hail Marys, the Our Fathers, and the Glory Bes. The check list takes the place of the beads. Just click after each spoken part, click to keep track of where you are, and click the final box when you are done. The five mysteries all have related pictures, by the decades, to add a visual experience as well.

With just another click, those who are unfamiliar with the rosary can see it written, or click again, and it is spoken. The website states that it is convenient for work or school. We certainly need the extra power of Mary during *those* times.

You can have the option of joining others around the world in an online rosary group or have a private session. Downloads are possible for MP3 players, phones, tablets, computers, or purchase a rosary DVD or Blu-ray for home. Apps, podcasts, and YouTube, are yet other options.

Media rosaries can be available multi-lingual, so language will never be a problem. Background music, such as Gregorian chants, are available for your rosary enhancement.

Whew, there is just no excuse for not being able to say the rosary any more; it is as easy as a click, touch, or swipe away. But, if the computer crashes, the electricity goes out, and your beads get lost, you can always use the old standby of your ten fingers to keep track of your rosary devotion.

The Miraculous Medal of Mary

One time, out of the blue, I received a Miraculous Medal of Mary in the mail. I immediately went to my jewelry box and found an unused gold chain so I could hang the new medal around my neck. I wasn't ignorant of its significance; I had heard about the miracles that occurred for the people who wore this medal. I was so thrilled to have one of these powerful pendants of my own. Unfortunately, I had never even seen one up close until that amazing day when Mary sent it to me for free.

The Miraculous Medal was originally called "The Medal of the Immaculate Conception." It was designed by the Blessed Virgin herself! There were three sightings of Mary in the story of how this came into being. The first apparition happened on the night of July 18th, 1830 in Paris, France, and because of this first sighting, it is said, that 1830 was the beginning of the Marian movement.

As the story goes, Sister Catherine Laboure was a barely literate, 24 year old novice in the community of the Daughters of Charity in Paris, France. On the night of July 18th, a mysterious five-year-old boy woke her while she was sleeping in the Motherhouse and asked her to go to the chapel. The boy was dazzling white, she recalls, and Catherine was afraid he would wake the other novices in the dormitory. He said to her, "Catherine, come to the chapel; the Blessed Virgin is waiting for you. Be calm, it is half past eleven, everyone is asleep; come, I am waiting for you." She finally followed the child into the chapel and began to pray.

As Catherine was praying in the chapel, she heard a rustle of a silk dress and she saw a beautiful woman sit in the Father Director's chair next to her. The beautiful woman had on an ivory-colored dress with a blue mantle and covering her head was a white veil that draped over her shoulders. Bright, jewel-like colors radiated from her hands. The boy-child announced boldly, "Here is the Blessed Virgin."

Catherine knelt before the Virgin and placed her hands in Mary's lap as she looked into her eyes. Then Mary spoke to her, "The good God, my child, wishes to entrust you with a mission. It will be the cause of much suffering to you, but you will overcome this, knowing that what you do is for the glory of God." They talked about the perils of France and the world as Mary spoke of the future and the next 40 years. Mary didn't expound on the mission that first night and it left Catherine bewildered what sort of mission was planned for her.

The second apparition happened in broad daylight in the chapel during the 5:30 p.m. prayers four months later, on November 27th. Sister Catherine saw Mary standing on a half globe, holding another golden globe in her hands and lifting it to heaven. The word "France" was written on the globe she held. Mary explained that even though it had only one country's name written on it, the globe symbolized the whole world. Again Mary was wearing a white robe of what seemed to be silk.

Streaming from Mary's fingers were rays of light and she said these rays symbolized the graces she provides for those who will ask. She also explained that some of the gems on the rings she wore, which were dark in color, were the graces no one asked for and remained available.

The third vision showed Mary again standing on a globe, crushing a snake beneath her feet, with her arms outstretched and dazzling rays of light shining forth from her fingers. There was an inscription: "O Mary, conceived without sin, pray for us who have recourse to thee." The vision of Mary turned around and the design on the back had 12 stars encircling a large "M" which rose from the cross. There were two flaming hearts and rising from them was a heart, circled in thorns, and another pierced with a sword.

Mary then told Catherine to have a medal created from this model and anyone who wore it, especially around his/her neck, would receive wonderful graces. Mary's final instruction to Sister Catherine was, "Now it must be given to the whole world and to every person."

Catherine explained these visions to her priest, Father John Marie Aladel, who secretly did not believe her. But finally, he had her write down, in great detail, the visitations, then took it to the archbishop in Paris in 1832. The archbishop immediately believed Catherine's report and gave permission to create the medal. It was a big hit. Before long, many healings, wonders, and deathbed conversions happened to those who wore the medal. Common people began calling it "The Miraculous Medal of Mary." Also, after these apparitions, Mary began to be called the "Queen of Heaven and Earth" – from the vision of her standing on the world.

Finally, in 1836, a Canonical investigation in Paris concluded that the apparitions were genuine. Sister Catherine remained anonymous as the one Mary called to the mission until just before her death, 47 years later. The sisters in her community were shocked to hear it was Catherine, who the Virgin came to see, since she had spent her life being "cold and apathetic," and unassuming. Sister Catherine died the last day of 1876 and was buried in the convent chapel in Paris where she first saw Mary.

You can purchase a "Miraculous Medal of Mary" easily these days at your local Catholic gift store or at numerous Miraculous Medal websites. There are various qualities and prices for these phenomenal medals of Mary. Some are even free, like the one I received, or you can purchase the more expensive medals and pay as high as several hundred or even several thousand dollars. These expensive medals are for those who want the turbo-charged medal of gold, with inlaid diamonds or jewels. All the different medals have the same design and equal power whether they are made of tin or gold with diamonds. Mary doesn't seem to care which medal you prefer – that is up to you, your taste, and wealth.

They are mighty, potent gifts – giving someone the opportunity to receive graces, healing, miracles, abundance, and love from Mary of the Miraculous Medal. They are accessible to anyone who cares to own one; even for me who just opened the mail one day and there it was – without even asking.

Hail Mary

In American football, there is a play called the "Hail Mary." This play is executed by the offense and is usually the last play at the end of the 4th quarter of the game. All the receivers run to the end zone and the quarterback throws the ball, hoping one of them will actually catch it in this last ditch effort to score. It is a pass made in desperation with only a hope and a prayer for success – the kind of play that would only succeed with the Divine Mother's intervention. The play has actually worked on quite a few occasions, to the great jubilation of the fans.

The first publicized Hail Mary play was on December 28, 1975 at the end of the Dallas/Minnesota playoff game when Dallas Cowboy quarterback Roger Staubach threw a pass that was caught by Dallas receiver Drew Pearson that won the NFC division title. The expression "Hail Mary" was coined for that play and posters of Drew's catch sold like hotcakes.

There was another divinely guided play in football named after Our Lady. It happened in the last few seconds of the divisional game between the Pittsburgh Steelers and the Oakland Raiders. The Raiders had the lead and there was only enough time for one last play, when Steelers' quarterback Terry Bradshaw threw the ball down the field. It bounced off the helmet of a player and Franco Harris caught it in midair, staying on his feet and running it in for a touchdown to win the title. The term "Immaculate Reception" was coined that day by Pittsburgh TV sportscaster Myron Cope and it has stuck ever since. You can see both of these amazing game-winning catches on YouTube in all their glory.

A "Hail Mary Shot" is when a photographer holds the camera high over his or her head in hopes the subject he or she is aiming at will actually appear in the photo. It can work particularly well in the case of large crowds, where the photographer is unable to have a clear line of vision or get close to the subject. When it works, it seems to be a case of pure luck or divine intervention, with Mary given the credit in the name itself.

A "Hail Mary" effort is now used in politics, war, and business to indicate a last-ditch, valiant, wing-and-a-prayer effort. Presumably, when her name is involved, the Divine Mother lends her spirit to the effort. It doesn't always guarantee success, but it just might help.

So when you are in great need and making one last, All-In effort, just say a prayer to The Virgin, put all your energy and resources into this do-or-die great attempt and Mary just may send you on to victory!

Mary, Mother of God

On June 22, 431, the Roman Catholic Church at the Counsel of Ephesus declared Mary, Mother of Jesus, was now to be known as the Mother of God.

"If anyone does not confess that the Emmanuel is truly God and therefore that the holy Virgin is the Bearer of God (Theotokos) since she begot according to the flesh the Word of God made flesh, anathema sit."

"Anathema sit" means excommunicated, eternal punishment, and condemnation. Strong words for opposing a theological concept, but, from then on, all counsels and Church doctrine officially refer to the Virgin Mary as "Theotokos," the "Mother of God."

This Catholic decree also states that Jesus was fully God, as well as fully human, thus, of two natures, Divine and human, united in a single person. Because of this, his mother is considered and declared to be the Mother of God.

After the Reformation and the beginning of Protestantism in 1517, a differing thought about who Mary was emerged on the theological horizon. The Protestants preferred the term "Christotokas," "Bearer of Christ," defining Mary as mother of Jesus in his humanity, not his deity; stating that God has no mother.

I remember seeing a bumper sticker once, "My Goddess is Your God's Mother." Before the Patriarchy, there was a Matriarchy and all deities were female Creators. Many believe that Mary was a Goddess and that only a Goddess could conceive such a holy child. Ancient myths speak of Goddesses conceiving male children by virtue of the Gods. Mary conceived the baby Jesus, as it is written, by virtue of the "spirit" of God. The Goddess scholars also know that is it possible for a Goddess to remain a virgin *and* mother at the same time. It is a feat that many may proclaim, but it is only the divinely touched that are called to such feats.

The New Age thought is that Mary is the feminine Christ Consciousness; that only a Christed person could beget a Christ. Only an ascended master or mistress could conceive, carry, and birth so much Divine light and love into the world.

We don't know the depth or the exact sacred nature of Mary, but her holiness is well known and widely regarded. The very fact that she continues to interact with us, even though she no longer walks this Earth in human form, is beyond our comprehension. We hear of no other person who continues to appear as much as Mary does to bring love and healing to this planet.

What does that say about her? We all have our various experiences and opinions: Mary as Bearer of Christ, Mother of God, The Goddess, or ascended, feminine Christ consciousness -- but does it really matter? What we all agree on is that we are astonished and deeply touched when she intercedes in our lives and that feeling her love for us is beyond anything imaginable. Thank you Mary, lover of God, Mother of us all.

The Long Quest to the St. Mary's Spring

On Haida Gwaii/Queen Charlotte Island in British Columbia, Canada near the town of Skidegate there is a natural spring dedicated to the Virgin Mary. It is said that if you drink from this spring, you will return to that place again within your lifetime.

The Queen Charlotte Island is now called Haida Gwaii because almost half of the population are Haida people. But most of the printed information calls the islands Haidi Gwaii/Queen Charlotte Islands to avoid confusion during the transition of the name.

The Haida Gwaii/Queen Charlotte Island St. Mary's Spring isn't well known throughout the world, but is well worth the trip. One woman who was returning to spread her husband's ashes by the spring says it is not an easy trek. From the northwest United States you drive to Port Angeles, Washington, on the northern edge of the Olympic Peninsula. (A side note: In 1791 a Spanish explorer Francisco de Eliza dubbed the port, Puerto de Nuestra Senora de los Angeles – Port of Our Lady of the Angels. Mary is indeed everywhere. It was later shortened and anglicized to Port Angeles Harbor.)

Take the 90-minute Black Ball Ferry ride to Victoria, British Columbia, Canada. You then travel across land to the next port, for a fifteen hour ferry ride, which takes you to another ferry for an additional 8 hour trip until you reach the British Columbia peninsula. It is quite a journey to return to Haida Gwaii/Queen Charlotte Island and the spring of St. Mary. It takes 25 plus hours from the most Northwestern corner of the United States to the spring. So if you do not live in northwest Canada, it can be quite far.

Be assured that Our Holy Mother will protect you the whole way. But remember, if you drink from the Haida Gwaii/Queen Charlotte Islands St. Mary's Spring, you are making quite a commitment for a long, arduous return journey sometime in the future. It is a glorious and beautiful pilgrimage, but you may want to bring a warm coat as it can get quite chilly on those holy nights way up north at St. Mary's Spring in Haida Gwaii, Canada.

Our Lady of Guadalupe Dashboard Magnet

One day, while at the Grotto gift shop in Portland, Oregon, I purchased a pewter, Virgin Mary dashboard magnet on a round, cherry wood base with a double-stick tape bottom. I like the thought of Mary guiding and protecting me as I drive, as well as the security from theft she may offer my vehicle.

With Grotto gift bag in hand, I walked out the door and saw a dead bird on the ground by the large display window of the gift shop. Apparently, the bird had flown into the window, with a terrible thud, breaking its neck, falling to the ground – dead. After offering a prayer of blessing for the bird's transition, I reentered the gift shop to tell the sales associate about it. She said, "Thank you," and assured me that she would call someone to take care of it; which probably meant a quick toss into the sacred Catholic dumpster by the grounds crew. Nevertheless, I was hoping the bird's body would be in loving care at this Monastery of our Sorrowful Mother, whose whole mission is about grief and death.

As I was walking out this time, a Sorrowful Mother priest in priestly black robes entered and we exchanged pleasantries about the cold weather. Since I believe and watch for synchronicity as a sign from Mary, I instantly thought about my newly purchased Virgin Mary car magnet and asked the priest to bless her for extra power. He graciously agreed and blessed my small icon. I was touched by the sincerity of his prayer, as if baptizing a newborn baby. Thanking the priest, I left again, passing the dead bird on the sidewalk; but this time I paused to thank it, for it caused me to return to the store and that ended with an official, cleric-blessed, Virgin Mary dashboard magnet.

So now my super-charged Lady of Guadalupe is stuck permanently to the middle of my dark gray dashboard. She helps me navigate life's traffic and roads of wonder. Mary's strong beacon of hope and grace gift my life with her powerful, pewter blessed presence.

Illness Strikes and the Medal of Healing

I got the annual flu again this year. It was a bad one. This flu took me out for three weeks, and I am still feeling the aftermath of its wrath as I write this. I was feeling so bad, I put my Miraculous Medal of Mary on a chain around my neck, asking for healing . . . or death. At that point I didn't care which came first. This Miraculous Medal looks like gold, but the plastic box that it came in says it is pewter. Gold pewter, huh, never heard of it. Must be a new blend of metal, whatever it needs to be, it is the medal's power I was seeking, not the quality of the metal at that point.

So it is working; each day I get a bit better from this scourge that hit me so hard – avoiding death, yet again. Each day I take shorter and fewer naps. At first, the routine was: up for breakfast, cold pills then a two-hour nap, lunch, two-hour nap, more cold pills, two-hour nap, dinner, two-hour nap, cold pills, and then bedtime, just to survive.

Finally, I only have to take one two-hour nap. After sanitizing it, I put my Miraculous Medal back in the plastic box, thanking Mary for her presence during my time of need. I also thanked her for a bed, sick time with pay, and the ability for my body to heal itself when all seemed hopeless.

Years later . . . I never opened the box again until my friend, Ambika, was taking a spiritual journey to Israel to finish her latest book. She allowed friends to give her a prayer or something to take with her to the Wailing Wall of this powerful city.

I gave her my gold-pewter Miraculous Medal on a chain. Ambika, a beautiful Jewish woman, told me later that she put it on at the beginning of her journey and did not take it off until she gave it to a woman in Jerusalem who had great need. She said it protected her from many a danger and fear while traveling throughout that war torn country. Mary now is back in her home land, helping another Jewish woman with the grace, healing, and strength of a powerful Jewish Mother.

Virgin Mary Sheds Tears of Blood

Dateline, Sacramento, CA – *News Flash* – Wednesday, November 17, 2005 – The outdoor statue of the Virgin Mary at the Vietnamese Catholic Martyr's Church at 10371 Jackson Road began to shed tears of blood from her left eye. The parish priest, thinking it was a hoax, wiped the tears clean, but over the weekend, they returned. The church maintenance man said he saw the tears flow miraculously again on Sunday morning around 8:30 a.m. He said he touched the statue and the tears were wet. In fact, there were so many tears, they stained her stone-white robe and pedestal on which she stood.

The parish priest took a sample of the tears and sent it for analysis. The Catholic Diocese has been contacted and a request made by the local priest; an investigation is under consideration.

As the days go by, Mary keeps crying and the crowds grow larger and larger, praying and staring at the statue. Pictures are taken; all are pondering the significance of the phenomena. Young, old, feeble, and healthy, all come to the Vietnamese Catholic Martyr's Church statue with prayers, candles, flowers, or just to see the sight.

No matter why the people come, all wonder if it is real or a hoax. Many are speculating that Mary is upset, sad, calling us to prayer for the present state of affairs, or in grief about what the future may hold. Some think it is an elaborate hoax of the Catholic Church to bring back the lost sheep. Others say it is someone playing a joke and standing in the bushes, laughing at the fools who believe. No one knows for certain, but just in case it is a miracle, people are giving it the benefit of the doubt that she is making this statue cry for some very good reason. They may even be tears of joy over how well we are all doing. But since there is no direct contact in words, we are left to our own conclusions.

This isn't the first time that an icon, statue, or painting of the Mother of Jesus has shed tears. On February 18, 2003 in Chittagong, Bangladesh, it was reported the Mother Mary statue at the Church of the Virgin Mary's Birth was crying red tears. Scientists, looking for a scientific explanation, said, that since the statue was enclosed in a glass case, the tears were probably condensation flowing down the face of Mary. The believers did not believe the scientists. She has been under glass for a very long time with no tears flowing before; this was definitely a miracle.

Bangladesh is 90% Muslim and once the newspapers printed the story with the photos, the overwhelming interest of the Muslims to see this statue cry made for throngs of visitors in this obscure, tiny Catholic church. That was a miracle in itself.

At the time of the crying Virgin, Bangladesh was seeing terribly violent times. It was said by the parishioners that Mary was moved to tears by the horrific conditions of the country and her people. The tears seem to stop flowing for a bit; then everyone wondered about that too. Again, people stopped to ponder, pray, and focus on the phenomena of Mary. At least they ceased fighting long enough to ask: "What could this mean?"

Several years ago, June 30, 1985, the Virgin Mary statue owned by Julia Kim in Naju, Korea, began to weep. At first it was clear liquid and when tested by scientists, it was found to be human tears. Later on, this same statue that had wept clear tears, began weeping red, bloody tears. This continued for some time, but then, miraculously, the tears turned into a flow of fragrant rose oil.

Again, everyone was looking for an explanation. Julie Kim's house became a shrine and strangers would knock on her door to see and pray in front of the crying Virgin Mary statue in her living room. Julia knew if Mary had chosen her statue to cry, it was crystal clear Mary wanted her to open her house to those who sought her. Joy filled that house from morning to night, with guests from many countries seeking the grace of the Virgin. I often wondered why Julie didn't just set the Virgin Mary statute outside for easier access for the masses. But instead, she just opened the doors of her house in holy hospitality.

Red tears, clear tears, rose tears, what, oh Mary, does it all mean that you would go to such trouble for us? We listen to your messages with great concern, knowing you love us so. Open our ears, our hearts, to have an inner knowledge of what your message is and please give us the strength to do what needs to be done to stop your grief and ours as well.

Thrift Store Mary

When I shop with Mary during the week and my money is low, we go to thrift stores. While living in Portland, Oregon, I find Oregonians very committed to recycling. They recycle everything: plastic, appliances, paper, glass, clothing, pets, books, furniture, and cars. I have even seen the homeless people recycle – putting their trash into the blue or green bins. It is not uncommon to be driving down the street and seeing a washing machine in front of someone's house with a "Free" sign on it. When you return that afternoon, it will be gone. Everyone is very generous with his or her unwanted surplus.

So, when I say to you Mary and I went to a thrift store, it isn't just a small store in a run down part of town. In Portland and surroundings, they have Thrift Super Stores. They are huge: six dressing rooms, a book section that is larger than most independent bookstores, and a drive-thru, drop-off station with an attendant to take the stuff out of the trunk, who hands you a donation tax slip without you even getting out of your car. Wow! What a find when Mary showed me these stores.

One store in town even has an Outlet Thrift Store! For the bargain, bargain shopper. This large thrift store "chain" throws everything in large bins for customers to dig through. It is wise to wear gloves as you rummage through looking for great bargains. Locals call this place "The Bins." They sell everything by the pound: a pound of shirts, a pound of pants, a pound of scarves, etc. Handbags are 50 cents, belts are 10 for a quarter. Most items are sold depending on their weight – "Mary bargains" by the pound.

Downtown has a designer thrift store amid the high-rise buildings. On a lunch hour one could pick up a pre-owned Coach, Louis Vuitton, or Balenciaga purse for pennies on the dollar. It is quite different from any other thrift store; more like a designer boutique instead of the usual warehouse full of unwanted items.

Mary and I love to go to the local thrift stores. She always teaches me to look for quality as well as value. The one advantage with thrift shopping is that you can actually see how a piece of clothing or fabric stands up to repeated wear, washing, and drying. Some don't do so well, others are like new. What a thrill to find a garment or item that is perfect in every way, for just a few dollars or cents, as the case may be. When I am wearing my thrift store find, I strut, knowing what a deal I got and I thank Mary for her great thrifty, shopping sense.

Edible Virgin Mary!

The Virgin Mary image seems to show up at just the right time, and, sometimes, even in unique culinary places . . . but please try not to eat her!

Toasted Cheese Mary

Diane Duyer took a bite of a grilled cheese sandwich she had made for herself one day in 1994, and when she bit in, she noticed a face. It was the Virgin Mary looking up at her from the toasted bread of the sandwich. She was so shocked that she didn't eat the rest of the sandwich, but put it in a clear plastic box, surrounded by cotton balls (?). She placed the box on the nightstand by her bed and left it there for 10 years!

Surprisingly, the sandwich did not deteriorate during those years of sitting on her nightstand. No mold or decomposition of any kind. You probably wouldn't want to eat it, but it was still intact, nevertheless.

After 10 years, Ms. Duyer was willing to part with the Virgin Mary sandwich and placed an ad on eBay. At first, eBay rejected the ad, thinking that it was a hoax, but Duyer convinced the eBay police that, indeed, there was a picture of the Virgin Mary on her old grilled cheese sandwich and she was, indeed, ready to sell it.

Finally, eBay agreed that it fit with their standards of practice and the sandwich was auctioned off to an online casino called GoldenPalace. com for $28,000. The representative for GoldenPalace.com stated they intended to sell it for charity sometime in the future.

Mary in the Watermelon

Mary Lou Robles was working at the snack bar at the Calipatria State Prison, when she cut open a watermelon and saw the image of the Virgin Mary. She knew something good was going to happen now that the Blessed Mother had appeared to her. Her co-workers urged her to just throw it away, but Mary Lou's mother and daughter were more supportive. They knew a miracle when they saw one. Apparently, she has kept it to this day. We all wonder what shape it may be in by now, but only Mary Lou knows for sure.

Virgin in Lemon Mold

Marty Nance was cutting lemons in preparation for his shift at Texas Billiards, near Dallas, Texas, when he noticed the mold on one lemon was in the shape of the Virgin Mary. He cut off the mold and froze it. Marty's parents, who own the bar, were proud of his find. Marty showed his sacred slice of frozen fruit to a chaplain who frequents the bar, but he just stammered around and left without saying a coherent word. Marty and his wife knew it was a message to him, a special gift he now keeps in his freezer for others to see and photograph. He feels blessed by the touch of Mary.

Additional food reports include: a pancake with the image of the Virgin seen by an individual in Glendale, Arizona; a peanut that looks like Mary was found by a man in an undisclosed location; the Virgin's image was seen in a piece of hard, Christmas candy in Toledo, Ohio.

Mary in More Unlikely Places

The Virgin Mary not only uses food to communicate her messages to us, but ...

In south Burbank, California – Shirley McVane, an 81 year old woman claims the pattern on the underbelly of one of her pet turtles looks just like the Virgin Mary. As the turtle developed, the image came into even better focus. At first, her friends didn't believe her, but when they turned the turtle over, they agreed . . . it looked like the Blessed Mother. Shirley McVane changed the name of the turtle to Mary – and the companion turtle she named Joseph.

In Limerick, Ireland – a freshly cut stump is shaped like the figure of the Virgin Mary.

In Durham, North Carolina – the image of the Virgin Mary appeared on the guest bedroom door of the Martinez's home while a friend was spending the night. Mrs. Martinez mentioned the image to three neighbors, and by Sunday, 300 people came to look at the door. The homeowners welcome all who want to come see the Virgin miracle and Mrs. Martinez said many are still bringing flowers and candles, kneeling and praying at her blessed, guest room door.

In New Mexico – a woman found the likeness of the Virgin in the marble above her bathtub.

In Bogota, Colombia – the Virgin's form appeared on the surface of a grocery store parking lot.

In Virginia – parishioners saw the appearance of the Virgin Mary in the church's baptismal pool.

In California – Mary's image appeared on a restaurant food griddle.

In Bronx, New York – the Virgin Mary's likeness is on a tree trunk.

In Monterey, California – after a motorcycle accident, the man's road rash on his knee cap looked just like the Virgin Mary. It is a gruesome sight but on the internet for all to see.

In your hometown . . .

Holy Mother

While friends were over at my house visiting one day, the subject of the recent news of the Virgin Mary statue crying tears of blood in California came up in conversation, just out of the blue . . . I didn't even bring it up. One man said, "I just love Mary." My ears perked up, but then the conversation went on to other subjects since several people were talking at once and the focus of the group was continually changing.

I remembered, and when there was a lull in the conversation, I asked him, "You said you loved Mary. I love Mary also. Did you have a Mary experience?"

"Yes," he said after a moment of thought, "I was a pot boy at the St. Joseph Hospital in Northern Ontario. I was about 12 years old. One night, after I finished washing all the pots in the kitchen, I joined the nuns in evening prayers in the chapel. My life was very difficult at the time. My father was a binge drinker and I was so mad at my mother for failing to protect me from him. That night was particularly hard; I was sobbing in the pew as the nuns were praying. I looked up at the Virgin Mary statue on the right side of the altar and suddenly a bright white light surrounded the statue. Mother Mary actually said to me, 'It's going to be alright, I am your Mother.' An incredible calm came over me," he said. "I knew from that time on that Mother Mary was my mother and all would be ok and you know what? It was."

He said he kept the vision to himself for quite some time before sharing it with anyone else. He finally told his favorite nun what had happened that lonely evening in the chapel. She confirmed his vision and said, "Miracles do happen." He was lucky to have such a nun confirming his Mary experience.

My own mother died several years ago. Sometimes we all just need to talk to our mother, tell her about our day, feel her unconditional love, be praised, or ask for advice. Maybe we didn't have such love from our birth mother, but we can have tremendous love and peace with this Holy Mother. I can feel Mary's motherly love, caring, and healing touch anytime I ask. It may be why many are curious and search out Mary, mother of Jesus; she seems to embody the celestial mother we all need.

When Jesus was dying on the cross, he told Mary that John, the beloved disciple, was now her son and to John he said that Mary was his mother. Many take this offering to mean that Jesus gave Mary to us all, as our mother, and we were given to her as her children. Others think this was Jesus' "coming out" to his mother on how important John really was to him. This is the point they became family.

We all need a home base, a stabilizing sanctuary of never-ending love – family. When we see her as the Holy Mother, her maturity, wisdom, strength, and love are ours. As a virgin, her youth and innocence are apparent. How much she can change in our many seasons of knowing and understanding her. Her universal spirit sooths us as we feel agony, distress, and weakness. She strengthens our fledgling spirits, sees and continues to love us even at our worst, puts us back together again, bundles us up, and sends us out into the world again to face, sometimes, a very difficult life. Then we return to tell of our triumphs and she is proud of our bravery, rejoicing with us with tenderness, knowing that her place in our hearts and lives is vital in our unending growth.

Happy, Holy Day, Mary! Thank you for being there.

Joseph, an Old Friend and Guide

Many years ago, when I was first exploring my ability to receive guidance from angels, guides, and higher dimensions, I asked if there was someone of the light of God who was for my highest and best who would talk and work with me. I sat at my computer and waited. Not very long after my prayer, I heard words coming into my consciousness and as I paid attention to them I began to type whatever came to mind. They were lovely words of guidance. Then the message came to an end and I asked for a name of who had been talking to me. The name surprised me. "Joseph," was what he said. I thought I may have made it up. But I knew I didn't have such wise and powerful things to say.

Joseph has been consistent from that day forth and always, as the communications ended, he would close with a salutation, "Joseph." I didn't really know which Joseph he was, but I had a sense that he was the husband of Mary. I communicated daily with Joseph for several years. I have it all saved on an old, black and white, Apple Power Book computer. It was one of the first laptops ever and I was thrilled to have such a convenient portable computer so I was able to record my conversations with him.

But, life happened; as time passed, I got busy and distracted with activities and had less and less time to devote to my writings and guidance from Joseph. The connection just faded away; I didn't even notice that I missed it. I went to school, began my angel work, and was very busy talking to other Divine beings. I just forgot about Joseph.

Years later, I had a bad flu bug which turned into a lingering sinus infection and bronchitis that required two rounds of antibiotics. I was so sick that I just couldn't do anything but the basics to survive: eat, sleep, work a little, sleep, eat, work a bit more, sleep, sleep, sleep. I didn't want to quit working all my jobs, so I continued to do what I could to get by.

One day, I was at the metaphysical bookstore where I did angel readings, telling them I was still too sick to work when the crystal healer walked by me. She stopped in her tracks as she passed and said, "Kermie, there is a man in front of you with his hand stretched out on your upper chest telling you to stop, similar to a mid-city traffic cop holding back traffic in a busy intersection. You are so sick, he said, that if you don't stop working and just do bare essentials the worst is going to happen. 'You haven't seen anything yet,' he says." That got my attention! I knew it was true. I had been fighting this illness, but continued to go to my part-time day job as best I could and hadn't taken the complete rest I needed to heal myself.

After a few weeks of concentrated rest, I was feeling better and I asked the crystal reader to reconnect with the man she saw and ask how I was doing; was I on the road to recovery? She tuned in and gave me another message from him. She said he had backed off a little and was standing over to the side. The man said he was going to be working with me again and he was an old friend. I then asked her his name and she said, "His name is Joseph."

I was awestruck and began to cry. I was so glad he was present and made himself known to me again. She said he was telling me to "take care" and he had a cloth over his head to guard against the wind and cold. It was cold out, just coming up to Thanksgiving. I had scarves, but hadn't begun to wear them yet, just too busy to bother, but I heeded his message and began to wear my scarves as prayer covers to stave off the cold weather. I have been talking to him ever since. What a joy to talk to them both, Mary *and* Joseph.

Joseph, Husband of Mary

We don't hear much about Joseph, the husband of Mary and the man who raised Jesus. In one Catholic homily he was titled: "Joseph, Jesus' foster father." He is probably considered, by our modern day labels, to be Jesus' step dad. That is, of course, if you believe Jesus was conceived by Mary and the fertile spirit of God. That being the case, did Joseph have to adopt Jesus or was it a family secret Joseph wasn't the biological father until after Jesus' death and the Divine progeny truth emerged? We really don't know and is it really that important what paternal name Joseph had during his lifetime?

What we do know, however, is one of the chief roles Joseph performs as Mary's husband is protector of his small family. The biblical story states an angel of the Lord, in a dream, tells Joseph not to be afraid, to marry his pregnant fiancé, and not to send Mary away. In another dream, after the three wise, Magi-men leave Bethlehem, an angel directed Joseph to quickly flee to Egypt with Mary and baby – to keep Jesus from being murdered by King Herod.

After Herod died, Joseph again listened to an angel dream informing him it was safe for them to return to Israel. But Joseph, being worried about Herod's son, who was the new ruler, had one more angel dream where he was directed to go to Galilee and live in the security of a town called Nazareth. So we *do* know Joseph kept them out of harms way by listening to angels in his dreams! The question might come up – why did angels have to come to Joseph in his dreams when Mary had a full-on, awake visitation, complete with dialogue including questions and answers with her angel Gabriel? Our special Mary, uh huh.

Nevertheless, Joseph was a very significant man in Mary's life – her husband, provider, and protector; yet at best, we can only speculate about him further. It is common, biblical scholar theory, however, that Joseph was an older man, a carpenter who taught Jesus that trade and died when Jesus was still young. We think Joseph died sometime after he found Jesus in the temple listening and questioning the teachers when he was twelve years old.

We also assume his marriage to Mary was arranged probably by the patriarch of the family or the temple authorities, as was customary at the time in Jewish life. Boy, he didn't know what he was getting in to . . . or did he?

I was sitting at an event in a church right after Thanksgiving one year. I was bored and tried not to stare at anyone while my mind daydreamed. I noticed, after a while, I was absentmindedly gazing at a faceless, gold, paper mache figure with a staff sitting on a table alone. Somehow, I knew that it was Joseph. But where was the Mary and Child? I usually see Joseph at the manger scene this time of year, but this night, no mother, no baby Jesus; he was just standing by himself holding his protective pole.

I started to think, why do I instinctively know this is Joseph, the husband of Mary? I knew it wasn't a shepherd, even though he had a shepherd's stave. So in my dreamy, bored state, I pondered why I recognized this rough, artist's rendition as Joseph.

Curiously, when I talk to Joseph, I have a tingling on the back, left side of my head. It is his way to let me know he is close. When I was looking at the paper mache man and thought it might be Joseph, the back left side of my head began to tingle – a lot! I said hello to my old friend, and thanked him for my visceral confirmation and for being the focus of my mindless gaze, bringing my attention back to him.

When I finally got up to leave at the end of the event, I did see a gold, paper Mache Mary behind a box in the corner as I passed. Ahhh, it really was Joseph and there was Mary to confirm my speculation – not far from her man.

Thanksgiving with *My* Holy Family

My partner and I decided to have Thanksgiving my way this year since we had her family visit for the holidays the last two years. I like a cozy holiday, usually with my beloved, staying warm and enjoying holiday feasts. So, when we were offered the use of a coastal Oregon cabin for a few days by a friend who was going out of town, we jumped at the chance. We loaded up all our Thanksgiving groceries, suitcases and off we went to the rainy, chilly, and pristine Oregon coast for Thanksgiving by ourselves. Or at least, so we thought.

It turned out to be an enchanted little cabin with a hot tub outside in the woods. We were in a bit of heaven after such a busy and stressful year. The night before Thanksgiving, my partner fell asleep on the couch with her head on my lap. I had bought Lady of Guadalupe and Sacred Heart of Jesus candles at the grocery store when we were grocery shopping and had them lit in the living room. Some Christmas lights were on and scattered throughout the house and yard. Our hostesses leave them up all year for the festive feeling they give. It was like a magical fairyland inside and out and one could see, through the large window in our secluded getaway, colored lights twinkling in the gentle rain.

I was half meditating and praying my thanks as I massaged my lover's head while she slept when I noticed the flames of the two candles flickering without any cause. No breeze anywhere. But I knew intuitively that Mother Mary, Jesus, and Joseph were all in the room with us. Their presence was very powerful and love flooded the space. What a surprise to be visited by all three at once. I basked in their presence and was deeply touched that *my* family, my Holy Family, had come to be with us for Thanksgiving. I cried, talked, and prayed with them that evening – just as if we were meeting again for the holidays after a long absence. My partner slept and I leaned back and was bathed in Divine love. I cried softly with so much love in my heart. I later told her that we had holy visitors; she understood the significance of their coming, grateful that I had time alone with them as she slept.

I kept the candles lit the whole Thanksgiving holiday. The flames of the candles shown brightly in the woods through the windows and greeted us as we came back from our chilly, coastal walks, welcoming us again to our enchanted sanctuary. There was a presence that weekend which was soothing and quietly intense. We both felt renewed and revitalized as we returned to our daily lives in the city.

Indeed, we had been with our other family, *my* family this holiday season. I even found a small, white, ceramic statue soon after of the Holy family with Joseph hovering protectively behind Mary and child with tiny pink roses draped around the scene. His strong presence in the figurine was as if to tell me that he was also protecting me as he had just re-entered my life after a long time apart due to my lack of attention to him. Their presence extended far beyond that particular Christmas because this figurine has been the focal point of my Christmas holidays for many years since.

Writing This Book

While writing this book, I have had very limited funds for any extras in my life. I am working as a per diem Occupational Therapist and that seems to cover my mortgage payment and some household expenses. My readings and teaching classes cover the TV show, school, and business expenses I have. That is about all there is. The rest of the time I write. I love writing and it is a gift to have the time to do this. Working with Mary is worth living with low funds.

I try to save my pennies and go to garage sales whenever possible so I can actually buy myself something once in awhile. Then I don't feel like I am doing *all* volunteer work or in too much deprivation. I will stop at a thrift store, occasionally, to see what they have in the way of skirts or some clothing I need for under $10.

Mary and I went to a thrift store the other day and it was a very big stretch for me to purchase three skirts and a jacket. It was going to take all the money in my pocket, but it was one of those many good days with Mary. Someone had donated several pieces of quality clothing that happened to be my size and color.

So, I trusted and went to the check out stand, refiguring my purchase to make sure I had the proper amount. As the friendly cashier was ringing up my purchases, she commented on what great deals I was getting. I looked at the prices she was ringing up and they all rung up *half* the already low ticket price! How did that happen? Apparently, everything I had put in my basket was marked with a blue tag which meant half price that day!

The total was a few cents over $10!! My thrift store budget was still in tack. Mary is the best. She teaches me again and again that it is all about trusting – even if it seems it won't work out, but walking forward, by taking the action; that is all that is required. I love my new clothes, especially since they come with a small financial miracle.

Ceremony in St. Mary's Chapel

After performing a rite of blessing for a musician and her instrument at the St. Mary's Chapel on The Grotto grounds in Portland, Oregon, we were packing up to leave when we noticed men in the aisle, holding unlit candles, crawling on their knees towards the statue of the Virgin Mary. It was a good 1500 feet from door to altar railing and they grimaced in pain with each knee step they took on the solid marble floor which led to the Virgin's feet.

I wondered how many times they must have done this kneeling pilgrimage. They were Latino men followed by adolescent boys, maybe family members, who participated as well in this sacrificial parade. They were quiet and prayerful as they slowly proceeded up the aisle.

There were three of us in our ritual ceremony, me (the officiator), the beautifully clad musician with her flute, and her boyfriend, who was also the photographer. It was a moving and quiet ceremony, with a certificate of bonding marking the seven years this sacred musician had been with this beloved flute – showering music and healing to adoring audiences – big and small. It wasn't really a flute but a Shaw, low D, Irish whistle, she explained. During the ceremony, the musician played her whistle, and with the phenomenal chapel acoustics, the music could have been recorded that very minute; it was so beautiful.

But then to have men walking up the center aisle on their knees after the ceremony was icing on the blessed, ritual cake. Mary was there that day greeting all who came to her. Thank you, Mary, for the devotedness of your followers, ever reminding us to continue to come to you – whether we run, walk, crawl or are carried.

Keep What You Love, Get Rid of the Rest

Feng Shui experts are in agreement about the importance to love everything that you own. If you love everything you possess, it will nurture you. If someone keeps something which isn't loved, or saves it out of obligation because it was a gift, the object drains the current owner's energy. The gift doesn't nourish – it does the opposite – it makes one weary.

Saying that, one of Mary's biggest lessons I am learning from shopping with her is that I need to *absolutely love* the item I am about to purchase; or I am better off leaving it in the store. It is true with relationships, cars, jobs, food, and all else in my life, as well.

Price has nothing to do with it. I bought a Coach purse for $25 at a garage sale, a beloved and functional item. Later I bought a beautiful scarf at a thrift store for 50 cents. The price wasn't what swayed my decision on any of my purchases. I loved them so much and was thrilled to be able to own them both. But, even after saying this, I *do* get a thrill paying less money for quality items I adore.

I think Mary probably gets a kick out of helping me find these treasures, and when they are affordable to me, I am so tickled. I am grateful to have such richness in my life. It is hard to remember this lesson when the price is so *very low* or the item is *almost* right. I have to say no and trust something better will come along which is *totally right*. And you know what . . . it always, always does.

Mary's Miraculous Medal in the Mail

I received another package in the mail today; in it were *five* sets of Mary miraculous medals and a form to sign up to be a promoter; the cost was only 25 cents. (!) For merely a quarter, promoters have prayers said for them several times a year at the altar of the statue of Mary at the Miraculous Medal church in Pittsburgh, Pennsylvania. Not only that, but the enclosed letter said a "Pittsburgh priest and other approved fathers" take an annual pilgrimage and more prayers are said for you at the original Miraculous Medal Chapel in Paris, France. (!!)

The Miraculous Medal package also included a computer letter signed by Sister Francoise, Daughter of Charity, and a small book about Catherine Laboure, *The Saint of Silence*. It is the story of Catherine Laboure's life – with much detail regarding the instructions Mary gave her which led to the making of the miraculous medal. The book has color photos of the chapel, a narrative by Catherine explaining what she told her confessors, and a copy of a page of her hand written journal detailing the conversation with the Blessed Mother. (!!!)

In the form letter, Sister Francoise invites me to visit the chapel whenever I am in Paris. I just may do that. If you want to go, the address is 140 rue du Bac, 75340 Paris Cedex 07, France. It is good to know they will let anyone visit and one does not have to be an "approved father" to say prayers at the altar. The Paris nun invites all to come see the statue and the holy place where Mary beamed her multi-colored graces from her out stretched hands onto Catherine Laboure.

Holding one of the medals, I could feel those generous graces, not only from Mary, but also from the Daughters of Charity and the Pittsburgh priests. Thank you for such a bright and marvelous gift on this gloomy, Portland day – all for 25 cents. (!!!!)

Mary's House

Mary's house miraculously moved from Nazareth on May 10, 1291 and landed in a field by Dalmatia at Tersatto – all in one piece. The governor of Dalmatia sent investigators to Nazareth to the Basilica of the Annunciation which covered Mary's home before they found it sitting in their field. All they found was the foundation and it matched exactly the 15 by 30 foot house in Dalmatia. It was even made from the same building materials as the original home.

Then, just as miraculously as it came, it moved again, in 1295, to the middle of the road near Loreto, Italy. This time it stayed . . . so far. This house is called the Santa Casa and inside is an altar, a hearth, and a statue of the Virgin Mary. It has a single door and one small window. A later Pope sanctioned the addition of more doors to accommodate the many visitors coming and going. Also a fortified church was built around the Holy House, called "The Santuario della Santa Casa." If you want to go see Mary's house in Loreto, Italy, you had better hurry before it takes off again; Mary's incredible flying house.

Writing Retreat

My partner and I were asked to go with friends to a cross country ski weekend in the mountains of Oregon. It was the middle of winter, so I thought, "Oh great, two days of uninterrupted writing while my partner and the hostesses go cross-country skiing. Ahhh . . . silence . . . in a cozy cabin nestled in the snowy mountains." It didn't happen.

First day, I slept in late and my partner said, "It's snowing and I need to go get chains or I will worry about getting snowed in. I have to make sure I can be back to work in a couple of days." I actually agreed; so we dug out and off we slid to Les Schwab in the nearest little town to buy chains. We ended up going grocery shopping for the group and sliding, digging, and slopping around the resort town all day. No time to write *or* be in solitude.

Next day, it continued to snow too much for good cross country skiing so everyone stayed in and played games, cooked, and talked. There was too much noise and activity in the cabin to spend any time writing, contemplating, or meditating. So it was a social day – a time with friends, eating, laughing, and loving the snow and each other. It was great, but not what my soul craved. I craved alone time – a time to write, to be with Mary, and a time to be in Divine presence.

I got the message loud and clear. If I want a writing retreat . . . go alone! I can do that. Just get out, show up, and find places to write that offer meals, or, even better – a kitchenette. Quiet time to plug in my computer and write, hike, write, walk, write, be in nature, and write, write, write. Ahhhhhh . . .

I found a retreat center close to Portland called Mt. Angel Abbey. It is available for large groups and private retreats. It also has a theological library for study and research. Wonderful! I visited one day to check it out and to take pictures of angels for my TV show, *Kermie & the Angels*.

They only had two angels; one was a guardian angel statue under a leafless, winter tree and the other was a relief on the wall above an entrance. I expected a retreat center with the name "Mt. Angel" to have many more angels about. Wrong again. Mt. Angel was the mountain nearby. But I did find a statue of the Virgin Mary, on a pedestal overlooking a pond, ringed with mossy stones, set against the wooded, Oregon backdrop. She had her hands palms out, as if unloading her graces into the still waters of the small pond. But, alas, even though the Abbey was beautiful, catered to all food restrictions and individual needs, I never had or made the time to actually go to such a perfect retreat center.

Still pondering back home about where my writing retreat would be and where would I find the time to go, I visited my favorite Portland tea shop to write. This tea shop also serves lovely vegetarian dishes and a sundry of domestic and exotic teas. You can stay there for hours, sipping tea and snacking on a variety of culinary goodies. As I was sitting, absorbing the Zen atmosphere, soothed by the waterfall wall, and watching young couples come and go, I kept writing. I began to think, this "writing retreat" in my hometown has cost me a mere $8 for cranberry-orange tea and a hummus plate with cucumbers and kamatra olives. The candles illumine the wooden tables with bamboo placemats and the sound of Peruvian music softly drifts in the background. My writing retreat time has begun – unexpectedly!

I realized at that moment, I would catch time to write . . . whenever . . . wherever it is presented to me. My *scheduled* retreat writing times have had the same result as the cozy cabin in the mountains – just never worked out; not that it wasn't a grand idea, but here I sit, writing in between life. Or does life happen in between writing? YES. I can have a writing retreat for a few hours wherever I am. I don't have to stop my life so I can write, but write – no matter what! And this is all within budget.

Thank you, Mary, for showing me this wonderful writing retreat life that I live now every day. As someone wiser once said, "Writers really don't need the time, money, or a room to write, they only need to write." Amen sister.

I now have two writing bags, one for my mini-computer and the other that holds a small journal. Writing on the go means stopping to write wherever I am: in a parking lot waiting for a friend, on a plane, under a tree, in a church, in the waiting room, at the mall, before a concert, while attending a party, or just at home in between the laundry, dinner, and taking out the trash.

Thank you, Mary, for my multitude of mini writing retreats. Someday, I will be able to put together the time and money to go with you to an actual retreat center. But, I may just get distracted by the lovely grounds, contemplative activities, or by examining all the spiritual books at the retreat library or bookstore.

Mary Pendulum

I always wear my Miraculous Mary Medal around my neck and sometimes I use it as a pendulum. When I need to make an important decision about something, I take off my necklace, let the pendant dangle loosely while I hold it between my thumb and middle finger and ask a question. If it moves in a circle, that is a yes, if it goes side to side, that signifies a no. Sometimes it doesn't move at all, which I take as, no comment. This is kinesiology, a form of energy information that many in the field of alternative medicine use, but I use it to talk to Mary sometimes when I am in a place where we just can't sit and chat.

One Sunday while out for brunch, the server greeted us at the table and announced the special of French toast with blueberries and walnuts. I took off my necklace, held the chain between my index finger and thumb, dangled the Mary-pendent over the table and asked if it was for the highest and best to eat the French toast? Mary has never once swung in a circle "Yes" over my French toast with blueberries and walnuts request at Sunday brunch. I am forever hopeful, though, that Mary will grace me with a positive circle swing on the sweet confection . . . maybe next Sunday morning. But it is true French toast is not good for me: the wheat flour, the sugar, and the fat. Even though I know that, I check to see if she ever changes her mind. It never happens . . . so far.

I know, of course too, I have total free will and can and do make my own decisions, but it is good to have her as my consultant on these iffy questions. The server came back to the table to take our order and asked what the pendulum said. "No, to the French Toast," I said and ordered a nutritious and delicious brunch. We all nodded in agreement, knowing how hard it is to do the right thing for our bodies sometime. But I always have Mary along as my swinging guide to help with better purchases.

Joseph with the Baby Jesus

I was reading an article in *Time* magazine recently and it talked about the increasing popularity of Joseph, husband of Mary. The article said Joseph was a modern role model for men, being the first "Promise Keeper." His claim to fame is he took Mary to be his wife even though she was pregnant with someone else's child, supported her, and raised Jesus to be his own son; giving him a trade and a secure home. The article talked about Joseph's Divine calling to care for this special child, for Mary, his wife, and for bringing them all together as one Holy Family. I would imagine his bravery to break social and religious cultural structure influenced his son, knowing it is of the highest work to take the way of spiritual truth over the human made, religious laws of the times.

I have found several pictures and statues of Joseph over the years. Today I am sitting in front of a statue of Joseph holding the baby Jesus in his left arm. He has stalks of lilies gripped in his right hand and it is outstretched, as if bringing Mary a bouquet. Joseph, in this image, is bearded and young. He has no candles at his feet venerating him, though, unlike the Virgin Mary statue on the other side of the chapel where many people are sitting, knelling, and praying. There are candles galore at Mary's feet, burning prayer bright in the afternoon light.

Actually, I was intending to sit in front of Mary's statue to write today, but there is no room left, and, as fate would have it, there is an electrical plug for my computer on the floor next to the pew in front of Joseph. It was meant to happen. Joseph's statue has much more room to spread out and work undisturbed.

The acoustics of this chapel are so good that you can hear my fingers typing from choir loft to altar. I hope I am not disturbing anyone. Everyone seems to be in prayer or contemplation within themselves and, hopefully, they don't even notice my tippy, tap, tap, tippy tap, tapping.

Outside, on the way out the door is a relief, in stone, depicting Jesus being baptized by John and a male, bearded God coming through the clouds with his finger pointing towards the sky, I assume, towards heaven. God, in this relief, looks a lot like the Pope in the movie *Brother Sun, Sister Moon* in the scene when the Pope is so touched by St. Francis' words of scripture that he shifts into Divine (un)consciousness and his index finger begins to rise slowly up into the air, pointing towards the roof.

Another Mary cement scene is outside the chapel on the corner in a nook, two stories up, out of reach. Joseph is no where to be seen out here, only the one statue inside. It is good to sit with Joseph periodically, even though I am beginning to talk to him on a daily basis. He has always been Mary's silent partner in all the spiritual drama; I am glad he is rising in popularity for his own honorable deeds. So I leave him now, feeling his fatherly love and protection as I reenter the world on this Oregon damp and misty day.

Carpet Stain Mary

We are selling our house to move to England where my partner has received an amazing job promotion. It starts in only a month, so there is much to do. I hope to find work, write, and visit any and all sacred sites of Mary in Europe. We will be there for 6 years – the length of her contract.

We received an offer on the house fairly quickly, but the following weekend a very large rain storm hit from the north. It rained horizontal sheets of water and winds gusted up over 110 miles per hour, the news reported. Some say it was a storm like none before. "Rain came into places that had never seen rain before," people said, and this is the Northwest; these folks know their rain.

The next day a friend and I went to an early lunch and while we were eating at an Indian restaurant, the server informed us that the kitchen and some of the dining area had flooded during the storm last night and they needed to wet-vac on the other side of the room before the lunch crowd came. They apologized for the noise and inconvenience.

We had window seats and apparently the water had not come in those windows, only through the north side of the building where the kitchen was. They too shook their heads saying, "We have never seen a rain like that before." We nodded in agreement, amazed this restaurant had opened at all. They apparently hadn't assessed the total damage, thinking it was only the kitchen that had water on the floor. The kitchen with tile floors was easy for them to clean, but then they found water halfway into the carpeted dining area as well. They were all a scurrying, moving tables, and vacuuming the excess rain.

The day after, I too was moving some furniture to vacuum my office and noticed a damp spot on the carpet under my desk on the north side of the house. I investigated further and, to my horror, the carpet was wet all along the north wall. I called the real estate agent and he advised me to call his contractor. The contractor pulled up the soaked carpet and said it was damaged from the storm. We both nodded without saying . . . it was a storm like no other.

I informed the real estate agent of the contractor's verdict, he then called the potential buyers informing them that there was some storm damage to the house. To make a long story shorter, the buyers withdrew the offer and we called in our insurance adjuster to further investigate. Being very thorough, the adjusters found a boat-load of damage from roof, walls, floors, basement to the bay windows. All needed to be removed and replaced. My partner and I were shocked and a sick feeling of desperation fell over us as we had such a tight time line.

We were in the midst of packing up and the movers were coming to pick up our stuff within two weeks for the trans-Atlantic move. We decided my partner would go ahead, secure a flat for us, move in our stuff, and begin her new job. I would stay behind, fix the house, and come when all was repaired and the house sold. I would live, for the time I was still in Portland, out of a couple of suitcases since I would be flying to meet her in England.

When the first contractor came and pulled up the carpet I saw an enormous wet spot. We had left it up to dry hoping that we might be able to clean it and tack it back down again. But it was ruined. One day I was looking at it from the other side of the room and I realized the very large, now dry, water stain looked like the image of the Virgin Mary. I took amused notice of it but didn't really think much about it until a few days later when I sat down to write and asked Mary what she wanted me to write about today. She said, "Write about the carpet stain that looks like me and tell about the storm."

Before this move, I had the perception Mary was guiding me each step of the European journey from start to finish, port to port. I didn't know what an ordeal it would be and this carpet stain image of Mary turned out to be an important sign of her presence in my life.

The storm actually delayed my move to England for a very important reason which I didn't know at the time. As time went by and walls were exposed, the roof came down, and windows were taken out, I was often reminded of that early carpet stained image. It was just enough to give me a glimmer of hope during a difficult time.

"Go Visit the Virgin Mary"

It's a dreary day in Portland and I had been thinking of visiting Mary at the St. Mary Chapel at the Grotto today. But, as usual, my life began to take over. Being in the middle of reconstruction of the house, there were constant delays and demands. The contractor calls, opening the house for workers, grocery shopping, Home Depot runs, and errands of all kinds caused me to disregard my inner guidance to go visit the Holy Mother. On the way to my local market, though, I stopped at a red light and the car in front of me had a purple and white bumper sticker that read, "Go Visit the Virgin Mary." I couldn't believe it! That is the only time in my life, before or since, I have ever seen that bumper sticker.

So, being the reluctant, but obedient, devotee I am, I went to go sit and visit the Virgin Mary in her chapel at the Grotto. I realized how much I needed this time with her to calm my frantic mind and to remember she is with me each breath I take. So, here I sit, glad to know I am not doing this overwhelming job alone.

I have a friend named Annalee and, periodically, when I am overburdened with responsibility and not knowing which path to take, or decision to make, she will ask me, "Have you seen Mary lately?" I sheepishly say "No" and then I get over to one of my many sites to visit the Virgin, feel her strength, calmness, and love. Not that Mary doesn't make house calls or isn't with me wherever I am, but it helps to go see her in beautiful, spiritual surroundings, to talk and feel her presence without my life interfering.

She will call me to her in many ways, just to remind me she is present, to help me breath and calm down into her serenity. The Blessed Mother will even stop me at a red light, behind a beloved Marian, with a reminder sign on the rear bumper.

Jewess

"It is said that half of Christendom worships a Jew and the other half worships a Jewess." - Anonymous

A strong, independent and brave Jewess friend of mine took me, an American-German, to the Holocaust memorial in Portland, Oregon. Outside the main area of the memorial is a brushed brass bench to sit upon before you approach the tall, dark stones which make up the memorial.

Sitting there, it becomes apparent the stone pavement is laid to resemble train tracks with small bronze sculptures imbedded, depicting everyday possessions littering the walkway. These items seem tossed as if dropped or lost by the push of the soldiers herding the Jews into the trains which delivered them to concentration camps. One small bronze sculpture is a pair of men's wire rimmed glasses, another a child's doll, a scholar's book, all symbolizing the variety of ages and genders that were taken. All personal items had to be left, disposed of like the Jews themselves.

My friend tells me the details of the construction of the memorial and points out other symbols that tell the story of the genocide. We approached the main, towering structure, in silence, stepping closer to read victim's names etched into the stones, marking this unthinkable tragedy which occurred not so very long ago.

I sit down, heavily burdened by the weight of this reality, with tears in my eyes as she gently and reverently touches *her* family name carved into the stone. She explains who was lost and who survived. The profound miracle that any of her family survived and she was actually born does not escape us.

I can't help but think my German ancestors could have been part of the persecution if they hadn't brought their family to America to find farm land and opportunity prior to that time. And I am aware also, I, a gay woman, would have been forced to marry a man or rounded up and taken as well.

My friend speaks of the one family member who survived – her grandmother. She tells me about how young her grandmother was when she was taken to the concentration camp and about her miraculous release when allied troops came and liberated the prisoners.

I think of this young Jewess, and she brings to mind another Jewess, Mother Mary, who fled to Egypt with a small child, keeping him safe from death and persecution. This Jewess also raised a family and survived to tell the tale for future generations to remember. She was with her son every step of the way, from birth to the deadly cross and finally the tomb.

Jewess, grandmother, mother, daughter, granddaughter all survived the appalling injustices of life to tell the story and birth a new way based on love and hope.

The Virginity of Mary

One of the many definitions for "virgin" in the *Merriam-Webster Dictionary* and the *American Heritage Dictionary of English Language* is "The Virgin Mary." Other definitions in each dictionary offer various definitions, all with the theme regarding a woman who has not had sexual intercourse. One can surmise from these authoritative texts that it is so well known when using the word "virgin," one might be speaking of Mary.

We know it all started around Mary's own innocent lack of sexual encounter with a man when the angel Gabriel approached her; she is described in scripture as a "virgin". There are many perspectives regarding the virginity of Mary and these perspectives have actually expanded throughout the ages.

Not only is it believed she conceived her son Jesus with the spirit of God, but she, herself, as stated in Catholic tradition, was brought into being without intercourse between her mother, Anne, and father, Joachim. There was "no original sin," and Mary's conception is what is called "Immaculate Conception."

It is a quite common misconception that the term "Immaculate Conception" refers to Jesus' conception when, in fact, it refers to Mary's. Remember what Mary said to Bernadette of Lourdes, "*I am* the Immaculate Conception."

In strict Catholic tradition, Mary also is said to have remained a virgin *all* her life. They call this her "perpetual virginity." Furthermore, Mary is believed by the Catholic Church to be a virgin "physically" even after the birth of her child. This is called *in partu* virginity. This indicates that Mary's "maidenhead" was never ruptured during the birth; quite a feat in itself.

Even though there are references about Jesus having brothers in the New Testament scriptures, some Christian scholars believe these were Joseph's children from a previous marriage. No one really knows for sure and all is open to . . . perpetual interpretation.

So when we talk about the virginity of Mary, we are possibly talking about her being a virgin in four ways. This is why she is considered one of the main definitions of the word "virgin" in our contemporary dictionaries, Virgin Mary x4, if you will.

To summarize:

1) Virgin birth herself by her parents – the Immaculate Conception or Nativity of Mary

2) The virgin birth of Jesus – Nativity of Jesus

3) Her perpetual virginity throughout life – *Aeiparthenos*

4) The birth of Jesus that left her hymen intact – *In Partu*

By definition, this case is about as iron clad as possible, stating that our Mary is *The Virgin* of all virgins.

Mary at AAA

My move to England was fraught with mishaps, tasks that are usually smooth and simple, became arduous and time consuming. I was getting used to the weird events which slowed my forward progress to a sluggish trudge. Taking passport photos was no different. I had to go to AAA (American Auto Association) more than once just to get these photos.

The AAA-passport-photo-taker (AAAPPT) was embarrassed as she explained the digital passport camera was inoperable. "It has never broken before," she said, puzzled by this small disaster. "Welcome to my world," I said to myself as I gave the AAAPPT an understanding nod. Somehow, I felt bad that my karma had rubbed off on the passport camera.

The AAAPPT was not familiar with the old, clunky, Polaroid backup camera, fumbling with the buttons. She snapped a picture. Click. Then realized there was no film in it. She put in film and asked me to pose again. Click. This time the black cover paper she needed to remove was still in the camera and nothing spit out of the long slit in front. One more try. Click . . . and nothing happened. She removed the faulty picture. Click. Faulty picture. Click. Faulty picture again. Click. Click. And finally … running out of film, she took one last shot. Click . . . and it WORKED! Out came a gray, moist print with a whirl. Thank you, baby Jesus! She asked me to wait in the AAA reception area for my image to emerge. She wanted to make sure it was right. I don't know what she would have done if it wasn't; there was no more film left.

I stood at the walk-up receptionist's desk waiting and lazily glanced through the *AAA Winter Get Away* edition of their latest magazine. Yes, this is what I need, a winter get away. As I was turning pages, I abruptly stopped at an article with colorful photos of Mexico City and there she was – Our Lady of Guadalupe, on the tilma with conveyor belted people moving slowly by her! I was paralyzed in my tracks; my mouth dropped open. It took me going to the AAA office twice, several passport photo tries later and Mary again brought me up short; all this trouble just to get my attention.

I knew instantly she was reminding me to continue to write on her book, her gentle whisper pointing to our committed work together. Even though I was moving out of the country and had so many things to do, she wanted me to write first; move second. I knew what she meant. I was making errands, packing, and tying up loose ends more important than writing. Ahh . . . a moment of synchronicity.

In the magazine photo, the tilma was surrounded with a gold frame on a golden wall. I stood there wondering if I would ever see this image of Our Lady in person. It was the first time I had actually seen a picture of the tilma *in* the basilica. The photo was beautiful. I knew she would call me if she wanted me there, just as she had called me to this moment.

The *AAA Winter Get Away* magazine was free, so I tucked it in my bag. My passport photo came out well, and, after paying for it, I thanked the AAAPPT and the receptionist walking out the door, a bit higher in spirits. The Virgin still knew how to slow me down in order to get my attention, always encouraging me to keep my priorities in order.

The Blessed Mother Made Me Do It

The next day, in my morning meditation, I kept seeing myself writing at a table at the Tao of Tea, drinking a pot of my favorite cranberry/orange tea, and eating a toasted coconut, fig flat bread. I was having a mental argument with the vision saying, "I have food and tea at home, I shouldn't be buying anything out." But, as I continued to pray for guidance, I kept hearing, "Go to Tao of Tea," and seeing myself sitting at the tea table writing. So, I gave in and went, looked for a parking place, playing the "if you really wanted me to go, you would at least provide a great parking place" game. No go. I took a wrong turn, but did finally find a place to park a few blocks away. Spirit was not in the mood for games, I suppose.

As I walked in the door, I spotted the exact empty table by the window with an electrical outlet, just as I had seen it in my mind that morning. I sat, ordered tea and flat bread, then opened my computer to begin to write about what had happened the day before at AAA.

There were three women at the next table talking about a meditation class one of the women was teaching. The conversation continued as I wrote and I overheard one woman asking the teacher to teach at their center. The meditation teacher said she would have to meditate on it. Wow, a meditator, and she, like me, waited until she ran things through a meditation before making a decision.

The other women left, leaving the meditation woman alone. I spoke up, "Excuse me, I overheard you talking about meditation; do you meditate often?" She said she meditated daily. She looked me in the eyes so deeply that I felt her depth of spirit. Her name was Christine and she explained, she and her girlfriends, who had just left, had studied psychic development and meditation together in Boulder, where I used to live. They all happened to move to Portland and the other two had opened a spiritual center while she had become a meditation teacher.

She asked what I did and I explained that I was a writer and was currently writing a book on the Virgin Mary. She told me she had an old friend of the family, whose family would always laugh and say, "The Beloved Mother made me do it!" "Whatever 'it' was, the more outlandish the better. It was almost always on the edge of spoiling themselves, either with too much ice cream, shopping, buying a new car or sleeping in." she said with a giggle.

I didn't tell Christine I, too, had conversations with the Beloved

Mother. When I follow her guidance, wonderful things happen in my life. So even if it is said, tongue in cheek, or with great reverence, you never go wrong when you listen to what the Beloved Mother suggests. I was glad Mother Mary told me to come to the Tao of Tea that day to write, to meet meditative Christine, and to listen to *her* Virgin Mary story.

Eat and Drink a Virgin Mary

A Bloody Mary Cocktail was originally concocted by Fernand Petiot, a bartender at Harry's bar in New York City in the 1920s. It is a combination of vodka, tomato and lemon juice, drops of Worcestershire and Tabasco sauce, pinches of celery salt, pepper, all stirred with a stalk of celery.

There was an attempt to change the name from Bloody Mary to "Red Snapper," but the Bloody Mary name was so popular that any attempt to change the name failed. It is thought to be named after Mary Stuart, Queen of Scots, who was violent in her rule. Bloody Mary Tudor was the nickname given to her by her detractors.

The Virgin Mary is a Bloody Mary made without vodka or any alcohol whatsoever. It is said that the Virgin Mary was untainted, some say, by the sin of liquor. So much so that if you go to any American bar and ask for a "Virgin" of any alcoholic beverage, the bartender will automatically know that you would like your drink without booze.

But this raises the question of whether Mary ever drank or was she against alcohol? The Marriage at Cana gives us our answer.

The very first miracle Jesus ever performed was changing water into wine when the wine the host provided ran out. Our own Virgin Mary was the one requesting that Jesus do this alchemy; she obviously knew he could do such feats. Mary even instructed the servants to do whatever he wanted them to do. And it was said, at this same party, the wine Jesus changed was *the best* wine of the evening.

John 2:1-11 - "On the third day there was a wedding in Cana of Galilee, and the mother of Jesus was there. Now both Jesus and His disciples were invited to the wedding. And when they ran out of wine, the mother of Jesus said to Him, 'They have no wine.' Jesus said to her, 'Woman, what does your concern have to do with me? My hour has not yet come.' His mother said to the servants, 'Whatever He says to you, do it.'

Now there were set there six waterpots of stone, according to the manner of purification of the Jews, containing twenty or thirty gallons apiece. Jesus said to them, 'Fill the waterpots with water.' And they filled them up to the brim.

And He said to them, 'Draw some out now, and take it to the master of the feast.' And they took it. When the master of the feast had tasted the water that was made wine, and did not know where it came from (but the servants who had drawn the water knew), the master of the feast called the bridegroom. And he said to him, 'Every man at the beginning sets out the good wine, and when the guests have well drunk, then the inferior. You have kept the good wine until now!'

This beginning of signs Jesus did in Cana of Galilee, and manifested His glory; and His disciples believed in Him."

Surprising isn't it, to think the namesake of our non-alcoholic beverages was the one asking for the water to be converted into wine. Jesus really did not want to do this for he said it wasn't his time to begin his work. But his mother, Mary, implored him and he relented. The power of our Mother Mary . . .

These water vessels contained around 30 gallons of water and he changed six of these into wine. Since we know the servants filled them to the brim, the total was approximately 180 gallons of wine. That is a whole lot of wine!

Our modern wine bottles generally contain 750 ml. This means 180 gallons would fill 908 bottles with the finest quality wine; a massive wine fest or drunken brawl for sure.

So if anyone tells you our own Virgin was a teetotaler and was against drinking wine, bring up the Cana marriage feast story. Mary and her son were a big hit that night, saving the host family embarrassment and providing for the party of the century. On that feat alone, his disciples believed in him and Jesus began his ministry with a bang. So much so, we still tell the story some 2,000 years later.

Mary in Roman Catholic Church Herstory

The first we read about devotion to Mary in church history is in the 5th century. It happened, scholars believe, after the Council of Ephesus in 431 AD proclaimed Mary to be *Theotokos*, literally, "God-bearer," or, popularly known as, "The Mother of God."

The first known church that was dedicated to Mary in the city of Rome was built in the 5th century and the earliest Marian shrine, near Constantinople, was constructed in that same century. At the time, many pagan religions were growing in popularity due to female deities and the Church wanted to lift up their own holy woman to show they too had a godly female. The obvious and best choice was Mary, the Mother of Jesus.

Also, during this time, around the 5th and 6th century, a rumor first surfaced that Mary Magdalene was a prostitute. There is no scriptural reference in the Bible regarding this and the teaching is totally erroneous. Even to this day, though, many churches are still teaching that Mary Magdalene was a sex worker and current popular thought is she was also, Jesus' lover.

What we do know about Mary Magdalene, however, is that she was a wealthy woman and that Jesus cast out seven demons from her. She, along with other women, helped finance the ministry of Jesus. This is based in scripture, but very few will bring to light that Jesus was financially supported by the women around him. So, as the Virgin was exalted, Mary Magdalene was trashed by the fathers of the Roman Catholic Church.

We find, toward the end of the 7th century, the earliest feast known for Mary was the Virgin-Purification Feast, closely followed by the Feast of the Assumption, the Annunciation and the Nativity of Mary. This rise of Mary, this crowning into church history, is significant for before that time she was only considered the vehicle, the womb, and the parent of the Christ child. But now she has been raised to new spiritual and liturgical heights as the Immaculate Conception, the Queen of Heaven and Earth, the Goddess, and the Holy Mother of God.

Mary in the Writing Group

Here I am in my women's writing group at Sister Spirit Pagan Church in Portland, Oregon. Above the altar, filled with Goddesses, Native Symbols, construction paper prayer requests, candles, incense holders, paintings, and pieces of nature (leaves, wood, stones, and such) is a very large, framed poster of Our Lady of Guadalupe. I note that it is above the heads of two women in my group who are probably unaware that the Virgin Mary is looking down upon them as they speak. She seems to be prayerfully listening while giving them blessings.

Her picture is next to a photo of Stonehenge and a Native sacred art piece constructed from feathers and deerskin. She likes it here – to be a part of the whole – one of many sacred pieces surrounding this diverse and inclusive altar. Holy amongst holy.

She doesn't get to hold the talking stick as we do, passing it to each woman, signaling it is time for her to share and for all others to listen about writing experience, angst, and the enthusiasm of new projects. Mary is silent, being one of the many feminine, holy women holding the sacred energy for this eclectic woman's group.

I notice the paper under the frame which holds the image of the Virgin has been yellowed, stained, and lightly folded as if it had been rolled up at one time for travel or storage purposes. She has found her final resting place, now protected behind glass above this magical altar. She is revered here as the Goddess, Mother, and Virgin – her own trinity.

As I sit in the corner, typing on my computer, I am sure the members think I am recording their important input. Well, I am, but mostly I am taken in and listening to the Virgin Mary. Thank you, Mary, for being here. I think I will return to this diverse writers group, knowing they love you too.

Behold Thy Mother

Sitting at the feet of Mary at the Grotto, I am in despair. My house has toxic mold; in the living room, the roof is missing; it is January and I am sleeping in the old coal room in the basement on a borrowed air bed with only a small space heater for warmth. Brrrrrrr. Thank God for friends who lent me this small heating appliance for my windowless bedroom. It is the only room, other than the garage, where I can sleep at this point. I am grateful I can still close the door to keep in what warmth is generated.

The contractors have given me bids that are three times as much as the insurance will cover. All my earthly belongings are in England – moved in hopes I would someday be there to follow my partner and my dream. All looks bleak on this gloomy and cold, Portland winter day.

I come to the Mary Chapel to sit at her feet, glad to be in the warm, well lit sanctuary, safe in this moment. My gaze is drawn to the ceiling by some unknown force and my attention fixes, unconsciously, upon something I have never seen before. There, on the ceiling is a painting, in the form of a banner, held by two female angels. Written on the pennant with bold, golden, gilded letters:

BEHOLD THY MOTHER

Indeed . . . I pondered . . . my eyes riveted to the words. I have sat in this same seat at the St. Mary's chapel many times. I have taken photographs of all the angels and Mary in this place, on the walls, the ceiling, inside and out, but this is the *first* time I have actually seen this part of the ceiling. I know this was not recently added. "Behold Thy Mother" is somehow illuminating my mind and heart, crashing in on my gray gloom with its brilliant, golden letters and glorious message. I am not alone ...

As I sit, I notice music in the background, soft voices singing Gregorian Chants. I was directed here by my own wild mind, seeking purpose and relief from my unending chatter and mounting problems, seeking a refuge and a deep knowing that would make life seem bearable. There it is . . . if I but allow it. A Holy Mother's touch.

I notice, once again, the protruding heart of Mary on this statue in front of me, right in the center of her chest, on the outside of her alabaster tunic; showing the world her love for all. Her outstretched hands with palms toward me as if she is saying, "Come my dear, I will help you." I didn't know at the time it was just the beginning of my difficulties, that there was more devastation ahead. But for now, I am ok, in fact, grateful for what I do have at this moment: a car, a basement room, food, and a strong body.

I have come to you *my* Mother. Thank you for your help. I will accept and rejoice in all that comes to me at this time. I can now go on, feeling your maternal presence within me.

The Virgin on the Garage Door

At 6 p.m. on August 15, 2007 in Minersville, Pennsylvania, someone noticed that the reflected, late afternoon sun light formed a likeness of the Virgin Mary on a neighbor's garage door. Apparently, the sun light bounced off a neighbor's window across the alley and hit the garage door, just right, to form an exact image of the mother of Jesus.

One neighbor told another and pretty soon folks from miles around would bring their lawn chairs, in the late afternoon, to wait in the driveway for the figure of Mary to be beamed upon the large door. A hush would come over the crowd, each in their own thoughts and prayers about the daily phenomena. It was a big event in this sleepy little town of 4,500. The townspeople say, even on cloudy days, she continued to appear.

Local and national papers picked up the story. TV news reporters traveled far and wide to take photos and interview the lawn-chair congregation waiting for the Virgin's image. Posts were made on the internet, trying to figure out the reason for the sudden appearance of the Virgin Mary in Minersville. Many said it was a "sign," some said it was a good optical illusion, and others said that people will believe anything. But the devoted in the driveway knew it was the Virgin, giving each one of them a message. Another fact which added fuel to their miracle was that she began appearing on August 15th, the day of the Feast of the Assumption of Mary. There you go.

It reminds me of something a wise woman once said not so long ago: "I would rather believe and find out it wasn't true, than not believe and find out it was." Isn't it just like Mary to reflect her Divine light onto the ordinary, the accessible, and the practical surfaces of our lives.

Mary, the Metaphysical, the Mystical, the Magical

"Metaphysical" means beyond the physical. A "mystic" is one who believes that direct knowledge of God is attainable through intuition or insight. "Magical" is extraordinary power from a supernatural force. Mary is definitely metaphysical, mystical, and magical; she is doing such dynamic work from beyond the physical plane and continues to remind us of the accessibility of the Divine. Mary, herself, beams through the ethers and appears to us in an assortment of ways.

How it upsets our traditional, ecclesiastical authorities, steeped in ancient beliefs, dogma, and constructs, thinking that the holy is what happened *then.* Along comes the Virgin Mary, busting through the tissue-thin veil of time and space, chatting with us openly and all in our native languages.

The organized religious may, reluctantly, begin skeptical investigation to deem her messages and appearance as true miracles . . . or not. It can take years of doubtful inquiry these days, not like a few centuries prior, when Juan Diego just opened his cape to reveal the magnificent painting composed by Our Lady to the Bishop and *all,* instantly, believed. Now, it may take years before the church will deem an apparition worthy of honor. And sometimes, no matter how many people saw or heard what she said, the religious authorities still won't bang their canonical gavel and pronounce that, indeed, this was a true apparition, a holy miracle worthy of our reverence.

It can be shocking to us when a being of light, who is supposed to be either a myth or dead, begins to communicate with us. But there they are . . . present, dressed up, ready to convey profound proclamations or just remind us that we are not alone. It is a gift. But it can be a startling gift to those who have this metaphysical, magical experience right in the middle of ordinary, everyday lives. Poof, there they are. Hello!

As we know, the magical often happens when people are doing mundane, daily tasks: picking up wood, going to town, sleeping, or tending the sheep. Mary has appeared on everyday objects such as garage doors, windows, a pizza, and even in a cheese sandwich; meeting us where *we* are. Statues of the Virgin cry, open and close her eyes, smile, and almost sing Alleluia.

When Mary shows herself on Earth, it causes quite a stir. Our minds and hearts try to grasp the significance of her presence, the extraordinary in our ordinary, the unplanned in our caffeine driven, conventional lives. It reminds us that there is a whole lot more going on here (or somewhere) that we miss. We realize we have more support than family, friends, and service providers. Invisible support *is* all around us. We *know* it . . . but, we either forget it, because it is not a daily occurrence, or, we doubt our own experience once the glow of awe has dissipated. "Oh, that couldn't have happened," or "Now I will be considered cuckoo, like I believe some of those New Age or spiritual people are."

But, we do grasp, if only for a moment, the knowing that our prayers are not in vain and that synchronicity or God-incidences do occur. Those series of well organized events, in cooperation with our higher purposes, are indeed taking place for all to see. Our paradigms shift and we sit back in astonishment about this brand-spanking-new, expanded reality. What? How could that be? We grasp the idea that our universe is bigger than work, play, sleep, cars, manicures, and football.

It is easy to forget again, though, and we go back into our daily grind: putting in gas, paying our bills, having our teeth cleaned. The vision that was so pearly bright and breathtaking now recedes, allowing us to get on with our lives, our responsibilities, and activities, with just a faint glimmer of light. What we once knew *for sure,* is now just tucked away in a sweet drawer of memory.

But, by chance, once again, we see a movie, hear a song, or read a book and we are transported to that same feeling – knowing deep within – yanking that drawer open and letting that awe bubble to the surface with tears and hope. We know, for another moment, that the spiritual *is* real. The metaphysical *is* physical; the mystical *is* available.

Once it has happened to us, it is easier for it to reoccur. This big fat, love surrounds us from somewhere within and without and we just cannot deny it. We welcome and stay open to these uncommon events, lightly attentive to the unusual and to synchronicity. The more we remember, the easier it is for us to ascend, again, into a higher place, breathing in… Divine presence.

Mary is like that, bringing up all the good in us, reminding us to love the Divine, one another, and ourselves. She cleanses all the petty, replacing it with the grandly mystical. After awhile, we look for her, as if on a scavenger hunt, going from clue to clue to find our way back to her and the magical experience again.

Inspiration is an essential need of ours, like breathing and eating.

We feed off of it to stay in our passion and joy. Thank you, Mary, for showing up in all these interesting places and nourishing those parts of ourselves that crave the otherworldly, the mystical, the magical, and the metaphysical.

Mary's Music

There are many songs that have been written to honor and adore the Virgin Mary. Some are so old that the composers have been long forgotten and others are fairly new to us. Other countries that have had significant Mary apparitions on their shores have set her miracle and devotions to music: Our Lady of Guadalupe in Mexico, Our Lady of Lourdes in France, etc. A few of the more common compositions for or about Mary are:

Magnificat by Bach
Gabriel to Mary Came by John Macleod Campbell Crum
Hail Mary, Full of Grace by Marnie Barrell
Mary's Little Boy Child by Jester Hairston
Mother Mary by Rita MacNeil
Mary, Did You Know? By Mark Alan Lowry
Vespers of the Blessed Virgin by Claudio Monteverdi
Stabat Mater by Pergolisi
Songs for the Blessed Virgin Mary by Hildegard Van Bingen
Virgin Mary by Giorgio Moroder and Pete Bellotte
Mother Mary by Joe and Athena Will
Be It Done Unto Me by Bob Herd
Breath of Heaven (Mary's Song) by Amy Grant and Chris Eaton
Alma Redemptoris Mater by Joseph Rheinberger
Regina Coeli Laetare by Joseph Rheinberger
Ave Regina Coelorum by Joseph Rheinberger
Salve Regina by Joseph Rheinberger
Rejoice, O Virgin by Sergei Rachmaninoff
Ave Virgo Gloriosa by Russell Walden
The Way of Mary by Russell Walden
Annunciation To Mary by Russell Walden
Virgin Mary Had a Baby Boy – Unknown

And of course, *Ave Maria*

Ave Maria

One of the most beloved hymns to Mary is the *Ave Maria*. It is the rosary sung in Latin. Different composers have written music to the Hail Mary: Giulio Caccini (1516-1618), Edward Elgar (1857-1934), Charles Gounod (1818-1893), but the most popular version is by Franz Schubert (1797-1828).

This Franz Schubert version of *Ave Maria* was composed around 1825 when Schubert was 28 years old. He originally wrote it for voice and piano and used the words by Sir Walter Scott from a poem called *Ellen's Prayer*. In this poem, Ellen prays to the Virgin Mary in her time of need, within Scott's larger work called *The Lady of the Lake*. These initial words from the poem were translated into German.

Later, an unknown person set Franz Schubert's music to the Latin *Hail Mary* and this is now the most common version. The angelic words spoken to the Virgin Mary by the angel Gabriel and Schubert's inspired composition have withstood the test of time.

Many have recorded Schubert's *Ave Maria* and, on YouTube, you can view Luciano Pavarotti, Maria Callas, Andrea Bocelli, Bobby McFerrin, Charlotte Church, Celine Dion, or even Beyonce singing this cherished piece.

In 2016, Pope Francis took a papal trip to Mexico. One of his many stops was at a pediatric hospital. As the Pope and the crowd of hospital dignitaries, doctors, and entourage walked around the hospital blessing patients, he came to a cancer patient, 15 year old Alexia Guaruno, who asked if she could sing him a song. Pope Francis said yes and she sang an emotional rendition of *Ave Maria* that stopped the Pope and silenced those present as they remembered, tearfully, the song of Mary.

Hearing Mary's blessed anthem brings tears to our eyes whether preformed by the simplest of voices, by rock stars, or by instrumentalists like Joshua Bell on the violin or Chris Botti on the trumpet.

Somehow Latin words sound more majestic with the music that we love. Here is the exact translation from Latin to English of the *Ave Maria*.

Latin	English
Ave Maria	Hail Mary
Gratia plena	Full of grace

Maria, gratia plena	Mary, full of grace
Maria, gratia plena	Mary, full of grace
Ave, ave dominus	Hail, hail Lord
Dominus tecum	The Lord is with thee
Benedicta tu in mulieribus	Blessed are thou amongst women
Et Benedictus fructus ventris	And blessed is the fruit of thy womb
Ventris tuae, Jesus	Your fruit, Jesus
Ave Maria	Hail Mary
Ave Maria	Hail Mary
Mater Dei	Mother of God
Ora pro nobis peccatoribus	Pray for us sinners
Ora pro nobis	Pray for us
Ora, ora pro nobis peccatoribus	Pray, Pray for us sinners
Nunc et in hora mortis	Now and the hour of death
Et in hora mortis nostrae	And at the hour of our death
Et in hora mortis nostrae	And at the hour of our death
Et in hora mortis nostrae	And at the hour of our death
Ave Maria	Hail Mary

Mary, Lover of Sophia

We are told that the Holy Spirit, which is commonly known as a feminine energy called Sophia or wisdom, came upon Mary and the power of the Divine overshadowed her, thus conceiving a baby boy.

Luke 1:35 "And the Angel answered and said to her, 'The Holy Spirit will come upon you, and the power of the Highest will overshadow you; therefore, also, that Holy One who is to be born will be called the Son of God.'"

This impregnation by feminine energy, Sophia, and the power of the Highest would lead us to believe that Jesus was a blend of double feminine love stuff and the Divine. If one believes that the Divine is both male and female energy, then it is possible that Jesus was conceived by mostly feminine spiritual energy – with a dash of the masculine.

In feminist circles, this theory is highly regarded. It is understood that the Christ consciousness, the male body and being of Jesus Christ, was conceived and birthed by the gentle, loving, creative, Christ/ess, feminine consciousness of Mary. This brings in the new age to the planet – a revolution of love, creativity, and cooperation. Glory Be!

At Mary's Feet

Mary isn't usually a big talker. She seems to communicate with me in short sentences, probably so I won't get confused with long discourses. She just answers my questions and fills me with love.

Mary calls me "dear one" a lot. "You are welcome, dear one," "Just keep going, dear one," "I am with you, dear one." And my favorite, "I love you, dear one."

I don't really know why she calls me "dear one," but I assume she calls me that because she loves me as one of her children, a daughter of hers – a "dear" daughter of hers.

So, here I sit, again, at Mary's feet and today she is talkative. "You have not been here recently, dear one. I have missed you saying hi . . . so close . . . yet so far. Your attention to your work and your worries have taken you away, yet, today I called you just for me, to sit with me and talk, sending everyone else away just so we could pray and love each other. I will give you a gift, so, once you are through with your computer, I will fill you with light and love. You are loved more than you can know or feel. I like your little book and it will bring hope, joy, and a giggle to the many who read it. It will serve well. I know that is your prayer for it – to be of highest and best service – as it is mine. Now put it away and let me strengthen you."

As I sit here at Mary's feet and open myself to her love and light, a silly question wanders, nonchalantly, through my mind. Why are Mary's feet always bare? Here the Virgin is waiting to fill me with graces and my thoughts are about her feet. What shoes *would* Mary wear if she lived in our present time? Birkenstocks – like Jesus, or a more feminine, ballerina shoe? Definitely, a ballerina type shoe or a simple, feminine sandal, depending on the climate.

Each time she appears she is barefoot, no polish, just lovely, slim feet. Many who have witnessed her visions say she is the most beautiful woman they have ever seen – beyond beauty – beyond beautiful feet.

Sorry Mary, my monkey mind is wondering and wandering. I will put down my computer and wait upon you, open to your gift of light and love. As I open my grateful heart, my hands are palms up to receive your presence again. I love you, my barefoot Virgin.

Mary's Last Home

Santa Casa in Nazareth was Mary's first home but, it is believed that Mary's last home was in Ephesus, Turkey where she lived with the Apostle John. While Jesus was dying on the cross, he gave John to be Mary's son and for Mary to be his mother. At that point John took her to Ephesus, Turkey and they lived together for her remaining days.

It is believed that Mary died 10 to 12 years after Jesus, somewhere between the years of 40-42 AD. Ironically, a few centuries later, in 431 AD, it was the Council of *Ephesus* that decreed Mary was now Theotokos, The Mother of God. Fitting.

The revealing of Mary's house was somewhat mystical. A nun, named Anna Katherina Emmerich, who lived in 18th century Germany, became very ill and was bedridden. On December 29, 1812, she was praying when she had a divine experience. She received the stigmata (the wounds of Christ) and she began to speak in trance. Emmerich began having visions about the Virgin Mary's life and death. A writer named C. Brentano heard about the nun's visions and began recording Emmerich. Brentano wrote Emmerich's narrative in great detail and published a book called *The Life of the Virgin Mary*.

In Emmerich's vision, Mary left Jerusalem with John and moved to Ephesus, Turkey. Ephesus is by Mount Aladag where the Christians had settled in tents and caves. John built Mary a house and Emmerich described the house in specifics, even though she had never been there. Mary stayed in Ephesus for about three years but wanted to return to Jerusalem for a visit. Both Peter and John agreed to travel with her back to Jerusalem.

While in Jerusalem, Mary got sick and lost so much weight that the disciples were afraid that she was going to die. Fortunately, she recovered and was able to return to Ephesus. She died at the age of 64 and Emmerich was told that Mary was buried at the site of her home there. Upon her death, the Christians who settled in Ephesus honored Mary by turning her house into a chapel.

Another nun, a Daughter of Charity, Sister Marie de Mandat-Grancey, read Brentano's book and, with the help of Muslim guides, people in the area, and her fellow monks and sisters, she searched Ephesus for and finally found the house of Mary. It was in ruins with a broken statue of the Virgin outside, but was exactly as described in the vision of Anna Katherina Emmerich.

The house has been repaired, with many stops and starts, but today it is a popular pilgrimage site for Christians and Moslems alike. Many healings have been reported from the springs that run under Mary's house; crutches and canes hang from the walls in testimony to its healing properties. One can fill cups and bottles with Mary's healing spring water. The whole area, including Mary's house, is now a park and nature preserve in Ephesus, Turkey – guarded closely by Muslim authorities, open for all to visit.

The Original Our Lady of Guadalupe in Spain

The original "Our Lady of Guadalupe" or the "Spanish Guadalupe" is a dark wooden statue of the Virgin Mary. No one knows who the artist was, but this sculpture is a famous Black Madonna.

The statue was originally in Seville, Spain but in 711 AD, the priests took this art piece with them as they fled the Moorish invasion. When they came to the mountain near the Guadalupe River in Spain, the priests dug a deep hole and buried the statue to keep it safe. Eventually, the Christians recaptured Spain from the Moors, because it was such a long battle, it was forgotten and location lost.

In 1326 a cowboy named Gil Cordero found one of his cattle dead near a spring and as he began butchering it, the cow stood up and returned to life! Gil was shocked to see his cow get up and the knife wounds healed instantly. As he sat there, the Virgin Mary appeared to Gil. She asked him to go to the priests and people of the village and tell them to dig at this place where the cow was resurrected for they would find her statue.

Of course, the priests and people laughed at him, thinking him crazy, but when he showed them the scars from the cuts he had made on the cow, and they could see that it was now very much alive; they were awestruck and believed him. The townsfolk ran to the exact spot where the miracle had occured and began digging. They found the sacred old statue, calling it "Our Lady of Guadalupe" after the Guadalupe River nearby.

A chapel to house the Our Lady statue was built at the very spot where it had been found. It is said that Christopher Columbus prayed to this Black Madonna before his first voyage to the New World. In fact, the first island he discovered in the West Indies was named Guadalupe, in honor of the Virgin giving him safe passage.

This first Our Lady of Guadalupe is the one that the Mexican Our Lady of Guadalupe is named after. After Mary healed Juan Diego's uncle, Mary told him her name was the Lady of Guadalupe and it has been the name of the image on the tilma ever since.

Mary's Fashion

When reviewing the Marian apparitions, common themes in the Virgin Mary's fashion and appearance are evident. More than one seer has called the Virgin "The Lady in White," meaning that she is sparkling white, brighter than anything they have ever seen. She maintains this powerful illumination throughout her visitations and then gradually fades from sight as she parts company.

Many Mary witnesses report Mary's brilliance as if she were surrounded by a dazzling ball of light, even "brighter than the sun," or holding an orb of light that was so blinding it "darkened the sun" in comparison. She has also been seen weeping inside a circle of light that "out shone the sun" or "inside a diamond of light."

Burning wheels of fire have also appeared with Mary, "flashing lights and intense rays of color streaming down to Earth." Mary says that these are her graces, her offerings of healing, strength, and uplifting light. This woman so dazzling is our own Virgin Mary.

Her clothing tends to be similar among the apparitions too. She is described as wearing flowing garments, a light blue robe with white tunic. Sometimes the white gown has a white or gold tassel cord around her waistline. We see countless statues and paintings of her full length, flowing white gown and light blue cloak.

The Virgin Mary as she appears to Juan Diego in Mexico, Our Lady of Guadalupe, however, wears a red gown with gold brocade and the blue or green mantel that is decorated with golden stars. Stars are popular with Mary. We have reports of silver and gold stars either around her or as part of the pattern in the fabric.

Mary wears her hair long, usually covered with her cloak. In Catholic art, she is depicted as wearing a crown, either on or above her head, as a symbol of her coronation into spiritual royalty and Queendom. To my knowledge, a crown or even a simple, tasteful tiara has never been part of her headdress in any apparition.

There are no reports to date about Mary wearing any accessories such as a necklace, earrings, bracelet, or sunglasses, but there is an occasional rosary. She obviously likes a simple outfit for warmth, piety, and comfort.

We do have reports that Mary sometimes carries or is standing on a globe of the world. When she appears with the globe, she uses it to make the point that her message is for *all* people and not just a certain region.

It gives us a visual cue of the breadth of her message.

She never shows up as elderly, only as a young maiden – the virgin. Even when we see art, for example the sculpture Pieta by Michelangelo, she is very young. Some art critics have questioned the artist – why did he sculpt her to look as a young mother when she had her 33 year old son Jesus in her lap? Michelangelo says that "She will always be the young virgin to us." Her apparitions seem to hold that same youthful truth.

Mary often holds her hands in prayer, with her head tilted slightly to one side, usually to the right, looking down. This is her prayerful pose, as if praying to God for us every moment of the day. Sometimes we see her with her arms crossed on her breast, covering her heart in love. Other times her hands are outstretched giving us Divine blessings and graces.

The presence and fragrance of roses is prominent in art *and* apparitions. In art, roses may crown her, float in the air about her, or be within the pattern of her fabric. Those present when she materializes physically, commonly say there was a strong smell of roses before, during, and after her arrival. As I write this sentence, I am aware of a potent rose smell. The rose scent is so strong I feel compelled to sniff the back of my hand to see if it is coming from the lotion I put on today. No, it is from her, the lotion is unscented. When I ask about this rose smell, she says she is reminding me not to forget her roses as I write this section. Done.

The image of the Virgin Mary, her pose, colors, and youthful appearance are so distinct to us that if we see even a faint resemblance to her, we know instantly that it is *The Virgin*, our beautiful, fragrant, bright, and powerful Mary.

Mary Breastfeeding the Christ Child

In Mary's day, wherever the mother went, so did the child . . . if it was going to be fed. No canned, bottled or pre-pumped milk was available. Occasionally, Mother Mary is depicted in art, holding and breastfeeding the Christ child. These pieces are profound and rare. Historians say that many of the early paintings of Mary nursing Jesus were destroyed because the image was thought "too unseemly" by conservatives of the time.

Padre Pio was a healing priest in Italy and it was said that he loved Mother Mary deeply. His favorite painting of Mary is over the altar at his beloved church. It depicts the baby Jesus with the bare breast of Mary, pointing outward, with a suspended drop of milk dripping from the nipple, as if to feed the world. When Padre Pio died, he was continually speaking two words, "Jesus, Mary, Jesus, Mary . . ." He loved both Mother and child.

But now there is a desire to embrace the humanness of the holy family. In 2010, the Vatican put out a call for more artwork showing Mary breastfeeding Jesus. Breastfeeding experts Dr. Elvira Henares-Esguerre, Director of Children for Breastfeeding, and Nona Andaya-Catilo, International Lactation Consultant, have commissioned a sculpture showing the Virgin Mary looking down with a mother's love at the baby Jesus who is in "full latch" breastfeeding position. It was commissioned to promote and help teach new mothers good breastfeeding techniques. The slogan used is: "If it was good enough for the baby Jesus, it is good enough for our babies!"

The Crowning of Mary – Coronation

There is a painting above the altar on the domed ceiling of St. Mary's Chapel at the Grotto in Portland, Oregon with Jesus and a holy man with a beard, either symbolizing God or the Pope, placing a crown on Mary's head. I don't think there was a modern Pope who had a beard, but curiously, this man's face is very similar to a recent, popular, and deceased Pope.

Mary stands gazing up into the ethers with her traditional blue and white gown draped about her, arms crossed over her heart in piety. Angels, of course, are winging in the clouds and a dove flies aloft. The painting is about early Church men's concept of crowning the Virgin Mary with Divine royalty in all her female humbleness.

The Catholic Church often depicts God as a bearded, old man, but I think there are other ways of showing the Divine, pure love and light, Creator of the Universe. So where did we get this version?

We know that Michelangelo and Leonardo da Vinci were both gay men and we see in their amazing art how they loved to paint very male themes when creating spiritual or traditional religious work. For example, the Sistine Chapel has an old, bearded man reaching out to touch a very male Adam. In the painting *The Last Supper*, there are all men – no women or children seen. Sort of like a Middle Eastern, gay dinner party. But we are told these are the disciples having the famous last supper with their rabbi, Jesus, on Passover, before they later all run away in the garden and/or betrayed him. So who cooked the Passover meal for them? Where are the other followers? Our ancient religious art tends to shape our beliefs more than we would like to believe and impacts our thoughts and images about God, religion, the role of women, and the world of spirit.

So Mary is crowned by Jesus, God the Father (or the Pope) into her Queendom. We are given these beautiful, holy images from ancient times which are indeed important – but dated. As we try to modernize and inclusify our art, we see more feminine presence.

I remember a devout parishioner once gave me a t-shirt of *The Last Supper,* but in this version, all the disciples were female. It was the same separatist coin – only the flip side. It was good to see a different perspective to show how exclusive our beliefs can be.

In the Bagel Deli

There's a New York Deli on 23rd Ave. in Portland, Oregon. The employees talk like they are from Brooklyn, they have pictures of the New York skyline everywhere, and the seating is very sardine-like. The food is fabulous!

Today I order my standard, smoked turkey Reuben with extra sauce on the side and potato salad. The rye toast has that greasy taste from being on the grill with piles of fried potatoes, burgers, and steak. The service is quick and blunt and you will hear complaints about people staying too long in their booths. Opps . . . I think that one is for me . . . as I plink, plank, plunk away on my computer.

So what does this have to do with the Virgin Mary? Well, I asked Mary today where to go to eat and write and she suggested this place. I know that New York has many devout Catholics and Catholics love the Virgin Mary, but why here? From past experience with her, I know there is always a surprise in store when I follow her suggestions.

I have overstayed my welcome, pack up my computer, and make my way to the Lady's room. Inside the women's bathroom, facing the toilet is a picture of the Virgin Mary on the wall! There she is, blessing the women as they take a few moments to themselves. I never know where she will show up, even though it may seem unusual, it is always perfect. Here she talks to us eye to eye as we sit in our comfort. Doesn't she just know how to get us alone and bless us wherever we may be? Oh, yes she does!

The Baby Mary

For many years I have collected "Baby Jesus" stories. When I was the pastor in Eureka Spring, Arkansas at the Metropolitan Community Church of the Living Spring, I would always include a new Baby Jesus story for the six sermons prior to Christmas. They were usually simple, fun little stories with a message that I would somehow fit into the sermon. The congregation would smile and nod as they heard the newest Baby Jesus tale, probably humoring me, but they did seem to enjoy them. Some congregants would even find and tell me their own Baby Jesus stories to add to my collection for next year.

Then, I ran across the "Maria Bambina," a story about the Baby Mary! Filled with glee, I read about a statue in Milan, Italy of the Baby Mary. It is a life-size, realistic, hard-wax image of the infant Mary created in approximately 1735 by a Poor Claire nun in Todi. Apparently, it moved around a bit until it found its final resting place with the Sisters of Charity of Lovere motherhouse in a novitiate.

As time passed, the wax body of the Baby Mary became dirty and discolored. It was then placed in storage. On the night of the Nativity of Mary in September 1884, one of the sisters asked Mother Superior if she could take this old statue of Maria Bambina to the infirmary to bless the ill. The Mother Superior agreed. As one gravely sick novice took the statue in her arms and prayed that night, her health returned and she was immediately cured of disabling paralysis. Two other nuns were instantly restored to health on that same night!

This being quite a miracle, the nuns gave the statue new garments and laid it in the chapel instead of returning it to the storage closet. Only the face was exposed amidst the bundle of swaddling clothes. The sisters reported that by January of the following year, the faded, dirty gray complexion of the statue slowly changed to warmer, flesh tones and took on the appearance of a very real baby. Soon the news of the Baby Mary self-cleaning herself, as well as the miraculous healings, became known to the townspeople who then wanted to view this wax statue. As the word continued to spread and her popularity increased, the sisters had a chapel built specifically to house the Baby Mary and to accommodate her growing public.

Wax copies were made and small images were given to special churches; prayer cards were designed. I ordered a prayer card on-line to add to my growing Marian collection of sacred objects. It is a beautiful prayer card – Baby Mary all dressed up in formal, baby-girl clothing, face as bright and beautiful as a real infant.

Many Catholic sisters, brothers, and fathers have devoted their lives to rekindle the flame of Maria Bambina and honor her throughout the world. We are grateful to them for the reminder of the infancy of the Virgin – the Baby Mary.

The Marian Prayer Book

Once while shopping at a bookstore with Mary, I picked up a small, white, hard back book with ornamental gold lettering titled, *The Marian Prayer Book*. It was published in 1984 by The Missionary Oblates of Mary Immaculate, Rome, Italy. I thought this must be *the* official Marian Prayer Book since it had such astute sounding publishers and came from the seat of the Roman Catholic Church in Rome. Inside it said that this copy was distributed from the National Shrine of Our Lady of the Snows in Belleville, Illinois; maybe a special branch of the papacy?

It was not the most sacred looking book on the inside though; it was filled with photos and only three of these were of sacred sites. These three photos were of the Annunciation Gardens with contemporary statues, the Lourdes grotto, and the Outdoor Altar, all from the National Shrine of Our Lady of Snows in *Belleville, Illinois*. The remaining photos were close ups of blooming flowers, landscapes, and sunsets. It did not mention if the nature photos were from Illinois or just placed in the book for a touch of color and beauty. I assumed the later.

I realized *The Marian Prayer Book* was a money making venture that any Catholic Church or organization could buy from the publishers and the purchasers were allowed the three changeable photos, so it looked like their own publication. The book had meditations, prayers for various needs, canticles, litanies, and the ever-popular Stations of the Cross. The print was large enough for failing eyesight and prayers were italicized so they would not to be confused with narrative; very user friendly, but boring. Not much even pertained to Mary. This used copy of *The Marian Prayer Book* had not seen much wear, almost brand new. I could see why.

The only evidence of human touch in the white *Marian Prayer Book* was a prayer card which seemed placed randomly between the pages. The prayer card was called *Prayer to Obtain Favors*. It also looked new. I immediately said the prayer exactly as it was written. I am always open to receiving favors – needing all the help I can get. I said this prayer a couple of times so I didn't miss a bit of what was being prayed for. Then I noticed these words on the bottom of the prayer card, in small letters in parenthesis *and* italic:

(It is piously believed that whoever recites the above prayer fifteen times a day from the feast of St. Andrew, Nov. 30ᵗ until Christmas, will obtain what is asked)

Unfortunately, it was February and I would have to wait to say the prayer for another nine months, November 30th at the feast of St. Andrew. It was doable, saying this prayer for those 26 days – November 30th to December 25th; 15 times a day is only 390 recitations in total.

I probably will forget about this prayer card, though, having to wait so long, and I think the owner of *The Marian Prayer Book* probably forgot too, suspecting this may be why this book and card were in such good shape.

I looked closer, reading all the fine print of the card and noticed that the Imprimatur was Michael Augustine, Archbishop of New York in February 6, 1897, who blessed it at the time. This little prayer card has been in circulation for over 100 years. It must work in order for it to still be in print. I will have to get back to you on this in December for the rest of the story, only, if I can just remember . . .

Mary Candle

I work as an on-call Occupational Therapist, among other things, to earn an income as I write. One day I worked with a patient, a resident at the nursing home who had fallen and broken his wrist. He had many other medical issues as well, but I was there to increase his independence in his daily living and to give him a series of exercises to rehab the injured wrist and make it strong again.

As we were working in his room, instructing him with arm exercises, I noticed a white, shiny Virgin Mary candle on one of the two shelves in his room. It had a small rosary draped over it. I asked him about the Mary candle. This normally rough, cranky, elderly man, shifted into his heart and told me that he was talking to a volunteer the week before about Mary and the next day she brought him this Virgin Mary candle. It was evident that he was deeply touched by her generosity. As I looked around his room, it was obvious he didn't have many possessions left.

I asked how he knew the Virgin, and he said, "She is my Holy Mother. My real mother died when I was a year old and, since then, the Blessed Virgin has been my mother." I took a deep breath, breathing in the profound nature of this statement. I began to puddle up and asked if I could look at the candle. He shook his head in affirmation. I walked over and gently touched her waxy shoulder with my finger; she was smooth, clean, and white. I asked about the crystal bead rosary she was wearing – as if it were a sash around her. He said, "That is part of the rosary, you say the rosary five times using that."

I never know where I will encounter the Virgin in my daily life and how she has helped so many people. We sat in silence the rest of the session and, as we worked, we said the rosary silently, feeling her love. Finally, we were through and as I left, we said, "God bless you" to each other with tears in our eyes – knowing once again that we were in her presence.

Women Named after Mary

When we bestow the name of Mary, in any form, onto an infant or prenatal child, we call in a higher purpose and mission to that being's life. Namesakes are very powerful. Mary is aware of all who have her name and energy. So choose your female offspring's name with much care and consideration; the universe is listening.

Some parents will name their daughter after a female relative who was significant to them who just happens to have the name Mary. There are theories that the child's spirit intuitively communicates his or her name to the parents from beyond. It just feels like the right name for the child.

These are a few examples of Mary names for your next girl offspring: Maria, Mari, Mary, Marilyn, Merry, Miriam, Muriel. Then there are the two names together, for example, Mary Kathleen, Mary Grace, Mary Beth, Mary Ann, Mary Louise, and so forth. Sometimes the Mary is the second name like Ann Marie. Then finally, we hear of some direct derivatives as in Momma Mia and, the ever popular, Virginia Marie.

Mariolatry

The worship or excessive veneration of Mary is called Mariolatry. This practice has always been an area of controversy in Catholic Church history, many times originated by non-Catholics. Are Marion people worshiping or honoring the Virgin? Are they glorifying her for her participation in the birth of Jesus? Are they adoring her for the mysticism of being the lover of the Divine in producing a child? Is she blessed among women and set as an example for womanhood, motherhood, or the feminine aspect of the Divine? Is she the Queen of Heaven and Earth? Or is she even the Christ Consciousness in female form, as Jesus was the male equivalent? Usually yes, to all the above.

Some of these beliefs are accepted by the religious authorities and some not, but the people who know Mary, the ones who have had experience, are firm in what they believe her to be. There is no changing what they know, they stick to their truth even if they have to be silent about it.

In current times, Mary is being embraced by many people who have never been Catholic, but are involved with a spiritual path. They just love Mary and want to wear her t-shirts, pray to her, befriend her, have her little statues around the house, in the car, and by the baby's crib. They just love their Mary!

Mary is very active in the modern world. Her popularity is growing and many who never even thought they were spiritual are finding a connection and beginning a conversation with the mother of Jesus. I hear this so often, "I don't know why I love Mary so much, I just do" or " I am not religious, never have been, but I love Mary."

She has touched the hearts of so many who are surprised by this fact. Silently, in the sanctity of their homes, cars, and businesses, Mary is there. Look around, you will see her everywhere: hanging from car mirrors, on dashboards, on display in homes . . . some times hidden from view, but open a drawer, look in a closet, check in the glove compartment – there she is! It is the dawning of a new day of our evolution. Mary is here, bringing the feminine into this Age of Aquarius. It is a Mary revolution – Mariolatry.

Mary is my Homegirl

Rachel walked into the recording studio as I was finishing a sound check for a meditation CD I was recording. She was wearing a pink T-shirt with the words written in white: "Mary is my Homegirl." I told her I loved Mary too, and asked if she was Catholic. She looked surprised that I might know the same Mary she knew since I was considerably older than she and looked like a soccer mom instead of a cool, young adult. I could tell she liked that we could relate on this level.

She said she was a "Recovering Catholic" and that she selected from different religions only what worked for her. She picked Mary. I was glad. Some just throw out the baby Jesus, the holy family, and the Divine when they throw out the religious bath water. I am happy Mary survived the aquatic toss.

The picture of the Virgin on Rachel's t-shirt was in perfect Virgin Mary pose: head slightly tilted to her right, a cloak over her head, but, on this t-shirt, she had a halo. Her hands are stretched out as if to give graces, blessings, or a big motherly hug. This Mary was looking right at you, which is not typical. She usually has a downward gaze and you have to sit to the left and underneath her to catch those eyes.

Mary is a homegirl: humble, popular, and certainly well known. You go girl! Or should I say, "You Go Mary . . . my Homegirl!"

The Virgin in Marpingen, Germany

In July of 1876, three German girls were gathering berries in the woods near Marpingen, Germany, when they saw the Virgin Mary. Word spread throughout the town and surrounding areas about the vision. Growing numbers of believers came to this small hamlet, many claiming miraculous cures at the sight where she had appeared.

Because of this onslaught of activity, there was a major conflict between the Prussian government and the pilgrims who flocked to Marpingen. There was also a cultural war going on between the German Liberal Party and the Roman Catholic Church at the time. The poor villagers were hoping the apparition would end all strife and their town would become the Lourdes of Germany, but it just didn't happen.

A comprehensive work by David Blackbourn retells the story in *Marpingen: Apparitions of the Virgin Mary in a Nineteenth-Century German Village*. Blackbourn was critically acclaimed for his research and for capturing the atmosphere of this great time of struggle, miracles, and politically warring factions. The final blow, though, was on December 16, 2005. One hundred twenty-nine years after the initial Virgin Mary encounter, the official decree from the Holy Seat of the Roman Catholic Church declared that there is no substantial evidence that Mary appeared outside the town of Marpigen, Germany. Holy Bummer!

Germans are tenacious though, they do not need an official decree to tell them if Mary visited those three girls on that summer day in 1876. They don't even need harmony in their political surroundings. They know that, in their minds and hearts, she did visit, and Marpingen will remain a pilgrimage site for all who wish to honor the Virgin, no matter what. No human authority or authorizing body can dismantle the spiritual truth for them of what happened so long ago. Sometimes Mary chooses to reveal her truths and her love to the hopeless, the ones who need her most. They will be forever grateful for her presence during those trying times.

Virgin Mary Statue Survives <u>Mass</u>ive Church Blast

On September 10, 2004 at 6:45 a.m., a blast flattened the St. Mary's Ukrainian Church in Colchester, Connecticut. The cleaning woman, who usually works at the church alone during that time, was delayed unexpectedly, so no one was injured. Thank you, Mary!

*Mass*ive pieces of the church building were found within a large area around the church grounds, but the Virgin Mary statue located within the church courtyard was totally unscathed. She was still peacefully praying amongst the debris – not missing a beat.

The townspeople reported that the blast was heard for up to five miles away. Rev. Kiril Manolex, the rector of the church, stated it was a miracle that the statue was not destroyed. Many came to pay homage and to see the statue praying in the huge pile of destruction which was once a majestic church. The photos show her standing amidst the strewn bricks and splintered boards of the demolished building, peaceful as can be.

I tell you, you need to get that Virgin Mary statue inside – where she can protect the staff, courtyard, *and* the building.

Happy Mother's Day, Mary

I was awakened by Mary's voice at 7:30 a.m. today and was softly urged to continue to write. She asked me to devote the next year of my life in close contact with her, writing this book. This devotion would begin today, Mother's Day and would end Mother's Day of next year. At first, I thought of the work . . . Egads! But immediately, my heart began to sing, knowing I would have a glorious 365 days to work intimately with Mary. I saw her image move forward and enter my energy field. I knew instantly the book would be completed in its first draft at the end of this time. What a relief; it has been over a decade of writing.

Mary showed me, in a vision, taking one red rose to her statue at the Grotto today and she ended my meditation asking me to also focus on my personal spiritual path. I was to go to choral and spiritual concerts, listen to New Age, instrumental, and sacred music, visit spiritual sites, and listen earnestly to her guidance. I was then led to the words she imparted to Juan Diego:

Do not be troubled or weighed down with grief.
Do not fear any illness or vexation, anxiety or pain.
Am I not here who is your Mother?
Are you not under my shadow and protection?
Am I not your fountain of life?
Are you not in the folds of my mantle?
In the crossing of my arms?
Is there anything else you need?

– The Virgin Mary to Juan Diego

I gently came out of meditation and stretched. Then the realization that I had a very full day planned came crashing into my consciousness. I got ready and quickly scooted to the Grotto parking lot, without the rose, thinking that I didn't have time to go get it. Silly me, thinking I needed to hurry up and get this done so I could get on with my busy day. I can be so goofy.

The Grotto parking lot was jam packed, of course, not a parking space to be had. Families were bringing their mothers to the outdoor Mass in front of the Pieta. I chided myself for thinking I could get away with a

159

shortcut. I needed to go get the rose and find something to eat on the way, *then* come back. How could I think that I could bypass any detail of her instructions? I am so human and fallible Mary, please forgive me. Here I was so thrilled to have your guidance not more than an hour ago and then didn't even follow through. I don't know why you even talk to me; I am such a spiritual slacker at times.

I drove to Safeway and purchased the one last, single, long stem, red rose left in the bucket and had a bowl of soup. Why do I rush through this process? What more important things do I have to do? Here the Virgin is talking to *me* and I want to rush through this special time with her.

I have now laid my one red rose at the feet of the Mary statue here at St. Mary's Chapel as I saw earlier in my vision. A policing nun spotted it in her sanctuary rounds and placed it in the vase full of carnations and baby's breath sitting on Mary's pedestal, there to honor her on Mother's Day. My rose, as I see from this distance, is the tallest of all the flowers in the vase. I am proud that I still have a place of distinction among the carnation petals, stems, and baby's breath.

Since it is Mother's Day, the nuns have also placed a crown of white and pink baby roses on Mary's head, crowning her with love and blessing. Her candles at her feet are uniformly lit. The public candle lighting area is outside by the Pieta, in the open air. There you find the racks and racks of red and white candles lit for the Virgin. Today there is not a single candle in the racks that is not flickering to the Beloved Mother.

As the outdoor grotto mass ends, people begin to wander into the chapel to pay final respects before their brunch. Happy Mother's Day, Mary! We are so grateful for all you do and have done in our lives. It is nice to take this moment of time to stop and honor you. I am deeply touched to be working with you and will try harder to do what you ask of me this next year.

The Immaculate Conception Church's Mandatory Courses

The Immaculate Conception Church of Torrevieja, Spain is holding mandatory premarital courses for those couples who are interested in having their marriage ceremony at the church. These classes are: Spousal Love, Jesus Christ, Spirituality, Church, Responsible Fatherhood, and the ever popular, Married Sexuality. All classes are held in the Immaculate Conception room for a total of 22 hours.

The topic of how to have *Immaculate* Conception was not included within the topics taught at Immaculate Conception Church; it apparently is not a big draw. *Maculate* conception, however, is discussed under the material covered in the Married Sexuality course. With all this conception going on, the Immaculate Conception Church is growing by leaps and bounds.

Mary's Birthday Party

This December 11th was a particularly gloomy day in Portland. I was feeling aimless and was wandering from errand to activity with no great enthusiasm. "What is wrong with me?" I kept wondering. I began praying for help to relieve me from this shadow. Within five minutes of saying this prayer, I drove past a Mexican restaurant known to be one of the best in the city. It was even close to home. The thought came to me that I could go in and order take-out for lunch. So I circled the block, parked, and entered the restaurant.

I told the woman by the cash register that I wanted something to go and this was my first visit to this restaurant. She knew very little English, but we muddled through my order. As she headed to the kitchen, I noticed an altar with a large picture of Our Lady of Guadalupe on a shelf above the cash register. A Virgin Mary candle was flickering next to a small vase of fresh, red roses that were in full bloom.

I instantly relaxed, oh yes, this is about Mary. *She* wanted me to be here. I stood, waiting for my food, silently talking to Our Lady, enjoying the Mexican music, and feeling bathed in a knowing that she had called me to this restaurant in answer to my prayer.

When the server returned with my meal, I pointed to Our Lady of Guadalupe and said, "I love her too." The server smiled and said, in very broken English, "It is her birthday tomorrow." I couldn't believe it. I knew it was close to her fiesta day . . . but tomorrow . . . I didn't want to miss it. December 12th is the Fiesta of Our Lady of Guadalupe and is celebrated by those who love La Madre. "Oh si, big celebration at St. Anne's church at 5 a.m. in the morning." My server was so excited to tell me this great news. I asked for the address, but said, "5 a.m. in the morning?" "Si, they have hot chocolate, donuts, and mariachis. It is soooo beautiful!"

So with the address firmly in mind, I thanked her, saying goodbye. I left the restaurant and shook my head. I wanted to go . . . but 5 a.m. in the morning? I wrestled with it all night . . . 5 a.m.!?! "Ok," I told Mary, "If you want me there, please wake me up early so I can go."

Without the aid of an alarm, I awoke at 5 a.m., got ready and finally arrived at the church at 7:30. I drove up to an almost empty parking lot. The doors were open and I was ashamed that I did not have the discipline and devotion to wake up early enough to go hear the Mariachis sing Happy Birthday and to greet Mary on this special day.

As I entered the church, there was a large, blue-tiled, infinity water fountain bubbling in the center of the foyer. Holy waterfall! It was surprising to see such a beautiful, hot-tube-sized baptismal/holy water feature as I walked in. I touched the water, crossed myself and looked around the sanctuary. Jesus hung on a small cross over the Eucharist box on the back wall behind the altar, and on the left side of the sanctuary, was a larger than life, ornate picture of Our Lady of Guadalupe. The picture was at least 12 feet tall and 4 feet wide with five mini spotlights lighting Mary's forever prayerful face. Her image was framed by an ornate gold frame with two large pillars holding up a canopy in front of her. It was so striking to see such a grand area featuring the Virgin. It took my breath away.

The Our Lady showcase had flower bouquets at least five layers deep and more than 50 Our Lady of Guadalupe unlit candles lined up in front of her on the floor. The area for lighting candles was on the side wall of the church and all those candles were brightly flickering their prayers. Since the candles in front of her framed picture were not lit, I surmised that there was an announcement that no candles in that area could be lit due to the fire code. Mary was certainly the main and majestic attraction in this spacious, mostly Latino church, with or without candle light.

The celebration was over and women were putting the finishing touches on the kitchen cleaning. The last cup was dried and being put away. Large bags of trash were being carried out to the dumpster. There must have been quite a crowd that morning.

Parents with babies in their arms were having their pictures taken in front of the Our Lady. Late comers and those who just didn't want to leave her stayed to pray and touch the picture with a rose. The magnificence of the morning hung in the air. Petals and leaves were scattered on the floor and in the pews – as if a mighty wind had come through to rearrange the plant parts.

Mary was there alright. You could feel her. I felt ashamed I had not taken the extra effort to come for the earlier celebration. I found a flyer in one of the pew shelves and, even though I do not read Spanish, I could make out that there were still more celebrations, at noon and 5 p.m. that night. "I could come to the later concert mass if I wanted," I said to myself, to soothe my regret for not attending the dawn event.

I said my prayers and offered my birthday wishes to Our Lady as I sat in front of her. I was late, but it was actually good to have her with fewer devotees, so I could focus on her and not on the other congregational distractions. So, it turned out to be a private time with Mi Madre. On my way out, I stuck my hand in the blue, shimmering fount, crossed myself again, and left.

I didn't attend the 5 p.m. concert either, but was at home around 9:30. An urge came over me to go back to St. Anne's that night. I didn't want to leave the comfort of my cozy, warm house, but decided to return – to be with her without the fanfare.

This time the sanctuary was noisy with the last of the children and their families. The cleaning crew was vacuuming the sanctuary even though there were many still praying and taking pictures in front of Our Lady.

Some children had native dress on. One baby, no more than a few months old, was wearing the outfit of Juan Diego, with a little mustache drawn on with his mother's eyebrow pencil. His older sister held him. His Mexican, peasant hat was tied on and he had a pacifier in his mouth. Their mother took a picture of them – surrounded by the bouquets and Our Lady's love. It was awesome, and brought tears to my eyes.

This time it was ok to take a souvenir flower from the vast garden of offerings. So I asked Mary for a flower and a red rose caught my eye. I made the sign of the cross with the rose on the picture of Mary as I had seen so many other women do earlier as they said their last good-byes. Men were as numerous as women, praying and sitting with her, some alone, some in families. All of us were reverent and touched by her presence.

Mary loves so many and so many love her. I sprinkled myself with blessed water again as I left, knowing I probably wouldn't be back to this amazing holy place. But I do know that each year, on December 12th, there is a magnificent birthday celebration for her here. I am so pleased that I was able to be present in some small way. I know I can go there – in my imagination and in my heart. Thank you for that memory, and Happy Birthday, Our Lady of Guadalupe. I am so glad you came and graced us with your presence, tilma image, and love.

Mi Raza

I was sitting at my desk one morning when I looked up from my computer and saw the yard man wearing a black sweatshirt with a large, white image of Our Lady of Guadalupe on his back. She was bobbing and bending with him as he mowed, pruned, and snipped my plants. When he turned around, the front displayed the words in big gothic white letters:

MI RAZA

It means "My Race" in English. Our Lady of Guadalupe is a national image for the Mexican people. She has fought wars with them and gives Mexico great national pride after her visit so many years ago.

I was surprised to see her helping out with the yard work that day, blessing my plants as she and my yard man made their rounds. I never know when or how she will show up next.

Festival of Lights at the Grotto

At the end of an event one evening, a friend offered me four free tickets to the Grotto's annual Christmas celebration called the Festival of Lights. Every year I have intended to go, but just couldn't fit it into my schedule. So these tickets were like gold in my hand. She gave me the tickets at 8:00 p.m. and said they were only good for *that* night and the Grotto closed at 9:30. Better hurry! I asked two others to join me, they said yes, and off we went – with glee. The Grotto was very close and we made it there in record time.

We loved the Festival of Lights. There was a petting zoo and over "500,000 lights" that illuminated all the paths, statues, and buildings on the lower level, but we were too late for any choral music. The Festival of Lights is said to be the largest Christmas festival in the world with over 170 choral groups. There are five concerts each afternoon and evening at this popular Portland Christmas tradition. The singing ended, though, at 8 o'clock.

It was quite chilly that night, so after racing through the grounds, downing our hot chocolate, and touching the baby donkey, horse, lamb, and bunnies, I guided everyone to the St. Mary's Chapel to warm up. I made them sit smack dab in front of the Virgin Mary statue. While we were sitting there, looking up at the Virgin, one of my friends began to tell us a story.

She said that when she was young she had attended a parochial school. All the kids were given an Audiology test to check their hearing one day. My friend said she fibbed, saying she didn't hear the faint little beeps. "Didn't hear a thing," she told the audiologist. Because she failed the test, she was considered deaf for quite some time. It was quite an act. But once the teachers figured out that she really wasn't deaf, she got in a lot of trouble for lying to get out of school work and to be treated as special.

Later that year there was an incident at recess in the school-yard, she knocked out a fellow class mate's front teeth. She got into big trouble for that too. She said when the school Christmas play came around that year, the nuns made her the Virgin Mary because they thought it might be a good way for her to channel some of the Virgin's goodness. We all laughed. She said, "You know what, they were right."

Somehow, being the Virgin in the play that one night felt so good to her, she actually changed her ways. From then on she was nicer, didn't lie as much and deeply loved Mary. Even though she considers herself a "Recovering Catholic" now, she told the story with reverence and we were all deeply touched.

We sat there for the longest time, staring up at Mary with her hands out to us, trying to absorb the goodness and warmth that our friend had felt. Finally, they had to close the Grotto and we were asked to leave. We walked out into the cold night, knowing we all needed to hear the story and how the nuns and Mary had helped our friend become one of the most giving people we knew. She is in a profession that helps so many. Oh, the wonders that can happen, by being the Virgin Mary, for a night, in a school play.

Looking Up to the Virgin

My move to England was quite difficult and there was much to do for preparation. I had a TV show, had founded and was the director of the School of Angel Studies, and had a booming practice as an angel reader/clairvoyant. All had to be closed down and shifted on-line, not to mention the packing, moving, reconstruction, and selling the house. We were excited about the opportunity to live in England and travel throughout Europe, but we had to say goodbye to this beautiful country, family, and friends.

One night, during that hectic time, I was driving past an ornate church in Portland. I had time to stop and take a peek inside, if it was open. I knew I might never have the opportunity to do this again. As I came closer, I saw the parking lot was full and people were standing outside the church, as if they were on intermission. I mingled and, sure enough, the people were attending a free choral concert.

It was a packed house, but there was an empty folding chair in the very back of the darkened church. I was so glad to have a seat. The concert began again and as I listened to the choir of voices singing sacred songs, I leaned my head back, closing my eyes, resting on the pillar behind me. Ahhhh . . . peace at last.

The lights were turned a bit brighter at one point during the second half of the concert and I slowly opened my eyes. I looked up at the ceiling and saw a serene face looking down at me! I was staring up at the chin of the Virgin Mary. My head had rested between her feet on the pillar and her eyes fell upon me! I knew – just knew – I was supposed to be at her feet yet once again and I hadn't even realized it. She said for me to be calm, for she was with me. I closed my eyes, drinking in the experience of a beautiful church choir, while resting at my mother's feet and feeling her soft gaze upon my weary soul.

Rev. Jim and His Rosary

Rev. Jim is one of the most generous, open, caring, and radical pastors at Metropolitan Community Church. Not only is he a great preacher, he is also an inclusive, feminist theologian, dedicated to expand spiritual texts and wisdom to *all* people. Many times I have wished for his use of language and sensitivity when speaking. He listens intently, thinks on his feet, embraces diversity, and creates humorous and profound ways of preaching with Divine love in his heart.

Jim is HIV+; he has AIDS. He almost died a few years back. Jim is a big talker, good communicator, and has a lot to say. When he was in the hospital, he was so sick that they had to put a tube down his throat into his lungs so he could breathe – couldn't talk with that hose sticking out.

He remembers that time and how hard it was for him; not because he couldn't breathe, but because he couldn't *talk*. Poor Rev. Jim; people were having full conversations in his room and he couldn't give his opinion, advice, or comfort. What a spiritual lesson he had to endure.

Jim had a rosary in his hand the whole month while he was on life support. This radical, gay man, loves Mary, Mother of God, with all his heart. Mary saved him, you know. She has big plans for him. He knows that too. She had to take some pretty drastic steps to get him to shut up long enough to tell him, though. I think Rev. Jim will listen to her better now. He knows that when she has something to say, she won't stop until he listens to her.

Jim says that he is a Marian; someone who loves Mary; believes in her sacredness; knows that she is of the Holy too. He knows a secret. It is right out there for everyone to read; Jesus was the son of God, but Mary was the *lover* of God. She had *the* greatest Divine favor.

Our Lady of Prompt Succor

The name, "Our Lady of Prompt Succor," was given to the Virgin Mary in New Orleans, Louisiana when a nun received a quick and favorable response after she prayed to the Virgin Mary concerning a seemly hopeless situation.

It all started in 1809 when the French Ursuline nun, Mother Saint Michel, needed more French sisters to help with the struggling convent and school in New Orleans. The Pope was a prisoner of Napoleon at the time and the French bishop would not send any more nuns to America without the Pope's direction. All looked bleak for the fledgling school and convent. There was little hope a letter would even reach the Pope and, if by chance it did, he would not be able to do anything since the Catholic Church was under so much persecution at the time.

Mother Saint Michel prayed before a statue of the Blessed Virgin Mary and said, "Oh most Holy Virgin Mary, if you obtain for me a prompt and favorable answer to this letter, I promise to have you honored in New Orleans under the title of 'Our Lady of Prompt Succor.'" She sent her petition on March 19, 1809 and received a letter from the Holy Father on April 29, 1809 granting her request – just five weeks later!

At that point Mother Saint Michel commissioned a statue of the Virgin Mary holding the baby Jesus. She placed it in a convent chapel in New Orleans on December 31, 1810, a year and a half later, calling it Our Lady of Prompt Succor. Interestingly, it took longer for the statue to be carved then it did for the request to be granted. Maybe Mother Saint Michel needed to pray to the Virgin for a faster artist.

Nevertheless, many miracles have been associated with Our Lady of Prompt Succor. An out of control fire was raging towards the convent in New Orleans, destroying everything in its path. A nun named Sister Saint Anthony placed the small statue of Our Lady of Prompt Succor in a window and Mother Saint Michel prayed, "Our Lady of Prompt Succor, we are lost unless you hasten to our aid." Immediately, the winds began to blow in a different direction and the fire was quickly extinguished. The convent was saved.

Another miracle happened during the Battle of New Orleans in 1815. The American forces, led by Major General Andrew Jackson, were in a brutal battle with the British, keeping them from overrunning New Orleans. The Ursuline nuns, along with many of the faithful sat at the feet of Our Lady of Prompt Succor, asking for intercession – praying and crying all night and into the early morning. A service was being held in the chapel at dawn and a promise was made by the Prioress of the convent that, if victory was won for America, a Mass would be said each year at Thanksgiving in honor of the event. Right at the moment communion was being taken, a messenger ran into the chapel to announce that the British had been defeated! To this day, the promise is kept every Thanksgiving in honor of the Virgin's power to intercede in a rapid manner.

Our Lady of Prompt Succor is located in New Orleans, but she can be used, anywhere, for any impossible situation, that needs a speedy miracle. Don't hesitate; say that prayer now for swift results.

Pilgrimages to Mary

It is reported that Mary, the Mother of Jesus, has appeared over 20,000 times since she walked on earth in a physical body. Researchers who make extensive study of religious apparitions agree that the Virgin Mary appears more than any other non-physical entity. These are only the *reported* visitations, but there are countless other appearances unpublicized and undocumented for various reasons.

In 1997, Newsweek magazine stated at least four hundred of these visitations by Mary have been reported in the 20th century alone. This number is larger than any other century making that century, what Newsweek calls, "The Age of Mary." She is quite active in these modern times. Again, the operative word in this article is *reported* cases. But even so, this is still quite a large amount and the 21st century is gaining fast.

Wherever Mary appears, the location becomes a pilgrimage destination as people seek the essence of the Beloved Mother. It is said by Marion scholars that she has more sacred sites than any other being in the known world. Most are lovely places where churches, springs, gardens, basilicas, shrines, and even hospitals are built, all in the Virgin's name. She has asked many people to build shrines or chapels where she presents herself, making it a sacred site for seekers who can again be touched by her healing energy.

The veil between dimensions is thin at these sites, becoming holy ground. Here the spiritual and physical worlds connect. The power of Mary continues to emanate long after she has gone and her memory is renewed as we hear the story again and we feel the awe. The Earth has absorbed her essence and continues to broadcast it to us when we pray, meditate, stand, and kneel at these hallowed havens.

So far, though, only eight apparitions have been accepted by the Vatican, the seat of the Roman Catholic Church. This religious body gives Catholics a guide deeming whether a visitation by Mary is "not worthy of belief," "not contrary to the Faith," or "worthy of belief." These ecclesial decisions are based, also, on Mary's message being in alignment with the teachings of this church's theology.

The locations of the eight apparitions accepted by this denomination are: Fatima, Portugal; Banneux and Beauraing, Belgium; Syracuse, Italy; Manila, Philippines; Akita, Japan; Zeitoun, Egypt; and Betania, Venezuela. These are well known pilgrimage destinations for Catholics and non-Catholics alike. So are many "non-approved" apparition sites, as we see people flock to be with her wherever she has made herself known through the ethers.

Whether she is "approved" by one church, local official, law enforcement group, psychiatrist, medium or Boy Scout troop seems to make no difference to Mary. She just keeps showing up whenever and wherever she is needed – to Catholics, Protestants, Pagans, Agnostics, Atheists, Aunt Harriet or Cousin Ed . . . there she is. Poof!

Mary often appears during the height of economic, political, and/or social upheavals. She offers a way of peace and hope in these crises with such depth that only Our Lady can offer and be heard. The messages Mary brings to the world have very similar themes. They haven't changed throughout the years except that the information is always relevant to the given place and time. She speaks of Divine faith, prayer, healing, strength, peace, praying the Rosary, public or personal guidance, and always, *always* about love. Mary is very generous with her blessings, sending forth ecstatic love to those who see and communicate with her.

Some who Mary has direct contact with are so overcome with her passion that they are in rapture, frozen, and in an altered state of consciousness. In Medjugorje, Bosnia, the visionaries have given their permission to undergo extensive tests by investigators while they are in the presence of Mary. The investigators have concluded that each visionary is in the midst of a spiritual experience and they call this altered state the "ecstasy of apparition."

Sometimes we may feel deprived if we do not see and talk to Mary in this intense way and have the "ecstasy of apparition." But we see these visionaries have a difficult path to walk after Mary has visited them. It changes their entire lives. They are sought after by seekers and the authorities alike. Some come to scoff and others to be healed. The visionaries remain steadfast, though, in their message and knowledge of the Beloved Mother, no matter what trials or triumphs they endure.

With our modern technology, reports of Mary sightings are transmitted world wide in just a matter of moments – traveling faster than the speed of light on the internet, social media, TV, and radio. The images of Mary are captured in photos and videos, downloaded on YouTube, Instagram, Twitter, Facebook and shown on TV, making her accessible in record and for all time.

Our planet is being healed by Mary's lingering essence. She has injected compassion, love, and light, as a cosmic acupuncturist, activating the energy lines of Gaia's body for purification, renewal, and revitalization. We travel to renew and refresh ourselves and we gladly go on our spiritual pilgrimages to be blessed by our Beloved Mother's love and healing again and again.

The Healing Waters of Mary

Often there are famous springs at the sites where Mary has appeared which continue to hold her miracle healing powers. Some of the most popular ones are Lourdes, France; Banneux, Belgium; and Marpingen, Germany.

Lourdes, France, on February 11, 1858 – The Immaculate Conception appeared to a teenage girl named Berndette Soubirous and after a series of visitations, the Virgin asked her to dig in the dirt by the stone Grotto. A spring miraculously sprang where no other spring had sprung before. It is known throughout the world as one of the most curative waters that Mary has ever provided.

Banneux, Belgium, on January 15, 1933 – The Virgin Mary appeared to an 11 year-old girl by the name of Mariette Beco. She appeared to Mariette several times and during one of those visitations Mary led her to a ditch where the girl was asked to uncover a spring. The Beloved Mother told her that the waters were reserved for all nations, to relieve the sick.

Marpingen, Germany, on July 3, 1873 – The Mother of Jesus appeared to three children, Margaretha Kunz, Katharina Hubertus, and Susanna Leist in the woods near Marpingen, Germany. Mary asked the children to pray and to bring water to her from a nearby spring. She asked that a chapel be built on the spot where she was standing and the spring is known to this day for its healing properties. It is often called the German Lourdes.

There are Mary healing waters all over the world. Mary springs are present from Poczajow, Poland to Betania, Venezuela. Some towns have even built elaborate fountains over the springs for people to enjoy as they partake of the refreshing liquid. The Mary fountain in Aachen, Germany was built in 1650 when a girl found a painting of the Virgin Mary near the spring. Westroosebeke, Belgium's fountain was dedicated to Our Lady and has been in operation since the 1400s. Austria has Mary fountains in Mariabrunn, in Pateinsdorf, and in Leobersdorf. San Damiano, Italy has a well known Marian fountain known for its medicinal qualities. These are just a few of the more well known water sites of Mary.

The powerful waters of the Virgin Mary are abundant and free for all. Drink . . . Heal . . . and Live!

The Lit, Throbbing, Sacred Heart of Mary

As I was organizing and packing for my move to Europe, I ran across a tin picture of Mother Mary with her son Jesus, in a leafy, gold plastic frame I had bought years ago. It says **God Bless our Home** in bold letters across the top. Both Mary and her son are pointing to their hearts. There is a compartment on the back of the frame for two AA batteries and a small plastic switch. When you put in batteries and turn on the switch, red lights flicker on and off, appearing through the tiny, tin, pin-holes around Mary and Jesus, lighting up their halos and sacred hearts.

It is quite luminescent in the dark. All you see is the red outline of the two with their hearts, halos, and Jesus' pierced hands blinking in syncopated timing. The inside pamphlet reads that the picture is used to ward off any evil that may visit your home.

My friends think it is a bit scary that I even like this picture of the Virgin and her son, but I do. It is also decorated with some sweet, baby girl angels holding a banner at the bottom that reads,

"God bless the corners of this house, and be the lintel blest; and bless the hearth and bless the board and bless each place of rest;

And bless each door that opens wide to stranger as to kin; and bless each crystal window pane that lets the starlight in;

And bless the roof overhead and every sturdy wall, the peace of man (and woman), the peace of God, the peace of love on all."

Something in me wants to take it apart and find out how it works, to see if there is one light, two, or many shining through the holes in the tin images. To tell you the truth, I really can't stand to have the lights blinking for very long; it is quite annoying with its constant, quick, throbbing light. What I thought would be a soothing, peaceful picture is actually irritating to watch after awhile. That may be why it is so useful for warding off evil spirits – they can't stand the constant flickering either.

So it has been delegated to a box now. I pull it out on Halloween to scare off all the mean-hearted by putting it on the porch – seems to work well, only princesses, pumpkins, and super heroes of all types make their way to my front door.

A Room with the Virgin

During the long reconstruction of the house in Portland, Oregon it seemed like everything was taking so much longer then it should. Contractors never showed up, I wouldn't get calls back, the bids were off the charts, and finally I just gave up. I prayed about it many times and came to the conclusion that there must be a reason, out of my control, that the Universe was delaying my move. All the furniture was sold and boxes of personal items were shipped and on their way with my partner to England. One morning, like all the rest, I asked God if there was anything that I needed to do that day. Then I listened . . .

That morning, at the end of February in 2007, my hand was gently but firmly guided, by an invisible force to my right breast and I heard a voice say, "It is time you take care of this." I had found a lump a week earlier during my monthly breast exam, but put it out of my mind saying, "I can't deal with this now, I will wait until I get to England." That wasn't what the Divine had in mind. So I called my partner and told her what I had found and assured her I would call my primary care physician as soon as the office opened. She offered words of comfort and hope, not to worry until we knew for sure what it was.

The doctor saw me immediately and scheduled a mammogram that morning. Seeing something that concerned them, they next sent me for an ultrasound downstairs and later that day scheduled a consultation with a surgeon.

The surgeon wanted to perform a biopsy of the lump, but after informing him I intended to leave the country for six years as soon as I finished repairing the house and selling it, we agreed on a lumpectomy instead. A few days later, after this surgical procedure, I was diagnosed with invasive ductal carcinoma – breast cancer. That day changed my life.

I realized, at that point, the reason for the extreme delays in the house reconstruction. God's idea was for me to find this lump and to get the help I needed where I had friends, a good medical team and, of course, insurance. I didn't know where I and my two suitcases were going to live during the course of treatment since I was living in the cold basement of our storm-damaged home during the repairs. So I asked . . .

Each time I would ask God where I was to live during my chemotherapy and radiation treatment, I would get a vision of a top floor room of a very large mansion type home. So I trusted and worked hard. The repairs of the house went smoothly after my diagnosis; I was amazed. Finishing the house kept me busy, which helped me not worry about my breast cancer or the future.

A couple of weeks prior to the house closing, I received an email from Pat Schwiebert, author of *Tear Soup* and member of the Peace House community, offering to house me during the next several months while undergoing my cancer treatment. Peace House is a United Methodist community that practices peace, diversity, and communal ministry, focusing on healing and grief work. Many times they have housed people with terminal illnesses as they get back on their feet or . . . transition into death. At one time, the house was filled mainly with people living with AIDS, now those with cancer, old age, dementia or such, find a home amongst this community. I was grateful they were willing to add me to the list.

I went to see the house and go over payment and arrangements with Pat. Peace House is in the Northeast section of Portland with large stone homes, old mansions, and tree lined streets. I arrived to see which room I would be staying in this large, three story Victorian home. I was shown to a small room on the top floor which was about 8' x 15' with a large walk-in closet. Although narrow, it was big enough for a bed. Since all I had were two suitcases of winter clothing and toiletries, I would be comfortable with such a small space.

Generous friends gave me summer clothing, towels, an old TV, which only the VHS player part worked, and kindness. There was no room for a chair, but that was ok since I was quite tired throughout the treatment and just wanted to lie down most of the time. When up, there were large gardens on the property and Peace House was walking distance from a grocery store, pharmacy, and coffee shop. Since I had very few things, this small room was perfect for my spiritual work and healing.

When Pat first showed me where I would be staying, she pointed to a postcard-size Peruvian Virgin Mary and Child plaque right outside the door. She said, "Mary is already here." She held me as I cried and we both knew that this was the room for me. It was exactly the one I saw in my vision whenever I would ask where I would be staying.

Our beautifully, renovated house sold quickly after all was repaired. An hour after signing papers and handing over the keys, I took up residence at Peace House and the day after that was my first scheduled appointment to begin my chemotherapy infusion. Reminding me, again, the Divine and

Mary *always* have perfect timing.

The nurse who administered my chemo was an acquaintance and I had a stream of friends stay with me during the infusions and we would all pray before she injected the treatment into my body. Nurse Beverly was one of the kindest people I know and I was so grateful to have her calm presence, her team of doctors, and expertise during that time. Being so sensitive, I knew chemo would be a bumpy road for me. I was grateful to have kind professionals and loved ones who walked each step with me; from diagnosis, operations, through treatment, and beyond.

My small top floor room had two large windows looking out onto the newly-leafed-out trees of spring and I could hear the birds sing each morning around 4:30 a.m. It was so serene there, with only the soft clanging of a peace bell in the wind and birds chirping as I went through the process of treatment and healing. The members of Peace House community embraced me and allowed me to ask for help as needed, providing sanctuary, safety, and privacy.

My partner came for a week when I was first diagnosed, but we both agreed she needed to continue her work in Europe while I took care of my health. I would join her in the fall when chemo and radiation were over.

Even before breast cancer entered my life, I had a regular practice each morning of journaling and talking to Mary. Our loving Mother has walked me through with love and grace. I have been amply provided for over and over again.

For instance, one day, at an event, I just happened to sit next to a woman I didn't know. I introduced myself and we exchanged pleasantries. The event hadn't started yet so I asked what she did. She said she was a massage therapist who was in Portland for a month and she didn't know a soul. She was there to complete her lymphedema certification and she worked in a breast cancer center in Michigan. (!) I couldn't believe it. I quickly told her of my breast cancer and that I was recovering from a recent surgery removing my lymph nodes. After lymph node surgery, there is always a danger of developing lymphedema, swelling of the arm, and once it happens, it never completely resolves. We looked at each other, stunned at the synchronicity that brought us to sit next to each other in such a large city, knowing there was Divine providence at work. Her visit that month was filled with my friends and she practiced her lymphedema techniques on me nights after class. We were *both* amply provided for.

Lonely and grueling months later, the tree that I looked at from my bed day and night sent one small yellowing leaf between my screen and window, as if to let me know fall was here and I would be finished with my treatment soon. Not long after that, being bald as a Buddhist monk, I was called by Mary to continue with the book and to write this story.

I was especially grateful to be in her presence writing this book again and to be asked to resume our work together, even though she was with me every breath I took. During treatment she told me other things, like what to eat, drink, and to get the help I needed as I healed.

For so many days, weeks, and months I had asked, "Is today the day to start writing?" Each day silence, then I would hear a small voice saying, "No, not today. It will come again, dear," was the reassurance. "You have other things to do." And, indeed, I did.

The Virgin and I Meet Gabriel

The angel Gabriel appeared to Mary, having a historical conversation about the conception of a baby son named Jesus she was chosen to birth. It was information that would change Mary's life and the world as well. The angel Gabriel is a powerful angel of God, an Archangel to be exact. Angels and Archangels always come at the right time and place.

Memorial Day weekend happened to land in the month between my chemotherapy and the beginning of radiation for the treatment of my breast cancer. Some friends asked me to come on a small women's retreat they organized every year at the Kahneeta Indian Resort in Oregon. This Indian Resort has a variety of accommodations for visitors: RV park, motel, lodge with casino, and eight large, cement floor teepees which hold six to eight people depending on the size of stuff and people. All are priced accordingly. We were on a camping trip, so we reserved two tepees and a couple of rooms in the lodge for the ones who preferred indoor sleeping. The tepees were somewhat rustic, but at least there was a bathroom with showers within walking distance.

I am not much of a camper, even with a sturdy tepee, flush toilets, and hot showers nearby. Fortunately, at the last minute, someone canceled her reservation at the lodge and there was an open side of the bed available for free. The organizer of the camping retreat asked if I would be interested in sleeping in the lodge instead of the outdoor teepee since I was still very weak from my chemo. I jumped at the chance to have indoor plumbing, a soft bed, and a balcony overlooking the Oregon hills.

On Saturday, a kayak trip was planned down the Warm Springs River near the resort for those interested. Fifteen of us women signed up along with others from the resort. Each kayak holds two people and when all my friends quickly paired up, I was the odd person out.

Having just finished my chemotherapy, I was bald, pale, and even though I had been getting stronger each day, my strength and endurance were still very low. I did look a bit sickly and that may have had something to do with why no one wanted to be in my kayak.

My good friend Linda was concerned for me as we began to line up to receive paddles and instructions. She anxiously said that I needed to get a partner quickly from the other tourists so I wasn't left out! I told her that the Universe would provide and I would just see what would happen.

At that moment, a woman with two strapping young adult sons

approached the boat house and stood next to me. I overheard them talking about how they needed to find a partner for one of her sons. I said that I did not have a partner and she offered her son to be my kayak mate. I introduced myself and he said that his name was "Gabriel" or "Gab" for short. There was my angel's namesake, standing big and tall. He even turned out to be on his college's *rowing team* and was now a firefighter. Thank you, Mary!

I told him that I was in the midst of breast cancer treatment and would not be much help with the paddling. He was thrilled, saying that he could use the work out. He liked being of service to a woman who was in the midst of her breast cancer treatment and took great care of me, with pride. He asked that I let him take over most of the time and for me to enjoy the big outdoors. I was grateful for the caring escort down the river. I only paddled when we needed to avoid rocks, tree stumps, and branches that were sticking out of the water. Unfortunately, that was about all I could handle.

The other women were amazed at my luck for having such a strong, handsome man paddling me. They laughed and nodded their heads when I introduced him as Gabriel. They knew that I talked to angels and they just shook their heads in acknowledgement that, of course, I would have Gabriel as my paddling partner. My friend, Linda, realized a bit more that day how the Divine, indeed, does provide for us all.

Gabriel, the rower/firefighter, seemed to have a wonderful time with the other 14 women loving and laughing with him all the way as he paddled Cleopatra down the Nile. His mother and brother didn't have half the fun he did – ferrying this weak, bald woman through the soft rapids. In the deep areas of the river, he would jump in for a swim and I would stretch out, feeling the warmth and meditating with the trees, birds, and sky overhead. One of the women took a picture of us as we posed; with him reclining back as I looked like I was paddling hard down the river. It made us all laugh so hard.

Thank you, Gabriel the man, and thank you, Gabriel the angel, for sending your name's sake to look after me that day. I remember the angel Gabriel's parting words to Mary, "For with God, nothing is impossible."

Marian Prayer Center

One night as I was looking for the address of a particular bookstore, I came across the name "Marian Prayer Center." Oh, my Goddess, what a find this was. I put the address on my "To Do" list to go visit in the morning. I was surprised I hadn't known about this place sooner.

Bright and early I called the Marian Prayer Center to see if it was a retail store or a spiritual center for Mary. The ad stated they were open only a couple of hours a few days a week. I didn't really know what to expect. The woman who answered the phone was a bit spacey, which can be good sign for a spiritual center. She said that, yes, it was a store, open to the public and they also had places to sit for contemplation and prayer to Mary. I got directions. She said that they were just now having a meeting about the upcoming Rosary Bowl at Volcanoes Stadium in Keizer, Oregon. Please come in about an hour from now. I said that I would be there, thank you very much. I jumped in the car and off I went.

The Marian Prayer Center is in a little town named Milwaukie that is so close to Portland that it is almost a suburb. Don't tell them I said that; Milwaukieans are very sensitive about being their own little town. As I walked in, people were leaving the small, strip mall store. The salesperson seemed a bit confused. She did not seem to know why I was there. I identified myself as a writer of a Mary book and said that I was so thrilled to be there; I was the one who had called earlier.

She apparently wasn't the one I talked to that morning and she sheepishly pointed to the sign that had the store hours. Saturday 1-4 p.m.; it was Saturday at 11:30 a.m. She said I could look around, but asked how long I would be since she wanted to go to lunch soon. I said that, if I could take half an hour that would be great. I would come back another time for a more in-depth shop. She agreed, relieved that she could still grab a sandwich before the store *really* opened. So Mary and I did some quick power shopping.

She pointed out the table with free literature and holy cards, telling me to help myself, which I did. I was in heaven. There were large shelves filled with Mary books for sale, Mary jewelry, used books, a lending library, videos, and a gallery of Mary prints, cards, and paintings. In the back was an altar with a Virgin Mary statue in the middle of eight stackable chairs. They had a prayer basket and I put in my own and other people's names for the prayer vigil that met each Thursday at 1 p.m.

Small bowls, filled with Miraculous Medals that were blessed at Mejugorje, were on the counter for 25 cents. I bought ten. Rosaries, statues, even a Lady of Fatima watch were in the cases. It was Mary heaven. I bought and bought and bought. The prices were low and the variety was great.

The sales volunteer's enthusiasm grew with each purchase. She began to tell stories and gave me a pink rosary that was blessed and a picture of the pilgrim Mary for free. I didn't want to miss any of it, so wrote snippets of what she was saying on a scrunched up piece of paper. She was delighted to meet a new, enthusiastic Marian person.

I told her I was a Protestant minister who loved Mary. She was even more delighted and told me about a Baptist minister who would come in and buy rosaries for the hospitalized troops in Iraq. "Black rosaries," she said, "so there would be no reflection to alert the enemy where the troops were." We two ministers were sort of Mary converts in her eyes; she didn't realize Mary is not just for Catholics, but for all people. I didn't mind, I run into that a lot.

As I was quickly perusing the books, knowing that I had very little time to be there that day, I ran across The New Marian Missal with a priest's name embossed on it. When I had been at the Grotto recently, I realized that I needed a Catholic missal with calendar so I could keep up with the Catholic liturgical year. Here in my hands was something better than a mere missal. Here was a true, blessed by ordained hands, priest's *Marian* Missal, worn and tattered. It opened to various underlined passages and had frayed ribbons marking the pages. A true treasure, I was honored to hold it.

I asked the store volunteer if this missal was for sale; I had found it on the used book shelf. It looked like it might be in the wrong place, since it was so sacred looking. She said that she didn't know for sure, but would find out later. I encouraged her to ask Mary if I could buy it. She took a moment in prayer and she said that Mary told her it was ok and to sell it to me for $5. Thank you, Mary!

I have been back to the Marian Prayer Center many times, to load up with Mary provisions, as if going on a cross country journey and needing a covered wagon full of supplies. As my travels continue and my larder dwindles, I return to this humble and sacred store to stock up with new Mary items. The unique Marian products, the volunteers, and such love for the Virgin continue to draw me back to the Marian Prayer Center again and again.

Looking for the Best Virgin Mary in Town

On opening night of the Willamette Writer's Conference there was a free, open-to-the-public panel. Since I couldn't afford the conference, I had to look for opportunities that were available for non-attendees. The panel consisted of editors and agents who would listen to authors give a three minute book pitch. After the quick pitch, the editors and agents would give feedback. This was a perfect opportunity to learn how to improve my presentation to help get my books published. The kicker was that there were only ten slots open. Thinking that the majority of the attendees would probably want to have a shot at this, I was at the conference hotel early while the coordinators were still setting up for registration. I was able to put my name third on the list for the free book pitch later that evening. Yes!

Returning later, I managed to find a seat in the totally packed room with new and wannabe authors. There were two authors ahead of me. I listened to their feedback intently and quickly made the appropriate changes to my presentation. When it was my turn, I gave pitches on both my manuscripts very quickly – a minute and thirty seconds each. Whew! The panel was cool over my first book *How to Talk and Actually Listen to Your Guardian Angel*, saying there's too many angel books on the market. But my *Shopping with the Virgin Mary* pitch was a big hit. I received great feedback on my proposal and much encouragement. This seasoned panel loved the name and content – juxtaposing the Beloved Mary with the superficial, consumeristic shopping activity. Being such a new author at that point, I was elated.

On the way back to my seat I saw a co-worker I recognized from a rehab where I worked occasionally. I had heard she was writing a book, but since we worked in different facilities, I hadn't had a chance to talk to her about it. Seeing her at this writer's conference let me know she was serious about her writing.

Afterwards, I went up to talk to her and asked what her book was about. She said rather sheepishly, "Bloody Marys." We both laughed at the irony that I was writing a book about *the* Virgin Mary and she was writing a book about *the* best Bloody Mary in Portland. What great research we both had to do for our books.

She had heard that I was going to Europe and asked if I was back or just visiting. I said I hadn't gone yet, I took off my hat, pointed to my bald head and said, "I was diagnosed with breast cancer and am in treatment for it. Hopefully I will be leaving in October." She nodded, "Oh, I am sorry to hear that. Good Luck!" We left with a big hug good-bye. Laughing one more time about how we were both writing about the best spirit(s) of Mary.

Our Lady of Fatima

In the spring of 1916, near the village of Fatima, Portugal, three children: Lucia dos Santos, Jacinta, and Francisco Marto were tending sheep when an angel appeared to them. The angel appeared two more times to them, identifying itself as the Angel of Peace and the Guardian Angel of Portugal. The angel instructed the children on prayers and various other teachings. During the last visitation, the angel also gave the children communion.

The following year, on Sunday, May 13, 1917, a cloud appeared to those same three children above an oak tree near where the angel had previously spoken to them. This time, a beautiful woman, dressed in a white robe with gold edging, emerged from the cloud. Her hands were in prayer and she held a Rosary of shining pearls with a silver cross dangling at the end. She told them that she had come from heaven and, in subsequent appearances, identified herself as "The Lady of the Rosary."

The children's parents, the officials of the town, and their local church priest, did not believe the children when they were told of their vision of the Virgin. They endured much questioning and intimidation, but each stayed true to his or her story. Mary gave them secrets which none of the children revealed, even under terrible threats.

The Lady of the Rosary appeared regularly in the same way on the 13th of each month for the next six months. She asked for more dedication in reciting the rosary, prayer, penance, and communion to change the course of the war (WWI) that was in the land. The Lady also gave one of the children three secrets, two of which were able to be told later.

Each time they returned to the field to visit Mary, a larger and larger crowd of people would accompany them. The Lady also explained that, on her last visitation, there would be a sign for all who gathered. On the last visitation, October 13th, over 50,000 persons were in attendance. It was raining and at approximately 1:30 in the afternoon, the rain stopped and the sun began to shine through the clouds. But then, the sun began to dance and move as it cast colors onto the crowd. The children were in rapture from the presence of Mary at the time so were unaware of this erratic solar movement. Witnesses and reporters present stated that, even though it had just quit raining and the sun was doing a weird dance in the sky, all of the people became instantly dry.

Word spread throughout the land. The children were in great demand by many in need as well as by the curious. Lucia did divulge the three secrets to the church, under Mary's guidance, and the Vatican revealed the last of these three messages in 2000, as Mary later instructed. Unfortunately, these were not secrets of good tidings, but warnings of suffering and strife which did, unfortunately, come true.

Our Lady asked that a chapel be built at the oak tree saying she would come there to heal people's body *and* soul in the future. This is a major Marian destination and The Lady of the Rosary is now called, simply, "Our Lady of Fatima." Healing continues to take place in Fatima, but the sun has never repeated such a light show.

The Pilgrim Virgin

There is a famous statue of Our Lady of Fatima, and on the 30th anniversary of the first appearance of Mary, Bishop Leiria blessed two exact copies of the original. The idea was to send the replicas around the world, one east and one west, in order to bless those believers who were not able to travel to Fatima, Portugal. These duplicates are four feet tall and are called the "Pilgrim Mary" or, more commonly, the "Pilgrim Virgin."

So many requests poured in to have the Pilgrim Virgin visit towns, villages, cities, and countries that more Pilgrim Virgins had to be made. By 1987 there were over 190 official statues pilgrimaging around the world in order to fulfill all the requests. Even more are on the road now.

Volunteer committees began to form to transport these Pilgrim Virgins from place to place. One such organization is called the "Pilgrim Mary Committee." They have carried her around in buses, planes, trains, cars, and boats to bring graces to all who see her. There are many stories of miracles that happen as a result of people being in contact with the Pilgrim Virgin.

Once when the Pilgrim Virgin was being taken into Russia, the bus it was on was pulled over by the authorities who wanted to stop this religious image from entering the country. At the time, there was great religious disfavor amongst the ruling political party. The Pilgrim Virgin was carried in a padded box tucked right behind the driver's seat. This gave added protection to the driver as well as the passengers.

Apparently, the Russian authorities searched every inch of the bus looking for the Virgin. They couldn't find it anywhere and questioned the committee as to the statue's location. The committee members just looked at each other and shook their heads. Since the police could not find the statue on the bus, they assumed that it was being transported into the country another way. They released the committee to continue its travels. As the committee re-boarded the bus, they silently gazed upon the box that Mary traveled in, still in its proper place, right behind the driver's seat, in plain view. They knew they had again experienced another miracle from Our Lady.

Another transporting and caring volunteer group call themselves the "Guard of Honor." They had been recruited from an organization called *Ambassadors of Mary*. They bring the Pilgrim Virgin to homes or churches on Saturdays, kneel with the receiving hosts, and offer a series of prayers, the rosary, and instructions for families, congregants, and visitors. They leave the Pilgrim Virgin all week and the following Saturday they arrive again, recite all their prayers and rosaries one last time, then, pack her up and off the Pilgrim Virgin goes to another location for the following week.

One Pilgrim Virgin statue cried in Haiti at a Port-au-Prince chapel on May 26, 1976 and another cried in Damascus on July 20, 1977. Those tears were shed at the same time those countries were experiencing strife and political upheaval. On each occasion, it was said the tears streamed from her eyes for several days and it was widely believed she cried for the sorrow of what was happening at the time.

The Pilgrim Virgin is now available for sale to the public from the Fatima Gift Shop. There are various sizes to fit each need. One Mary is 21" high and is packaged with 25 rosary beads and brown Scapulars with an instruction book full of prayers and devotions – all for $129.99. It is suggested to use this Pilgrim Virgin in nursing homes, youth centers, schools, or for private and group devotion.

Another Pilgrim Virgin is a plastic lawn and garden statue standing two feet tall. Depending on your preference, the price is a reasonable $59.95 for the bronze-like or $89.95 for the wood-like plastic. Apparently, the Pilgrim Virgin is quite powerful in all her reproductions.

So, be aware, if you hear about the Pilgrim Virgin coming to your town or village, or, if a neighbor has just put one in her garden, don't miss the opportunity to be blessed – as she has traveled far and wide . . . just to come be with you.

Holy Names Drive

On my way to the dentist office in Lake Oswego, Oregon, I drove by Marylhurst College. It dawned on me as I whizzed by, that this was a school dedicated to the Virgin Mary, thus the name, Marylhurst. I made a mental note and decided to explore the campus after my dentist appointment. Coming back, I took the first street into the Maryhurst campus, but soon realized it was not the main entrance. It was called Holy Names Drive. Not knowing anything about the college, I thought is was a cute name and very Catholic. I followed this street around the perimeter of the campus. It was a beautiful campus drive on a warm summer day.

At the end of the winding drive was a newly built retirement community called Mary in the Woods. Being tucked in the furthest part of this sprawling campus, I doubted it was open to the public, but I turned anyway. It was a community for retired nuns and priests. I saw a couple of them walking about as I meandered through the well manicured, secluded village. I wanted to learn more.

It turns out that the nuns who founded St. Mary's College in 1893, were called "The Sisters of Holy Names of Jesus and Mary" from Montreal, Canada. They later changed the name to *Marylhurst*, meaning Mary in the Woods, when they moved to the current location and it was the first liberal arts college for women in the Pacific Northwest.

The Holy Names Heritage Center had recently opened on campus. It held a library and was also a rental venue for weddings, parties, and corporations. The library contained information about the order and history of the founding of Marylhurst. I was very curious and asked at the reception desk how I could access the library within the Heritage Center. The women at the desk were gracious and gave me a tour of the one room library. They made a special effort to point proudly to the locked glass wall that held a few old photos and books the sisters brought with them from Canada over 150 years ago. This library was dedicated to the history of the college, making it different from the other larger academic library on campus.

I told the receptionist I was writing a book on the Virgin Mary and asked if they had any books about her. She said she would ask the main librarian who was sitting at a desk in an adjoining office. I followed the receptionist into the librarian's office and, while introducing myself, I explained I was looking for resources for the Virgin Mary book I was writing. She also was very gracious and said, "Why yes, we do have books on her in the religious section." They then walked me to the section which consisted of four shelves against the far wall.

She turned to me as I pulled out a visibly ancient book called "The Life of the Virgin Mary" and said how she was so excited to have their first scholarly person utilizing this library, since it had recently opened. I didn't have the heart to tell her my book wasn't exactly "scholarly." I thanked her, putting back the book, and said I would be back soon, when I had more time.

Mary and those who love her are scattered throughout this country; one never knows when she or her loved ones will appear in such rich, scholarly ways.

Mary and I Move

I am finally done with surgeries, chemotherapy, and radiation and am moving to England. The preparation for this move has taken way over a year. On my way to England, I took the opportunity for furthering my education by taking a seven day course in Transitional Ministry in Edmonton, Alberta, Canada. The course was held at the Providence Renewal Center. This was a retreat center, but named for the renewal of the spirit. The Sisters of Providence run this renewal center. The course offered was training to expand my ministry to become an Interim Pastor.

Having arrived in Edmonton, I took a cab to the renewal center and checked in. They gave me a double room with both a double and a single bed. I don't have to share this space with anyone for the week I am here. After my many months of treatment, staying at Peace House in a small room with just enough space for a single bed; this was a little bit of heaven, well, actually . . . a *big* piece of heaven.

At the head of the hall stands a four foot statue of the Virgin Mary with a blue and white cloak, her hands in prayer, looking slightly down and to the right. The property has another larger statue of Our Lady of Fatima at the end of a stone walk. In front of this Mary was a wooden bench so one could sit and have a chat with the Beloved Mother.

There was no Jesus in sight at this center, except for the small crucifix hanging over the double bed in my room – little Jesus, large Mary. The sisters are here because of the son, but really love the Mother too.

Class begins tomorrow, but I arrived early, needing a bit of renewal after moving out of Peace House, giving my newly acquired summer wardrobe, towels, and broken TV to one of the many thrift stores, saying goodbye to beloved friends and flying off with a cancer free life. The plan is still to live in England for five years with my partner. By now, she has already fulfilled one year of the contract while I sold the house and went through treatment.

I got a call right before I boarded the plane that I was chosen to be the Interim Pastor of the East London church! So, with renewed life and vision of a brightening future, it was so poignant to have Mary at my first stop here in Canada.

I sat on the wooden bench tonight after supper and talked with Mary. As I was eating my "digestives," looking out on this vast property, I noticed three enormous, well fed bunnies hopping about. Earlier I had seen a wolf walk through the rolling, green grounds and I was wondering what on earth a wolf would have to eat here at the Renewal Center. Then I saw those gigantic bunnies. I knew instantly why a wolf would like to visit this protected area and enjoy the big bunny buffet.

After dark I went exploring inside the center and on the third floor of the housing building was a statue of Joseph holding the baby Jesus. It was comforting to see my old friend here too. I slept better and began to heal more quickly knowing that my Holy Family was holding their places at strategic locations around this center.

Bunnies, wolves, Mary, and Joseph – with a bit of Jesus hanging around – all made me want to sleep and drift into the safety of this place.

Morning . . .

Today is my birthday. I walked out of my room and the housekeeping staff had their cleaning cart parked in front of Mary, with a mop handle resting on her praying hands. Mary is cleaning up all that has been discarded from all the renewing that has taken place. She is not above cleaning up a bit of our messes – to refresh and restart our lives and faith. The sight of her cleaning while she remains in prayer with those loving eyes is an image I will always remember; the ever cleansing love of Mary.

The Coronation of Mary

I have finally arrived in jolly old England. We live in a flat in Brighton, a city south of London, where my partner has labored with diligence to arrange all our American possessions in an orderly and tight fit. She has done a wonderful job. My part-time employment as Interim Pastor in London is a two hour train, subway, and bus ride – on a good day. If there is a problem on any leg of the journey, it can be up to an eight hour commute. One never knows if there will be a strike or a problem on the rails, so I leave Brighton at dawn to make sure I preach the 5 p.m. Sunday service. I do most of my work from home and travel to London on Sunday for meetings and the worship service.

One day I arrived very early, no church meetings or problems with any of the transportation. I was able to tour around London a bit before services and went to visit the public art collection housed in the National Gallery at Trafalgar Square. It is a monumental building and sits in the back part of a large public square in the middle of London. The promenade in front of the National Gallery has large, beautiful fountains and statues. The National Gallery's columned façade and many steps leading into the entrance make for a very grand presence. After you climb the steps and look back towards the square from the front doors, you see Big Ben, Victorian architecture with streets full of double-decker buses lumbering along, and hoards of tourists taking pictures of loved ones in front of those gigantic, spewing fountains. The noise and bustle of this busy city surround this tranquil place.

Inside is art from many periods and it is said to be one of the largest public collections in the world. The admission is my favorite price, free. Since I am on a limited budget at this time, I am enjoying with great appreciation all free gifts. This was one of the best.

Paintings from the 16th through the 20th centuries are located on the second floor. I saw two Virgin Mary paintings that were exquisite. One of her in a vibrant blue gown with her hands folded in prayer gazing down to her right. I made sure to stand in her gaze so I could look in her eyes as she looked into mine. I want Mary to see me. I have noticed throughout the years, that the pews and kneeling benches that are directly within the Virgin's gaze are always the ones that are the most tattered and used. This indicates that I am not the only one who wants to be in the direct line of sight of the Holy Mother.

The description card next to the painting said that it was unusual because the artist, Giovanni Battista Salvi, in the 17th century used a very expensive, ultramarine blue paint to paint her gown. Thank you for the quality you executed in this painting, Giovanni. The color is still vibrant, as if it was still wet paint.

The other painting that captivated me was by Guido Reni called the "Coronation of the Virgin." Roman Catholic belief is that Mary was crowned after her Assumption into Queendom, thus her name Queen of Heaven and Earth. In this painting, Reni depicts the Virgin in the clouds, with angels placing a golden crown upon her head. Most of the other art of Mary's coronation show men placing this royal headdress upon her, either Jesus, a male image of the Divine, or, I have even seen it done by one of the Popes.

This painting, "Coronation of the Virgin" was truly celestial, with two baby putti angels holding the crown above her head while a multitude of adult angels sing and play instruments to exalt the installation scene. No men or humans present. It was a party that was glorious and this painting displays it beautifully. I had trouble moving from the spot. This painting was riveting and depicted the joy as she stepped into her role of Queen of Angels.

As I became aware that I was unable to move from in front of this painting for quite some time, being fed by this feast of beauty and majesty, I realized the only way I would ever be able to continue with my life was to take a picture on my camera phone so I would be able to view it whenever I wanted. There was one big problem. Sitting directly across from the painting, staring at me, was a bored, but stern looking security woman, making sure that no one touched, stole, or took photos of these priceless works of art. So it wasn't going to be easy for me to slip my phone out of my purse with my back to the woman, concealing the forbidden act of taking a picture. But if I didn't take this chance, I would never be able to leave this gallery . . . so I was desperate.

There were signs all over the Gallery: "NO Photos Allowed." So I practiced a "Hail Mary" shot without looking into the viewer and with the flash off. I only captured half the painting. Darn. But, on the second try, I had the whole painting on my phone! What joy! Life can continue; there is hope and a future outside of the walls of the National Gallery.

I walked away from the painting several times, but still I had to go back again and again to both paintings and say thank you to Mary and those artists. I said a prayer and thought that if this exhibition was in another part of the world, one that was fervently in love with the Beloved Mother, there would be at least one rose or candle left by a believer in front of either of these two paintings and one of the devoted saying the rosary on a nearby bench. But alas, it is England, so I had her all to myself and was blessed that day to have seen such beauty and to have it in my phone to view any time I need to see it.

Desperately Seeking Mary

Brighton, England is on the southern most coast of the United Kingdom and has a long, pebbly beach front with a pier that jets out into the water. Such a lovely place and a bustling resort town. While here in Brighton, I have scoured the area looking for Mary. Where is she? I have found many churches whose congregations have dwindled so much that the medieval cathedrals have been turned into community centers, restaurants, flats, or tourist attractions. The Christians have been so upset with the lack of human rights and hypocrisy within the Church that they refuse to go to Sunday services anymore. But I know Mary still lives on somewhere here. It is a treasure hunt and I am waiting for that next puzzle piece, the next cosmic clue on where to find her.

Lo and behold, I did find her in an obvious place – within Brighton's Church Directory – a church named "The Church of St. Mary the Virgin." It is referred to by the locals as just "St. Mary's." The congregation is elderly and very small. So much so that this winter they can not afford to turn on the heat in their gothic sanctuary, so they sit in their winter coats during services . . . shivering. The candles lit in front of Jesus and Mary are the only sparks of warmth in these hollow chambers. Dusty scaffolding rises on one side showing the lack of progress on replacing windows and renovation, slowed by money problems and a dying congregation. It is a gloomy place, this St. Mary's.

The brightest spot in the church, however, is a small chapel dedicated to the Virgin. The central piece is a lovely painting of Mary with the angels flanking her in mid-air flight. It is worthwhile to sit on frigid chairs for the time it takes to say the rosary and a quick mass.

I picked up the visitor's guide to St. Mary's one time when the doors were open for the Eucharist service. I poked in and one kindly woman said to go ahead and look around. I could join the winter frocked group in the smaller room off the foyer, if I wished. She said they met in there to keep warmer. She knew that, like so many others, I wouldn't join them, but it was nice to be asked. She limped in to join her holy remnant.

The visitor's guide had a story about when the church collapsed because of botched work from previous builders long ago. The organ and some pipes were salvageable for the new construction. I was interested in reading that the first Vicar of St. Mary's was a Rev. Elliott, whose sister, Charlotte Elliott, was the writer of many hymns, including *Just As I Am*.

Fitting for this church to now be taken . . . just as it is.

I made a point of visiting St. Mary's church more. It was within walking distance from my flat and full of history. I have no car and it is an easy walk for me to be with the Blessed Mother in her chapel whenever the doors were open. Those open-door times were limited, a few hours each week.

On the church website is a picture of the church family and, yep, they still have their winter coats on for the photo by the altar. God Bless this old and historical church. Mary is with you and we all pray that there will be better days ahead for you loving and chilled, faithful followers.

Mary's Other Joseph

There was another significant man named Joseph in Mary and Jesus' life. It is widely believed Jesus either had an uncle, disciple, or patron who was the wealthy Joseph of Arimathea. He seemed to come forth as the one who watched over Jesus and Mary after the death of his father. It is rumored he took them on many travels, understanding the need for Jesus to learn from, the then known, spiritual teachers and travel the world.

Joseph of Arimathea was a wealthy merchant who dealt in metal, tin according to some sources. He had great caravans which journeyed the ancient world and was able to provide Jesus with travel to many foreign lands. Legend says he took Jesus and Mary to Britain at one time. There is much speculation that Jesus came with Joseph to study with the Druids. Glastonbury was the location of the Druid Mystery School. It is said The Rock of Israel was in Glastonbury, on loan from the Celts, around the time of Jesus' visit.

After Jesus' crucifixion, Joseph of Arimathea returned to Glastonbury with the chalice Jesus used at the Last Supper which held drops of Jesus' blood at his death. This chalice, called the Holy Grail, was apparently buried by Joseph somewhere beneath the Tor. The Tor is a tower on a nearby hill which is known to be the entrance to the underworld or the gateway to dimensions. Soon after this act, a spring came forth in close proximity to the Tor, which is now known as the Chalice Well. The rusty, iron oxide water of the well is said to be from the rust of the nails in Jesus' hands.

Another legend is that Joseph laid his staff on the ground as he slept not far from Glastonbury and it miraculously took root overnight, sending forth leaves and blossoms and becoming a plant known as the "Glastonbury Thorn." People come from far and wide to look at the Glastonbury Thorn and hear the story.

I have visited Glastonbury and have heard these stories about Joseph, Mary, and Jesus, have seen a Glastonbury Thorn and the Tor. The Chalice Well, in the Vale of Avalon, has powerful energy that is almost tangible. Many consider this well to hold and represent the female deity – the "Mary Well," as some call it. I still have a bottle of water from this well. I sprinkle it on the ground, in rivers, creeks, and anywhere I am led as I travel to sacred sites; pouring this powerful red water of Mary's Well around the world.

I have to tell you, this is a journey of great spiritual significance for those who take the time and effort to go. Glastonbury, England has a deep and rich heritage for a variety of faith walks. Traveling from one end of the world to the other . . .

In India, a written manuscript was found documenting the arrival of a young prophet, named Issa, who came from the West. It reads that he learned from the great masters of India and upon returning home, taught, healed, and was put to death by crucifixion. This prophet was known to break the spiritual laws of the time in India, as well, and gave sacred teachings to the lower castes – which brought him much trouble. These holy writings were only for certain *worthy* people. It is also stated in this ancient manuscript the prophet had to escape in the dark of night so he wasn't killed for doing such loving deeds. He provided holy teachings to those who had previously been denied access to God. Sounds like our Jesus. It is said India was one of the common trade destinations of Joseph of Arimathea's caravans.

Joseph of Arimathea was very important at the time of Jesus' death also. He was *the* one who was given the dead body of Jesus from the cross; *he* anointed the body with myrrh and aloes and wrapped Jesus in the finest linen shroud that *he* bought and laid him in *his* tomb. Because of this, *he* is now called the patron saint of funeral directors. (!)

Both Josephs were very important to Mary and her son. We thank you both for your service to your holy family and to us, the future generations.

Mother Mary Taught Her Son to Read

Every Wednesday at half past noon, The Parish Church of St. Nicholas of Myra in Brighton holds a lunchtime recital. St. Nicholas was the bishop of Myra who died in 342 AD and was the patron saint of fishermen, sailors, and such. Brighton being by the sea and having a seafaring past, it makes sense that the first church was built in honor of St. Nicholas, to protect the founders of the town; the sailors, and fishermen. It is also called "The Ancient Mother Church of Brighton."

This church is said to have been built in the 11th century or earlier. On the inside wall are stone carvings of some of the ancient vicars, the first one dated 1091. His name was simply John of Brighthelmston.

Brighton was first named Brighthelmstron, but when the Regent Prince George IV lived here, it was shortened to Brighton, for his convenience. It was known in those days as quite the party town (and still is) so it was probably shortened by alcohol induced, slurred speech many years ago and it just caught on.

I do love these free luncheon recitals. The church brings in pianists, violists, cellists, duets, sopranos, tenors, and many other talented artists. It is a pleasure to sit on the cushy, modern pew-chairs and listen to their 45 minute performances while absorbing the ambiance of the oldest church in these parts. Each time I go, which is often, I see something else that I didn't notice before.

This time I found "The Lady Chapel" which is on the right hand side of the long main sanctuary. I was so thrilled to find another place to talk with Mary. As I walked in the chapel area, the central image of Mary was an ornate oak wood carving of her teaching Jesus how to read. She is holding the Christ child on her right knee, while instructing him, from what seems to be a sacred book, on her left knee. She is pointing to a passage of this hefty book and he is raptly studying what she is pointing to. What an insight; Mary taught Jesus how to read!

This learned prophet, Jesus, the one who opened scripture and debated with the Rabbis at the temple, was taught to read by his mother, Mary! Of course, it makes so much sense when you think of it. This was the theme of The Lady Chapel at the St. Nicholas Church. Please Mary, teach me to read holy words too.

Sorrow and Direction

After all the preparation, waiting, and longing to go to England, my partner and I decided that we needed to shift our relationship and just be friends. Yes, it was a mutual decision, but I was still heartbroken. Our relationship and my European dreams shattered all at once. Just recovering from breast cancer and having depleted my money, I needed to stay on for several more months to work and accumulate funds in order to return to the United States and begin my life over.

I remembered one episode on my Portland, Oregon public access TV show, *Kermie & the Angels*, when I interviewed Mark Dodich the astrologer, who showed how astrocartography worked. When the planets are placed on the map of the world corresponding to the time of your birth, a graph is created that indicates where your lines of planetary influence are the highest. One of his examples was Oprah Winfrey and why her career took off so well in Chicago where so many of her astrological lines converge.

As a gift for having him on the show, Mark sent me my astrocartography chart. He said that my most favorable place for writing and publishing was on a line that ran north to south, passing through the four corners area of the western United States. He said that the greatest influence of the energy of these astrological lines was within three hundred miles on either side, east or west.

I am a warm weather lover, so I looked at the most southern city that was still close to that line. It was Tucson, Arizona. So, when all was shattered in my life and I was free to go anywhere in the world to live and write, Tucson seemed the best choice for a home that had extra energy to fulfill my writing dreams.

I had lived in Tucson many years ago and remember that time fondly. I was painting and had an outdoor garage studio. It was a very productive time and the warmer temperatures were lovely. Tucson has cultural diversity and is a small city with a large state university which attracts creativity, culture, and knowledge. So with much prayer, meditation, help from others, and patience, I began making plans to move from Brighton, England to Tucson, Arizona. So, Mary, we are on the move again, but I remember a wise person once told me, the joy is in the journey. I hope they are right.

Struggle and Hope

It took several months to finally board a plane in London after packing and resending the remnants of my belongings back to the states. I was very ill from a flu bug, again, that just wouldn't go away. My English doctors were baffled. Apparently, my immune system had taken quite a hit from the chemo and the cold, windy weather of England. Many miracles and much synchronicity brought me to this day – Mary was in it all. Just when I thought I wouldn't be able to go through another day of sadness, illness, and pain, she would be there in some form. I didn't write much during that time, it was all I could do to just get up and do what had to be done for that day.

I had a small stress fracture in my left foot, from the chemotherapy, so I wore Crocs all winter long, walking as short a distance as I possibly could, fighting the pain. Thoughtfully, my ex-partner had secured a flat, with me in mind, in the center of town with a grocery store in the same building. I found wonderful spiritual healers who worked by donation close to the flat and I showed up at their doorstep whenever I could. I wore my Miraculous Medal daily, under layers of warm clothing.

Finally, in the spring, my foot healed, I could afford a bus pass and I began to take the bus to another part-time job in addition to my East London pastorate. I met many friends and loving people in England. I so appreciated their support.

I found stillness and silence to be my healing balm. I would sit for long periods of time, drinking in the ocean, the cold air, and this lovely English town of Brighton by the crashing sea. Mary was in the silence. I saw and heard wonders that I would have missed along my way. I would look, long and hard at the world, finding the Divine in the most unusual places. I listened, deeply noticed, and breathed in the goodness around me.

One day, I ventured to a psychic fair in Hove, a town adjacent to Brighton. An astrologer was sitting in the corner of the ballroom that housed the event. I told him, as I slowly passed by, that I couldn't afford his services, but I was going through a difficult period in my life. He asked my date of birth, then nodded saying that I was in a Saturn return and everything in my life would change. He repeated again, EVERYTHING was going to change, from my hair style to where I lived. He said I would get through this fire-walk time, and it was necessary for the pruning which had to happen in order for me to go to my next level. I was very grateful for his quick and free assessment.

I did spend the money for a psychic reading that day. Since I had to find the best, I asked the conference coordinator who she would recommend. She told me she was unable to pick favorites, but she nodded toward the woman in the corner and turned away to the business at hand. It took my last bit of money, accepting her nodding advice gratefully and, by strange and wonderful synchronicity, the psychic's next appointment never arrived. She smiled, knowing that the Universe had made way for me, and told me to sit down and shuffle the cards.

The reader said I would still have a couple more very difficult months in England, but the future was bright in the United States. She encouraged me to go through this time as best I could and all would be better than ever – later. She talked about my future books and that my health would improve. I carried the psychic's and astrologer's information with me, giving me hope which carried me through those next, tough months.

Finally, finally, I boarded the plane, very ill . . . but I was on. I saw there were seats available, together, in the middle of the plane. I was able to lay down the whole trip over the Atlantic, trying to calm my stomach and shaking body, telling myself . . . all would be okay once we landed . . . and it was.

At the end of my flight, I arrived back in Portland where I had friends and loved ones waiting for me at the airport. Here I knew the people, the places, and I had secured a traveling, contract Occupational Therapy job which was to start in a few days. My employer provided an apartment, and my friend, Annalee, after picking me up at the airport, took me to another friend's house where I was fed and quickly put to bed. I was so much better the next day. I had made it through. Thank you, God, and thank you, Mary!

I stayed in Portland for four months, fulfilling the job contract. I bought a car, received my OT license for Arizona, and regained my health. There was an athletic club just one block from my apartment, I went everyday. I played racquetball alone to build up my right arm weakened from the surgeries and slowly increased my body strength with the machines.

My friends, who supported me through cancer and the break-up, were so glad to see me again, and I was starved for their love and affection, having gone through a steep, rocky journey in a strange land. They surrounded me with love and support. I healed and became financially stable as well. Then, I was ready to strike out on my own and continue my trip to Tucson, my new hometown. I had no job yet, even though my traveling company was looking. Again, by synchronicity, I had heard that two friends had recently moved to a town near Tucson. They said I could stay with them until I had employment and a place to live. All was in place.

Another loving friend gave me a small bumper sticker my last week in Portland that read, "Relax, God's in charge." It was small enough to stick on the driver's side, back window so I could see it each time I entered the car. I would stand looking at the bumper sticker as I filled up with gas and would take a deep breath and exhale letting go of whatever was worrying me at the time. Maybe it was helpful to someone else who may have stopped next to me at a stoplight too.

At last, early in the morning, Annalee came by to help me pack the car and send me off. So, with a hug and a wave, Mary and I said good bye, turned to the future to see the great Southwest, and to find a new home.

Flagstaff, Arizona has Mary Too!

On my way to Tucson, I stopped to see an old friend, Laura, in Flagstaff, Arizona for the weekend. We spent the first night catching up on our lives. I told her I loved the Virgin Mary and asked if there were any Virgin Mary churches or shrines in Flagstaff. I, of course, expected none, but the next day we went to a church called "Nativity of the Blessed Virgin Mary Chapel" on west Cherry Street. That was the only place she thought might have the Virgin Mary in some form, which, given the name, you would think.

For such a beautiful name, there was very little Mary in that church. There were beautiful angels on the exterior walls, though, and attached to the church was a lovely little bookstore. We went in to do some icon shopping. A woman behind the counter was friendly and we wandered about the store searching for sacred items we might like to add to our altars.

I asked the saleswoman if she knew of a place dedicated to the Virgin Mary. She told us about a little church in town which had a lot of Mary. My ears perked up. She said it was closed now, only open for special events. Each time I asked where it was, she said she doubted we would get in. "It is closed!" she repeated, and wouldn't give us the address. Having asked her repeatedly for the location, I kindly expressed my understanding and assured her, even though it was no longer open, I still wanted to see the *outside*. She finally relented and began writing the directions, all the while saying it would be useless to go since it was closed tighter than a drum. I was not to be deterred by silly little things like being "closed" for good.

So I paid for a CD, said our goodbyes, and off we went, searching for this deserted church. The church's name was "Our Lady of Guadalupe Chapel" at 224 S. Kendrick. Laura said, come to think of it, she remembered driving by it once, but had never explored it. She had some idea where it might be, so we navigated the maze of streets until we finally found it. Once we located it, it seemed odd that it was so hard for us to find since it was one block off a busy main street.

As we approached the chapel we were shocked to see so many parked cars surrounding it. Apparently there was a special event being held there. It was a *sign*. My friend, being somewhat of a "good girl," said we couldn't possibly go in, but I was not swayed. I knew my Virgin Mary and if she had called us to this place, she would get us in . . . somehow. As it turned out, when we peeked in the front door of the church, the sanctuary was empty. The event attendees were all in the basement for a reception. We had the place to ourselves! Yep, there was Mary, big as day on the wall of the sanctuary. I took pictures on my phone camera and we said our prayers quietly, not wanting to disturb nor alert anyone downstairs that there were visitors upstairs.

When we were through with the inside, we walked out the front door and as we were descending the steps, we noticed a small grotto with Mary and several candles in it, tucked away on the side of the church. My friend, now in the spirit of searching and finding Mary, was ecstatic to discover her in this overgrown, garden grotto. She pointed excitedly . . . what a jackpot to find her again. We cleaned up her outdoor rock sanctuary and took more pictures. Mary with me, Mary with Laura, Mary with both of us, Mary close up, Mary from a distance, praying with Mary, lighting a burned out candle to Mary, loving Mary.

We then meandered a bit further outside the church's garden area and into a small grove, and lo and behold, we found a plexi-glass enclosed statue of Juan Diego and the Virgin, depicting the scene at Tepeyac in Mexico! Such a profound scene it was, surrounded by the tall pine trees of Flagstaff, Arizona. We stayed there for a time, again for prayer, pictures, and to continue our awe, until we had had our fill of Mary and the Divine.

My work was complete. I knew she would allow me leave, to travel to my new home with her blessing. Again, I was reminded that Mary is *always* open for business.

Villa Maria

Coming down the mountain on the highway north of Phoenix, I began to cry when I saw the first saguaro cactus standing straight and tall. I knew I was at a place I could call home. The desert is so beautiful in October.

When I arrived in Tucson, I stayed with friends. They welcomed me with open arms. "Stay as long as you want," they said. This warmth at the end of my journey touched my heart. Just a few days later my company called with a three month Occupational Therapy contract and the location of my new furnished apartment. What a blessing to have a job and corporate housing, with everything provided. All I needed were my clothes and a toothbrush to move in. That's all I had so I was set... home at last.

I hoped Mark Dodich was right, that my planetary lines would help me in some way to continue to write and actually publish my books. I needed all the help I could get to make that a reality. So, I sit here in Tucson writing, a more healthy and worldly person. I seem to be cancer free at this point and am so very grateful to have made it through those last two, incredibly difficult years.

I wasn't in town for more than a couple weeks when I was driving down the busy Grant Road, and all lit up in the night was a bigger-than-life, outdoor, tile shrine of Our Lady of Guadalupe at the Villa Maria Care Center. I am not sure the folks at the Villa Maria Care Center realized when they installed their sign with Our Lady by the driveway, that they were installing a sacred shrine, but it has turned into just that. I couldn't believe my eyes – I wasn't in England anymore! I didn't have time to stop that day, but I took down the nearest landmark and promised I would be back to see her soon.

That weekend, my new friend, Amanda, and I had some time at sunset and I asked if she would mind if we searched for the Virgin Mary shrine-sign. Amanda is spontaneous, always open for an adventure, so off we went, to find Mary.

There she was, in the twilight, with the spotlights illuminating her. Several candles were on the ground in front of her, dead flowers and all the evidence of adoration left behind by those who love her. I began to clean her area, taking out debris, an old dryer sheet (?), candy wrappers, cigarette butts. I continued by up-righting the fallen vases of flowers, petrified from a long, baking summer. I blew off some dust and grime from the busy thoroughfare and spruced up the area with much devotion and attention to detail.

We took pictures on my cell phone of Mary, me and Mary, Amanda and Mary, you know the routine . . . we watched the neon orange sunset from her vantage point and, finally, said our good-byes. I like having an outdoor place to visit the Virgin in my new hometown. Because it is on a very busy thoroughfare, one can drive by the Villa Maria Care Center and blow her a kiss . . . without even slowing down.

One day, 3 months later, I was asked to fill in for work at our new "sister" rehab facility and it happened to be at the Villa Maria Care Center! I was so pleased to work with Mary at her *own* Care Center. I was curious what the inside looked like, being so familiar with the outside-shrine-sign. When I inquired how the staff felt about working in a place named after the Virgin, they actually said they liked working under the watchful care of Mary. We all nodded our heads in understanding, knowing there was a different energy there than at any other nursing home.

I liked working there. It was a small rehab department, but I knew if there was ever an opening, I was going to apply for the job. No one would mind if I had a picture of the Virgin on my desk or wall. I will let go and see what the future holds.

A few months later . . . the company I was under contract with offered me a full-time job, same hours and similar pay. I accepted it, once my contract expired. Because I was no longer under contract, I had to move into my own housing. A cheaper, but larger apartment opened up right across the parking lot, so I moved in a single day over the weekend. I got settled quickly, since I didn't have furniture or much stuff. That night, Amanda and I ate dinner on an overturned box, covered with a scarf, sitting on a couple of pillows, with a Virgin Mary candle glowing on the kitchen counter. It was simple, but a good beginning.

One day not long after that, the census at my main facility was low and my manager asked if he could send me to work at Villa Maria Care Center again. One of their therapists was off for a couple of days and they needed a replacement. I jumped at the chance. On my way into the parking lot that morning, in the wee hours before dawn, I stopped by the Virgin Mary outside-shrine-sign and lit a candle, asking for blessings on all the patients I would see that day. I lit a few more half burned ones, just for extra emphasis and to restart the previous prayers someone else had said when originally lighting their candles.

The Virgin still had her Christmas lights on and there were flowers from her birthday celebration a month earlier. It was January and her area was much cleaner then on previous visits. The candles all looked somewhat new, with no bugs in the wax. Rain was predicted and I noticed a rock was covering part of a lit candle, so rain could not extinguish the flame and dampen the prayer. So I placed a rock on the top of the glass holding my candle, covering the opening enough so the flame had a better chance to survive the inclement weather. All is well now, tucked away in her sanctuary.

My work seemed to flow better than usual that day. As my company was beginning to cut hours due to the failing economy and low census, there was talk that we would have to go home early whenever we didn't have patients to see. I had gotten used to my full-time, take-home pay and benefits. Knowing our concerns, our managers told us that we would retain benefits, but we would have to take voluntary and involuntary days off throughout the week.

The therapists at the small Villa Maria Care Center were accustomed to less then full time work with full-time benefits. They went home early most days and actually seemed to like it. When I asked about that, one of them said, "I don't mind, I have other things to do." As if he had a life to live that didn't revolve around his employment. One therapist even had a standing 2 p.m. tee time, so would get upset if he had to stay his full eight hours. What a concept. I was reminded again that I too have a life to live, and most of all, a book to write. Mary again, subtly, sent the message for me to keep my writing priorities in order, to lighten up and go with the flow.

Now that I am settled, I can live on less and actually have a richer life. Just when I needed it, I got wise advice from the sages at the Mother Mary Care Center, to take what I perceive as a challenge and make it an opportunity. Taking the time off to smell and write about the roses . . . of Mary.

Pink, Rose Perfumed, Virgin Mary Candles

One of the best known ways to turbo charge a prayer or praise is to light a candle. The flame keeps the intention steady while the candle is lit. When I am talking to Mary, I frequently light a Virgin Mary candle. They are tall, glass enclosed candles in a variety of colored waxes. The labels on the outside have a prayer and a picture of Mary. Many options are available; candles that depict Mary talking to Bernadette at Lourdes, Mary and the three children in Fatima, and Mary with the Miraculous Medal. These candles tend to have blue or white wax, but I prefer the pink, rose perfumed, Our Lady of Guadalupe candles best.

Virgin Mary candles used to cost less than a dollar, but now they have almost doubled in price. Walgreen's seems to have a perpetual sale on these candles, though, two for $3. But, if you are stuck without one, you can find them at some specialty shops for up to $5 a piece. Eck! And those are not even the perfumed ones. Lighting specialized prayer candles to Mary is rising in price.

The Virgin is growing in popularity among many non Catholics and there are usually candles for her in many Protestant or non-denominational churches and metaphysical bookstores. In these parts, they are even sold in grocery, liquor, and convenience stores. These tall, glass candles can last a few days on altars, shelves, and at the base of statues.

My apartment is small and it was just too hot to have Mary burning in the house with temperatures well above 100 degrees. So I turned my empty fireplace into a small summer shrine. I leave the flue open so the heat, smoke, and perfume carry the prayers up through the chimney and out into the heavenly realms.

My fireplace-Virgin-Mary-shrine holds flowers, Christmas tree lights, ceramic angels, and all sorts of festive articles to spruce up this, now, sacred place. At night, when I come home and it is dark in my apartment, Mary is brightly shining in the fireplace, welcoming me home and protecting me from night fears. "Good evening, dear, I am still here."

Sometimes, I will wake up and go to the living room to talk to her by her candle light. When one burns out, I light a new one with a different prayer and thanksgiving for her constant attention.

One time, all the pink, waxed candles were sold out and only the rare, green wax, Our Lady of Guadalupe candles were left. I asked Mary about the green colored wax and she said that I could use those for any money fears I might have. I scooped up all that I could hold in my arms, always open for help in *that* area. I have grown to like the green ones, but, I always return to the pink wax, in all its femininity and softness, for my daily devotions. I think Mary likes the pink ones best too, providing that subtle, rose, warm glow, day and night for every season, concern, and gratitude.

Churches Named after the Virgin Mary

Many Roman Catholic Churches have been named after the Virgin Mary. Most are a variation of "Saint Mary Church" or "The Blessed Virgin Mary Church" until the name just becomes redundant. So I am pleased to pass on a few, creatively named churches honoring the Virgin Mary.

There is a church for Mary's baked goods and her disposition called, "Sweetest Saint Mary Church" in Detroit, Michigan. Showing Mother Mary's age is the "Old Saint Mary's Church" in Cincinnati, Ohio; or the longest name of a Mary church is, "Saint Mary's Catholic Church of the Purification of the Blessed Virgin Mary" in Ontario, Canada.

Egypt has "The Hanging Church of the Virgin Mary" perched precariously on a hill. Orlando, Florida, the home of Disney World, has a church called "Mary, Queen of the Universe Church." It also has a shrine, museum, Rosary garden, and gift shop – allowing dreams to come true.

Mary shares billing with the angels at: "The Virgin Mary & Archangel Michael Church" in Madison, Wisconsin; "Blessed Virgin Mary, Queen of the Angels" church in Bemowo District, Warsaw; "Church of St. Mary of the Angels" in Assisi, Italy, and "Our Lady of Angels" in Bronx, New York, just to name a few. The "Guardian Angel Church" in New York, New York is under the protection of the Virgin Mary and our Guardian Angels, as stated in their website and literature.

But I think the most interesting (or boring?) is "The Falling Asleep of the Ever Virgin Mary Church" in Chicago, Illinois. Zzzzz . . .

Tubac and the Virgin

Tubac is a small, artsy town just south of Tucson. It is known for its Mexican shops and art sales. There is a church in the town called "St. Ann's," named after the mother of Mary. I have been there a couple of times now, and each time I visit Tubac, I stop in at St. Ann's for prayer and respite. In the backyard of the church is a stone covered grotto with a statue of the Virgin Mary in it. At Christmas time, colored lights are glued (?) to the stones surrounding her. In front of her grotto is a wooden bench, so one can sit, ponder, pray, and chat with the Mother of God.

I stopped in Tubac one cold, December night to see the Virgin in her Christmas splendor. I took pictures and lit some old candles that had been left behind. (I need to put candles in my trunk – I keep forgetting.) I scraped out the dead insects and old leaves that had accumulated around each of the wicks and I lit as many candles as would hold a flame. I think she likes me to recycle, our Eco-Virgin.

Another day when I went to visit Mary in Tubac, I had a scrumptious lunch on the patio of a café in town. What a find. Mary loves to take care of me when I am on one of my pilgrimages to see her – eating with the Virgin Mary – yum.

Around the corner from St. Ann's church, in the front yard of a house, is a small, wooden, doll-house sized church sitting on a pedestal. It could be in front of a gallery or a residence, there is never a sign that identifies what the building is. I have never paid much attention to the occupants in the building, only the Virgin in the doll-house church. Mary looks just as majestic in a doll house as she does in the church grotto. I am so pleased that she seems to be everywhere I go in the vicinity of my new home. It gives me such comfort and joy to find her as I explore the Arizona/ Sonoran desert.

The Many Amazing Names of Mary

Wherever Mary appears or is honored, she is given a different name. Here are many that I want to share; they are all quite unique and beautiful:

Bride of Heaven; Blessed Among Women; Disperser of Grace; Fountain of Living Water; Lady of Victory; Mediatrix of All Graces; Mystical Rose; Mystical Body; Perfume of Faith; Sanctuary of the Holy Spirit; the Virgin of Virgins; Spouse of the Holy Spirit; Highly Favored Daughter of the Father; First Charismatic; Seat of Wisdom; Cause of Our Joy; Vessel of Honor; Mystical Rose; Mirror of Justice; Spiritual Vessel; Singular Vessel of Devotion; Morning Star; Health of the Sick; Comforter of Sinners; Refuge of Sinners; Comforter of the Afflicted; Help of Christians; Tower Unassailable; Wedded to God; Helper of People; Disciple of the Lord; Our Advocate; Daughter of Adam; The New Eve; Fountain of Salvation; Full of Graces; Treasure of the World; Victor over the Serpent; Highly Favored One; Daughter of Zion; Exemplar; Undefiled Treasure of Virginity; Rich in Mercy; Neck of the Mystical Body; Joseph's Spouse; Mediatrix; Pillar of Faith; Tabernacle Most High; Birth and Giver of God; Full of Grace; Fount of Beauty; Life-giver of Posterity; Adam's Deliverance; Co-Redemptrix; Lady Most Benign; Joy of Israel; Advocate of Grace; Nourisher of God and Man; Woman Clothed in the Sun; Never-fading Wood; Bride of Heaven; All Chaste; River of Flowing Water; Reparatrix; Lady Most Clean; Kingly Throne; Crown of Virginity; Comfort of Christians; Ark Gilded by the Holy Spirit; David's Daughter; Dove of Simplicity; Bride Unbridled; Lamp Unquenchable; Court of the Eternal King; All Good; Unlearned in the Ways of Eve; Minister of Devotion; Advocate of Grace; Only Bridge of God and Man; Daughter of Man; God Bearer; House of Gold; Splendor of the Church; Rose Ever Blooming; Theotokoas; Carrier and Bearer of God; Tabernacle of God; Reparation of the Lost World; Lily Among Thorns; Advocate of Eve; Created Temple of the Creator; God Bearer; Gate of Heaven; Chosen Daughter of the Fallen; Cause of Our Joy; You Who Took the Child Jesus to Jerusalem for the Passover; Vessel of God's Mysteries; Sanctuary of the Holy Spirit; Second Eve; Mirror of Justice; Seat of Wisdom; Loom of the Incarnation; Garden Enclosed; Formed Without Stain; Temple Divine; Model of the Church; Servant of the Lord; Throne of the King; Tower of David; Nature's Recreation; Lamp Unquenchable; Forth-bringer of the Tree of

Life; Light Cloud of Heavenly Rain; Aqueduct of Grace; Market Place for Solitary Exchange; Surpassing the Heavens; You in Whom the Word Became Flesh; Unploughed Field of Heaven's Bread; Salvation of the World; Fountain of Light and Life; Chosen Daughter of Israel; You Who Gave Birth to Your First Born at Bethlehem; Model of Widows; Splendor of the Church; Birth Mother of God; Spiritual Vessel; Woman Crowned with 12 Stars; Unwatered Vineyard; Immortality's Wine; Surpassing the Seraphim; Deliverer from All Wrath; Eastern Gate; Dwelling Place of the Spirit; Medatrix of All Graces; Forth-bringer of Ancient Days; My Body's Healing; Bridal Chamber of the Lord; Vessel of Honor; Glory of the Human Race; You Who Were Found by the Shepherds with Joseph and New Born Child; Helper of the People of God; Summit of Virtue; Mediatrix to the Mediator; Free From Every Stain; House Built by Wisdom; The New Woman; You Who Kept and Meditated All Things in Your Heart; Singular Vessel of Devotion; Dispenser of Grace; God's Olive Tree; Paradise of the Second Adam; Refuge in Times of Danger; More Glorious Than Paradise; All Fair and Immaculate; Dove of Simplicity; Reparatrix of Her Parents; Star That Bore The Sun; Most Excellent Fruit of the Redemption; Fountain of Living Water; Hope of Christians; Paradise of Innocence and Immortality; Dwelling Place of the Illimitable; Surpassing Eve's Garden; Jesus' Companion at the Marriage Feast at Cana; Nature's Restoration; Treasure House of Life; Advocate of Grace; Tower of Ivory; Perfect Follower of Christ; Earth Untouched and Virginal; Living Temple of the Duty; Healing Balm of Integrity; Olive Tree of the Father's Compassion; Consoler of the Afflicted; Mediatrix and Counciliatrix; My Soul's Saving; Most Perfect Image of the Church; Heiress of the Promises Made by Abraham; Flower of Jess' Root; Incorruptible Wood of the Ark; Forth-Bringer of God; Spotless Dove of Beauty; Sweet Flowering of Gracious Mercy; Associate of the Redeemer; Woman Crowned with the Stars; Called Blessed By All Generations; Archetype of Purity and Innocence; Paradise Fenced Against The Serpent; Inventrix of Grace; More Gracious Than Grace; Inviolate; Lowly Handmaiden of the Lord; Woman from Whom Jesus Was Born; Fountain Sealed; Preserved From All Sin; Bride of the Canticle; Minister of Life; Temple Indestructible; Ever Green and Fruitful; Destroyer of All Heresies; You in Whom the Almighty Worked Wonders; Bride of the Father; Chosen Before the Ages; God's Vessel; Patroness and Protectress; More Beautiful Than Beauty; Treasure of Immortality; Scepter of Orthodoxy; Tabernacle of the Word; Earth Unsown; Perfume of Faith; Temple of the Lord's Body; Supplicant for Sinners; Undug Well of Remission's Waters; Workshop of the Incarnation; Protectress From All Hurt; Dispenser of the gifts of the Redemption; Eve's Tears Redeeming; Paradise Planted by God; Exalted Above Angels; Fleece of Heavenly Rain; Deliverer of Christian Nations; Dwelling Place of God; You in Whom the Word Dwelt Among Us; Mary, Help of Christians; Ave Maria; Miryam of Nazareth; Marien; Marian; Mary Immaculate; Mary, Immaculate Heart; Mary Who Chose the Better Part; Mary, Mother of God; Solemnity of the Immaculate Conception of the Blessed Virgin Mary; Immaculate Conception of the Blessed Virgin Mary; Virgin Mary; Virgin Mother of Grace; Blessed Virgin; Mexican Virgin; Virgin of Tepeyac; Protection of the Virgin Mary; Virgin Most Meek and Obedient; Blessed Virgin Mary; Virgin Most Venerable; Virgin Most Renowned; Virgin Most Powerful; Virgin Most Merciful; Virgin Most Prudent; Virgin Most Faithful; Virgin of Zeitoun; Virgin of the Rose; Virgin Inviolate; Virgin Daughter of Zion; Virgin Most Venerable; Ever Virgin; Virgin Most Merciful; Immaculate Virgin; Virgin Most Powerful; Virgin, Mother of Emmanuel; Virgin Most Pure and Lowly; Source of Virginity; Milk Giving Virgin; Virgin of Hal; Virgin of Chartes; Virgin of Notre Dame-Du-Roncier; Lady of Perpetual Sorrow; Our Lady of Perpetual Help; The Immaculate Conception; Sweetest Heart of Mary; Sacred Heart of Mary; Goddess of the Americas; Mother Goddess of Christianity; Immaculate Heart of Mary; Dwelling Place of Christ; Little Black Lady, and Birth giver of God, Our Lady of the Internet and of the Highway . . .

The list is inexhaustible – ad infinitum – to infinity and beyond.

Holy Names of Mary

Mary has many "Holy" names as well. A few of these are: Most Holy Name Mary; Mary, All Holy; Holy Mary; Holy Mother; Holy Mother of God; Holy Virgin; Holy Name of Mary; The Holy Theotokos; Holy Virgin; Ever Virgin Holy Mother; Holy Virgin of Virgins; Holy in Body and Soul; and More Holy Than the Cherubim, the Seraphim and the Entire Angelic Hosts . . .

Holy Molie!

Shopping for Houses with Mary

I liked my apartment, but my dream was to buy a house or condo and begin rebuilding my life. In recent years, the housing market in Tucson had tanked, so there was a good chance to find something affordable, even with my current limited income. I hadn't worked much the year before, what with my breast cancer treatment and my move to England, so I was uncertain if I would even be able to qualify for a mortgage.

One of my first days in Tucson, I met a real estate agent, Pat Fox, who attends my new church. I told her my situation and she said she worked with a wonderful mortgage broker. "If there is any way of getting a mortgage, he will be the one to do it," she assured me. "Ok," I said, "I will call you when I save enough for a down payment."

When I thought I had enough money saved, I called Pat. We met and I told her I was writing a book on the Virgin Mary and I asked if we could pray together, asking to be guided to the house God wanted me to have. She said she rarely was able to pray with clients and was excited to do so. After praying, we hugged and she said she would let me know what she found. We both were aware that we had just opened a new adventure with spirit. We were willing and committed to go wherever it took us.

By now I knew which part of town was most convenient for work, play, access to the highway, health food stores, a mall, and, of course, Home Depot. Pat was right, the mortgage broker was able to pre-qualify me for a loan and we began our mission. We saw a ton of houses and condos and I began making offers on them, one at a time. As each one fell through, we would say to each other, "That one wasn't it, the *right* house is out there." Then we would plan our next weekend's house hunting.

A few months later, on a Saturday, my realtor had two houses for me to visit, both in the same block. We drove separately and when I pulled up to the first house, I liked it immediately, quaint and cozy from the outside. Sweet, I thought. In the sunlight, it almost had a pink tone to it. This one was cheaper, more run down, Pat said. She wanted to show me the least desirable house first.

When we walked in, we saw that the house looked like the owner had left, as if going to the grocery store . . . several months ago. All her possessions were still in place. We also assumed, from her belongings, that she was a very elderly woman. It also appeared that she had probably raised a family and still had adult children and grand children in the area.

There was a beautiful ceramic stature of Mary holding the Christ child on a table by the front window. As I looked around, I saw many pictures of the bleeding hearts of Mary and Jesus on the walls. It was obvious, this older woman was a devout Catholic and she loved the Virgin Mary. I was a bit distracted looking at all the pictures and statues. It felt that this woman prayed her rosary often and was, indeed, a holy woman. Mary was everywhere.

The house itself had "potential," even though it was a disaster by real estate standards. The bathroom counters were falling off the walls, everything was dirty from years of wear, and the plumbing, the electric, and who knows what else would have to be redone to code. I shuttered to think what was behind those walls. The carpet was worn and frayed; the linoleum flooring was new but buckled, all the work of an amateur installer. There was rotting food in the refrigerator, empty McDonald's bags behind and under the couch, and bugs, unfortunately . . . everywhere.

Out the back door were two old, broken, white, plastic chairs, no patio, only dusty dirt, dead weeds, and a variety of discarded car parts, including engines, and debris spewed everywhere. The yard had two rusted tin sheds with doors that couldn't close, filled with years of accumulation.

The house had an addition that, by the look of the open electric box high on the wall, was built without permits. The side door was a trailer door that barely shut. The sliding glass door to the back yard was put in backwards so it could easily be opened from the outside. Luckily, it was broken so no one could get in or out of it either way. None of the back windows matched. All the old, crank front windows were broken, with holes in the glass from random BB gun pellets. The appliances worked, but there was no handle on the fridge, the dryer wouldn't stop drying, and the washer leaked.

The roof was damaged from air conditioner leaks and the ceiling in the living room looked as if it might cave in at any minute. There was a large crack in the side wall, exposing cinder block. Either the house had settled or there had been a great, desert earthquake. I was so afraid that this was my God house. Oh, please God, no . . . but . . . I will if you want me to.

Apparently, the woman had lived alone for many years after her husband's death. Even though it appeared that someone had attempted to help with the maintenance, too many years of failing eyesight and insufficient help had led to this disaster. She just lived in these conditions. It was a total mess, but . . . she loved her Mary.

The other house, down the street, was a beautiful remodel with tile floors, newly updated bathrooms, fresh, stucco-like adobe and all new fixtures. It was beautiful. I made an offer on the remodel, but knew, in my heart, that my thoughts kept going back to the calamity of a house down the street. Oh no . . .

The deal with the remodel fell through, of course, and I even tried an offer on another property. No go. I returned to the extreme fixer-upper again and finally, finally, my real estate agent and I sat at the dining room table with the stained lace tablecloth and unopened mail, to sign papers for an offer. We prayed, asking for God's will, and I became willing to actually do it. Even with all its faults, there was a peace, serenity, and love that emanated from that house. I looked over at the stunning ceramic statue of the Virgin with Jesus on the coffee table; it became etched into my brain.

The other agent got back to us very quickly and said that the family had just accepted an offer three hours before we sent ours. Whew, I felt relieved this wasn't going to be the house for me, with all the massive work needed, yet, somewhere deep inside, I was strangely sad. But . . . that was over and I continued my search.

I found a condo that would be nice. No major repairs, some paint and we were good to go. I placed an offer on the condo. In the meantime, while we were waiting for the counter offer, Pat received a call that the deal had fallen through on the rundown house and they asked if I would be interested in resubmitting my offer. We waited until the counter offer on the condo came through. It was much too high, but I was slow to move forward, weary from all the wheeling and dealing, dashed hopes and dreams. Also, as I continued my search and I saw what else was on the market, the extreme-fixer-upper became even less appealing. It had been on the market for over 18 months with no offers, until now. Wouldn't you know, the price just kept getting lower and lower – I certainly knew why.

When I was last in the extreme-fixer-upper, I noticed a faded and skewed sticker on the front door window. Tilting my head at an angle, I read it. The owner had apparently given to foreign missions and stuck the poem they sent back in gratitude for her donation on this small, door window. It said that this was a house of light and all who entered would know it was a beacon in the darkness, the house was blessed. That was so true. It truly was very light and airy – within and without, even with the rotting food in the fridge, trashed yard, and scary bathrooms.

In prayer the next day, I asked to be shown which house God wanted me to buy and, in my mind's eye, immediately flashed the statue of Mother Mary holding the blessed child under the bowed-ceiling living room. Each time I repeated the request to be shown the house I was to buy, that statue would pop into my mind in full color. I would try to erase it and try again and there it was . . . again . . . and again.

Hoping that God wouldn't want me to buy such a house, I finally asked, on my knees, for one last sign. *Very* clearly I heard, "What more sign do you want?" flashing, again, the vision of that statue.

This was so true, so I sighed, knowing this was the house, for better or worse; it was Divinely selected. That is what I wanted and again, something deep down was thrilled to be shown a God house at last. I began to cry as I was filled with joy to have found my home. I knew if God had picked it, it must be the very best one on the market for me, even though it didn't seem like it outwardly. I made my decision, said a prayer of thanksgiving, and called Pat.

I wanted to meet her at the house to draw up the papers, to see it one last time before my re-offer, but most importantly, just to feel it. We both sat in silent meditation. It was a very powerful experience for each of us. God was there. The energy was exquisite. Tears streamed down my face as I felt the love of spirit and knew that no matter what, this was a holy house of God and I was honored to just be in it, let alone have the possibility of actual ownership. I gratefully signed the papers.

After the meditation, Pat said the energy had been so powerful that she almost fainted. We both were spacey when we stood up to leave. We had to ground ourselves in order to be steady on our feet. We both knew in our hearts this was the house I was led to buy. It held such Holy energy. That wonderful old woman had spent years saying the rosary, loving her Mary, and truly experiencing the presence of God there.

We left knowing it was out of our hands and we would both be led by this loving spirit. We thanked God, Mary, and each other as we parted – silently pondering what we had both felt in that exquisite mess of a house.

Sacred Heart of Mary Convent

One day I found myself with a few hours with nothing to do. I had completed everything on my list, I couldn't even think of an errand that needed to be done. I was in the waiting period to see if I was really going to qualify to purchase the old, holy house. I had done my part, now it was up to the owners to fix a few things (that were *really* bad) and wait for the lender's final ok . . . or not.

My mortgage broker was very kind, as well as efficient. He had asked me to write a story about my experience with breast cancer and why my income was so low (non-existent) last year. He said financial institutions do have a heart . . . sometimes, and he wanted to try anything he could to help me put my life back together. I really appreciated the extra effort he brought to the table.

So, I was driving in the foothills, heading back to my apartment in east Tucson. What was I going to do with these few precious hours I had before dinner? I realized I simply wanted to be with God; to be silent and feel God's presence. The turn to Sabino Canyon was coming up and it seemed like a perfect idea to go sit in the desert canyon and commune with the Divine in nature. I turned left and as I began ascending the Tucson foothill's road, I passed a convent with a sign, "Immaculate Heart Novitiate."

I had never seen this sign or the convent before. It was down off the road and the sign didn't stand out, but today I just *happened* to see it. I made a quick u-turn and drove down into the convent's empty parking lot. I got out of the car and looked for a place to be alone without being too conspicuous, not knowing if I would be welcomed or not. This may be a private novitiate, whatever that was. I spotted a chapel, walked up the steps, and quietly opened the door of the sanctuary.

There were a few nuns in full nunnery clothing, sitting quietly in the chapel, scattered throughout the pews. I took a seat in the very back row, again hoping for invisibility as I joined them in silent prayer and reading. It was perfect God space. Up front was a statue of Mary, one of Jesus, and another of Joseph with the usual row of candles, some lit and others not, waiting for the devoted to activate them with a flame and a prayer.

I meditated and sat in silence for quite some time. I alternated between kneeling on the bench that folded from the pew in front of me and sitting back quietly to meditate. After awhile, I opened my eyes and noticed more nuns had taken seats in the chapel, sprinkled around me. Silently they had come in to gather. Then one nun began to speak from her seat, softly, as to not shatter the silence, speaking words so quietly I could barely make them out. Then, as if choreographed, all the other nuns began reciting "Mary, Mother of God . . ." many, many times. I was in a worship service!

The Divine presence was thick, and to be within those sacred walls as the chanting continued around me in soft feminine voices, set me to thinking I was in the midst of angels. After about half an hour, a nun brought me a missal and pointed out where everyone was so I could join in. I thanked her and began reciting, not only the rosary I was now saying with everyone, but also the appropriate responses and chants.

The service ended as softly as it had started. The nuns began to silently leave, each in her own time. I eventually got up and handed the missal to one of the nuns sitting in back of me, at a table. I smiled and thanked her for allowing me to participate in their worship. She inquired about my being there and I told her I had been led to the chapel by my wish to be with God. I told the nun I loved Mary. She smiled and said she did too. We blessed each other as I left the chapel.

Mary had let me know during the silent time that this house was mine, it was her gift, and she was, indeed, in it. I was instructed to prepare for my move and this new chapter in my life with her. Tears began to flow, again, in awesome gratitude.

Mother Mary Names

Mary has an abundance of "Mother" names, and the most popular of all is the Mother of Jesus and Mother of God. But here are several more in case you are interested in adding to your names for the Virgin or are looking for a great "Mother" name to call her:

Mother of Perpetual Help; Mother of Mercy; Our Blessed Mother; Mary, Mother of All Graces; Mother of Divine Providence; Mother of Perpetual Help; Great Mother of Us All; Great Mother; Mother of All Humanity; Mother of the Savior; The Mother of God and Ever the Virgin Mary; Mother of God of Great Truth; Mother of the True God Teotl; Sorrowful Mother; Mother of Our Lord; Mother of the Church; Our Mother; Queen Mother of Jesus; Mother of the King; Mother of Divine Grace; Mother of Christ; Mother Most Pure; Mother Most Chaste; Mother Inviolate; Mother Undefiled; Mother Most Amiable; Mother of Good Counsel; Mother of Our Creator; Mother of Our Savior; Mediatrix of All Graces; Virgin Mother of Grace; Holy Protection of the Mother of God; Our Mother the Saint Virgin; Mother of the Mystical Body; Mother of the Church; Mother of the Heavenly King; Mother of Our Head; Mother Most Venerable, Mother and Teacher in the Spirit; Mother and Mediatrix of Grace; Mother of Reconciliation; Mother Most Powerful; Our Own Sweet Mother; Mother Of Mercy; Mother of Good Counsel; Mother Most Pure; Sister and Mother; Mother Whom Joseph took into Refuge in Egypt; Sorrowful Mother of the Church; Mother of Christ the King; Glorious Mother of the Messiah; Mother Standing at the Foot of the Cross; Mother of Every Christian Family; Mother of Divine Love; Mother of New Isaac; Mother Who Were Found Together with the Child by the Wise Men; Mother of Unity; Mother Most Undefiled; Mother by Act of the Holy Spirit; Mother Whom Jesus Obeyed at Nazareth; Mother of Consolation; Mother of Fairest Love; Mother of Jesus for Having Done the Will of the Father in Heaven; King's Mother; Mother of the Savior; Mother of Divine Providence; Mother of the Disciple Whom Jesus Loved; Glorious Mother of the Messiah; Mother of Men; Mother of Women; Mother of the Son of David; Mother of Divine Grace; Most Holy Mother of God; Mother Most Chaste; Mother of Christ's Members; Mother Most Faithful; Mother of the King of Israel; Mother Inviolate; Mother Most Merciful; Bountiful Mother; Milk Giving Mother; Good Mother; Alma Matra; and Notre Dame . . .

I Bought the House

After much faxing, writing, and attempting to show I was financially responsible, the day came when I did sign the closing papers. The mortgage guy and my real estate agent were there as I received the keys to this blessed house. I couldn't believe it.

The previous owners had cleaned out the rotting food in the fridge and removed everything, stem to stern. When I opened the door on my first visit to my new home, I looked quickly towards the living room to see if the Mother and Child statue was left behind. But no, it had gone with the empty McDonald's bags and car parts. It is still there in spirit, though, was my thought as I worked to console myself.

Along with all the cleaning supplies I could carry, I also took a scented Virgin Mary candle and lit it first, saying a prayer and inviting her, God, and the holy family in. I asked the angels to, please, help me clean and I set the intention of Divine love and light. I even asked the fairies to come and be at home in the front and back yards. As I thoroughly cleaned the empty house, I did find a few keepsakes in the recesses of the house: a ceramic plaque of Virgen Del Rocio and a refrigerator magnet of the Virgin holding her son. Mary wanted me to know she was still there. I was very touched. The refrigerator magnet is now covering the hole where the door handle used to be.

I put up a couple of Marian items and went shopping (with Mary) for what I needed to fix a few small things. She was now solidly in residence. It was indeed a spirtual house, not very beautiful, but certainly holy. This should be an interesting journey, I thought to myself that first day as I looked at all to be done, both with the house and with me – but I was so glad to be home at last.

I prayed to be led to the workers God wanted me to hire as the house was rehabbed, asking for guidance each step of the way. I wanted to tile the entire house with a terra cotta tile except for the bedrooms which were to be carpeted. I searched and searched for the right tile.

One Sunday as I was driving through an unfamiliar part of town, I saw a hand written sign, "Today Only – Tile Blowout Sale." I turned in and there was the *exact* tile and carpeting I wanted and *all* at incredible reduced prices. They knew of a great installer for me to call and, within an hour, I had paid for the materials and set up a time for the installation of my new floor, prior to my rapidly approaching move-in date. The installer just *happened* to have a cancellation for the next week, it was unexpected. He was grateful for the work. Being booked several weeks out, he said he couldn't move any of his existing client's times up on such short notice. Yes, he could start tomorrow!

The synchronicity continued. When I called the Home Warranty people to report some leaks, the plumbers they sent felt so sorry for me for getting stuck with such an awful house. You could tell they thought that someone had really taken advantage of me. They replaced all the broken faucets with out-of-date faucets they just *happened* to have in their truck. They said, "No one else would want these old models, they have been in the truck for years." I loved the faucets. They actually worked and were new to me.

When they examined the tub drain, the pipes were so rusted and broken that the water from the bathtub drained directly into the dirt under the house. They would pull out rusted-pieces of pipe-parts, shaking their heads, feeling more and more pity for me. They were so kind and charged me a much discounted price for all the work they did, out of compassion for the mess I was in.

I have to tell you, I had to re-do, not only the plumbing, but the electric, the roof, the paint, design new bathrooms, tear down walls, fix ceilings, and put rock in the yard to deter the many feral cats from continuing to use it as their own personal powder room – God was in it all. The miracles, the people who just showed up out of nowhere, all convince me that *all* was, indeed, in Divine order.

Mary was throughout the house. I prayed each day that the loving energy continued to be a blessing to those who entered. Sometimes, I thought it was too much to own a home, especially when something *else* went wrong. Then I was reminded again and again, this is so not my house, it is God's and I always, *always* got the help I needed. The house was very broken and waiting . . . just for me. This house is strong in spirit. Now her outsides reflect the beauty of the energy she holds inside. Holy, happy, and healthy.

The Assumption of the Virgin Mary

The book, *Assumption of the Virgin* (Liber Transitus), circulated in the 5th century AD. This ancient book states when Mary died, all deceased apostles miraculously appeared in the funeral procession. Also, during this procession, a Jewish rabbi tried to overturn the bier and found that his hands were bound to it until he confessed his faith in Jesus.

When the body of Mary was laid in a tomb, Jesus appeared accompanied with a band of angels and, at Jesus' command, the angels carried her off to heaven. Since the 5th century and the publication of this book, the bodily assumption of Mary has been a known Catholic belief.

To confirm this, on November 1, 1950, Pope Pius XII declared it "revealed dogma" that "the Virgin Mary, the Immaculate Mother of God, when the course of her life was finished, was taken up, body and soul, into the glory of heaven," thus, making the Assumption of the Virgin Mary official in the eyes of the Roman Catholic Church.

Queen Mary Names

Mary has been giving the royal name of "Queen" and some of the most common are:

Queen of Heaven; Queen of Peace; Queenship of Mary; Queen Mother of Jesus; Mary Queen; Queen of the Angels; Queen of Patriarchs; Queen of Prophets; Queen of Apostles; Queen of Martyrs; Queen of Confessions; Queen of Virgins; Queen of All Saints; Mary Immaculate, Queen of the Universe; Queen of Confessions; Queen of Heaven and Earth; Queenship of Excellence; Queen of Charity; Queen Unconquered; Queen of All Creation; Mother, Queen and Servant; Queen of Mercy; Queen of the Heavens; Queen Conceived Without Original Sin; Queen of Virgins; Spiritual Queen; Queen Assumed into Heaven; Queen of Families; Queen of the World; Queen Conceived Without Sin; Queen of Peace, Persevering in Prayer with Them; Queenship of Efficiency; and the popular Queen Mary I and II.

Mary on the Front Porch

Around the corner and down the block from my new house in Tucson is a well lit, life-sized statue of the Virgin Mary. It is standing on a small platform on the front porch of the house with lattice woodwork and Christmas lights all around! I about wrecked my car the night when I first drove by my neighbor's house. It was an unexpected sight to see the beautiful Mary calmly standing there, unassuming, blessing the neighborhood and all those who passed by. The yard was bare except for two weathered chairs and a swing set placed among the dead weeds that did not survive the summer heat and trampling little feet. I have since made this street my main road of travel whenever I go to the shopping areas on the nearby thoroughfare – just to pass this reverent shrine of the Virgin.

I have noticed she looks particularly lovely at night with all her multicolored lights illuminating her in prayer and grace. One evening I had to stop, get out of my car for a closer look, and honor her. A shadow looked out the window to see who was stopping in front of their house. It was me, a Mary devotee. They seemed to understand and, when they realized I was there for Mary and not them, they continued with their evening activities, closing the blinds to give added privacy – both to them and to us.

I noticed a new addition to the statue after Mary's Birthday celebration on December 12th. Brightly colored streamers cascaded and gently blew in the wind. There were also brilliant, neon colored tissue flowers and stoic candles at her feet. Now she looks festive and not as solemn in her prayerful stance on these cool December nights.

I would like to have a Mary statue in the front yard of my house too, I thought, in the corner this side of the hedge. My hair stylist shared with me soon after, that her husband had bought a beautiful statue of the Virgin Mary from Food City on Fort Lowell Blvd for $40, as her birthday present. She isn't Catholic or particularly spiritual, but she loves her Virgin Mary. I was so excited to hear about Mary statues being for sale that I went on a field trip to Food City to see for myself. Food City has much to offer to the Mexican palate, from cookies, various salsas, beans, and menudo to colored candles of favorite saints. It was fun shopping at Food City and I loaded up on the Mexican food that wasn't available in my local Safeway or Trader Joe's.

I finally found the $40 statues of Our Lady – above the canned chili's and condiments on the tippy-top shelf. I had to reach up high to slowly pull one of the statues down to look at the price pasted underneath. Yep, $40; this is the one and, yes, she is beautiful. It would have been the one I would have bought too, as I looked at all the different sizes and styles of Mary statues, but I didn't know how she would hold up outside in the Tucson monsoons and extreme heat. This seemed to be an indoor Mary. I will keep looking and see if another statue appears that is more all weather. Maybe cement would be a better choice.

Then I saw it, a smaller statue of the Virgin within its own ceramic grotto. It came with rocks and all, just like a real outdoor grotto. It was perfect. Being too heavy and too high for me to reach, I looked around for an employee or strong man to help me.

At the end of the aisle was a very strong looking, distinguished man and I asked if he would help me get the Virgin off the tippy-top shelf. He said he would be happy to and came over, lifted her down, and as he turned to place her lovingly in my shopping cart, I saw he had tears in his eyes. He said, "You don't know how much this means to me. My mother just died, and you asking me to do this is a sign from her." I began to cry too as we stood in the middle of Food City, having a spiritual moment together.

I am aware that all Virgin Mary statues are usually blessed by the priest, but I asked him if he would bless my statue for me. He beamed through the tears and consecrated that statue in such a way I will never forget, very powerful, and with much emotion. I said my thank you and blessed him. He held up his hands in prayer and departed back into the world.

It is good to be in a town that has the Virgin Mary in so many places. A friend of mine gave me a cardboard car freshener to hang from my rearview mirror of Our Lady of Guadalupe. The rose smell had been all used up and my friend now had a new one swinging from her mirror. She had just thrown the used one in the glove compartment, knowing that she would give it to a Mary lover who would appreciate having Mary swaying from their rear view mirror too. She figured right. I have a pink ribbon from my birthday party last year draped over my preloved Lady and it is very festive, like the front porch Mary with streamers.

One Sunday as I was heading to Home Depot and passing my favorite front porch Mary, there was a Yard Sale sign in the front yard. I stopped to thank the owners for keeping Mary alit on their front porch. Luckily, the young daughter spoke English, so she could translate for her mother and father what this middle aged, white woman was going on and on about, pointing to their front porch Virgin. They were quite happy to hear that I too was in love with Mary and invited me to next year's celebration on December 12th at midnight. The mother was smiling from ear to ear with delight to have me so interested in Our Lady.

Mary is loved and celebrated in this neighborhood and town. I belong here and in a neighborhood that will flaunt their love and devotion in such a bold way. The gated communities in the foothills do not have much of Mary on their front porches. I know, again, that I am also in the right house, with a ceramic Mary grotto tucked in the corner, this side of the hedge in my front yard. A candle is always burning, giving graces day and night to those who pass by.

Coming Back to Immaculate Heart Novitiate

I woke up today knowing I was called to write at the Immaculate Heart Novitiate. I had not returned as a home owner and found it was much further away than when I was living on the east side of town. As I entered the parking lot, I noticed a middle aged man changing into hiking shoes and clothing. I thought he might be planning a hike up the small mountain behind the chapel and was using the parking lot as a changing area. I got out of my car with my little computer bag and found that the chapel door was locked, so I sat on the stones in front of the Virgin Mary statue outside.

The hiker approached me and asked if I was here to write, looking at my computer bag. I said I was and he introduced himself as "John" and then explained that he hikes up the path which has the Stations-of-the-Cross. The nuns ask him to clean as he goes. So once a week, he hikes up the desert mountain in back of the convent and polices the area.

I asked if I could walk with him today on his rounds. He agreed and off we went, he in his shorts with his walking stick and me in my fashion boots and computer bag. He showed me a path to another statue of the Virgin which had a rock altar with a picnic area, a barbecue grill, and running water. He explained there had been, at one time, a retreat quarters and large meeting room in one of the buildings of the Novitiate. That peaked my interest and I wondered if it was a possibility to actually retreat here.

I followed him up to a couple of stations until the loose gravel path turned into a much harder climb than my fashion boots and feet could endure. I said "Thank you," and told him that I needed to stay on the lower ground due to my shoes. He continued on his mission as I came back to the benches in front of Mary at the picnic area.

John came down from the cross at the top of the hill and stopped to tell me that I probably needed to check in with the nuns in the front building and he gave me two names. I was glad to have this information so I could begin to address the nuns when I saw them.

I knocked on the convent door John had pointed out and an elderly nun answered. She was in a blue and white habit. I told her I was writing a book on the Virgin Mary and John, from the mountain, had asked me to stop in to tell them what I was up to. She looked at me quizzically and then asked if I would like to go to the chapel. I said I would and she led me through the back entrance of the chapel and asked me to sit in the back row. I asked about services and she said they were at 8 a.m. daily. The only exception was the service at 9 a.m. on Sunday. I must have attended a private service my last time there. By the look on my face, she seemed to sense I was not an early riser and wasn't as devoted to my faith as I probably should be, but she left me in the chapel to be in the silence.

As I was doing my usual alternating from kneeling to sitting and meditating, I asked Mary if there was something she wanted me to see or do. I have to warn you, if you are not totally sure you want to see or do something, don't ask the Virgin that question. She might have requested I get up early tomorrow morning to come to church at 8 a.m., but she didn't. She just wanted me to take photos of the statues in the sanctuary and to sit silently in her presence.

Sometime months later . . . I was with a friend and it was Good Friday. We were looking for a quiet place to be, somewhere away from crowds, and we thought about Sabino Canyon. On the way, I told her I preferred something a little more secluded; she agreed and we stopped off at the Novitiate instead. This time, I had walking shoes on and we walked up the hill, stopping at the Stations-of-the-Cross along the way to the top where a big Jesus was hanging on a cross.

Since it was Good Friday, there were others taking this same journey. My friend turned to me after a few stops at the stations and said she wished she knew what the stations were. We saw people saying words and doing a ritual at each station-stop, but, not being Catholic, we just paused and nodded as we lumbered by. We hadn't gone more than one more station when we approached two women who were reading and chanting. We stopped politely, listening for a minute and, as we quietly turned to depart, one of the women asked if we wanted the Station-of-the-Cross pamphlet. We were thrilled as she handed us the information and the words for each station. So off we went, armed with the official script for station-stoppage.

We finally reached the top about the time the sun was lowering in the west over the Tucson mountains. There was Jesus, hanging in twilight hues. The sun was beginning to set as it did so long ago when he died. It was quite moving, seeing the significance, even with our bumbling ways. We knew we were at the perfect place at the perfect time on this Good Friday.

All the climbers waited briefly at the foot of Jesus until the slower ones arrived. Even though we didn't know each other, we had somehow become united on our ascension to the cross. Without prompting, we all recited the final instructions as the last of the sun sank beneath the horizon.

With all the prayers, kneeling, and picture taking completed, we each silently clambered down that rocky path as it was getting dark; got into our separate vehicles and headed off to supper knowing we had just participated in a deeply beautiful and Divinely orchestrated Good Friday event.

Our Lady of Locations

There are even more Mary name possibilities. These are all based on locations:

Our Lady of Lourdes; Our Lady of Guadalupe; Our Lady of the Sea; Our Lady of the Mountains; Our Lady of Fatima; Our Lady of the Snows; Our Lady of the Canneries; Our Lady of Altagracia; Our Lady of Mount Carmel; Our Lady of the Copacabana; Our Lady of Knock; Our Lady of Walsingham; Our Lady of Cobre; Our Lady of La Salette; Our Lady of Pompeii; Our Lady of Akita; Our Lady of Pontmain; Our Lady of Czestochowa; Our Lady of the Desert; Our Lady of Belen; Our Lady of Toledo; Our Lady of the Alps; Lady in the Hawthorne Tree; Our Lady of Cape; Our Lady of Africa; Holy Mountain of Our Lady; Our Lady of Lujan; Our Lady of Kevelaer; Our Lady of Cana; Our Lady of Nazareth; Our Lady of Mariazell; Our Lady of Beauraing; Our Lady Altotting; Our Lady of Japan; Our Lady of La Vang; Our Lady of Limerick; Our Lady of Turumba; Our Lady of Pillar at Saragossa; Our Lady of Cenacle; Our Lady of Montserrat; Our Lady of Shongweni; Our Lady of Gundalupe of Estremadura; Our Lady of Einsiedeln; Our Lady of Saint-Victor; Our Lady of Mariazell; Our Lady of El Rico; Our Lady of Soledad; Our Lady of Kazan; Our Lady of Rocamabour.

Please feel free to add your own: Our Lady of (your home town). I will call her Our Lady of Tucson for awhile . . . it might even catch on.

Our Lady of . . .

Along with Our Lady of Locations, we have names of Our Lady Of . . .

Our Lady of Charity; Our Lady of Grace; Our Lady of Mercy; Our Lady of the Most High Rosary; Our Lady, Queen of the Apostles; Our Lady, Health of the Sick; Our Lady of Consolation; Our Lady of Divine Providence; Our Lady of Tears; Our Lady of Good Counsel; Our Lady of the Most Blessed Sacrament; Our Lady, Refuge of Sinners; Our Lady of the Angels; Our Lady of Prompt Succor; Our Lady of Light; Our Lady of the Roses; Our Lady of the Miraculous Medal; Our Lady of the Most Holy Rosary; Our Lady of the White Dove; Our Lady of the Immaculate Conception; Our Lady of Refuge; Our Lady of Incarnation; Our Lady of Sorrows; Our Lady of Perpetual Sorrows; Our Lady of Perpetual Help; Lady of Legend; Lady of Prayer; The Lady of the Cloud; Our Lady of the Visitation; Litany of Our Lady; Our Lady of Ransom; Our Lady of Victory; Our Lady of Safe Travels; Our Lady of the Hermits; and last but not least, Our Lady of Milk and Safe Delivery.(?)

La Fiesta de Guadalupe at the DeGrazia Gallery

Ettore "Ted" DeGrazia is a well-known southwestern artist who lived in the desert just northeast on the outskirts of Tucson, Arizona, until his death in 1982. During his lifetime he was an extremely prolific artist. The DeGrazia Foundation alone has more than 15,000 of his permanent works. While he was alive, he sold thousands of original art pieces around the world.

One of his paintings, "Los Ninos," was chosen by UNICEF for a 1960 holiday card. This led him to become an internationally acclaimed artist. On May 12, 1976, it was reported Ted DeGrazia burned many of his priceless works in protest of the Inheritance Tax that was to become law. The tax would be levied on the art work inherited by heirs of the deceased artist at market value. This protest led to much press on a national scale. He was a good father, protesting that tax on behalf of his descendents.

In December of every year, there is a festival for Our Lady of Guadalupe at his ranch/gallery/home in the foothills of Tucson. Visitors are able to park in the shopping center parking lot several blocks away and take the shuttle into La Fiesta. You can also take your chances, like I did, by parking in the bank parking lot, which is closer. You do need to arrive early for that luxury, as it quickly fills up with cars in the wee hours of the morning. This was La Fiesta de Guadalupe, and amazingly, I was there at the cracked pepper of dawn. Occasionally, it does happen, I show up on time.

People wander about his property and see the various structures he constructed from materials he found in the surrounding desert. The buildings include a couple of galleries, houses (including the one he lived in), and a chapel to Our Lady of Guadalupe. Inside the chapel, up front and center on the sanctuary adobe wall, DeGrazia painted a life-sized Our Lady of Guadalupe above the altar. Candles, pictures, and rosaries from the many visitors who have entered this sacred building are scattered in constant view of DeGrazia's Our Lady. In this chapel, it is all about Mary. Jesus does have a small room near the entrance with the cross and a few candles, but the main sanctuary is focused on his Mother.

On one side wall of the sanctuary, DeGrazia painted a permanent choir of forever-in-flight, singing angels. The floor is rough with abode bricks, flat rocks and various desert woods. The center of the ceiling has an opening with a simple cholla cactus cross pointing towards the sky and the Catalina Mountains.

DeGrazia dedicated the chapel to Our Lady and Juan Diego, who was the recipient of the famous image on his tilma. On the back wall is a short summary of the story of the meeting of Juan Diego and the Virgin; the atmosphere seems to take you to the very spot of Juan's visitation.

During the Fiesta, an outside stage is set up featuring dancers and local Mexican, Native American, and Jazz bands. The celebration is concluded in the late afternoon with a children's procession and the lighting of the luminaries at dusk. Every hour a piñata is broken – to the delight of the audience and youngsters attending. Off to the side of the stage and placed under casitas, are Native and Mexican-American food vendors selling fry bread, tacos, burritos, fruit, and salted prunes. Yum! It was so awesome to sit on a folding chair next to two Tohono-O'odham Native American elders and eat fry bread spread with honey, drinking iced horchata on this mild, sunny day in the desert. The stage was featuring a young, co-ed Mariachi band and there were Native Americans in traditional dance regalia waiting under an ocotillo roof for their hour on stage. Life was rich that day.

I went to the chapel twice during this visit to see Mary. I wanted to breathe in the artist's love for the Mother of God and to feel the joyful and creative energy emanating from the paintings and buildings. I took pictures with my cell phone so I could continue to get a glimpse of his art in my daily life. I was inspired to return to being creative with my own house and to build an outside grotto for Mary in the backyard too, using desert materials.

Thank you, DeGrazia, for continuing to inspire us – even in death. Viva La Fiesta de Guadalupe.

Meeting Our Lady in Mexico City

On February 27, 2011, I prepared to go to Santa Maria Basilica in Mexico City to see the image of Our Lady of Guadalupe on the tilma of Juan Diego! I didn't know if this day would ever happen. I am beyond thrilled to have the opportunity to see this image in person – the only art that Mary *herself* has painted.

A friend and I will be staying at the hotel where many Americans stay, thinking it may be safer since there has been much violence against tourists in Mexico recently. It is also only thirty minutes from the Santa Maria Basilica which holds the tilma of Our Lady of Guadalupe.

Our friends and family think we are nuts to be going into Mexico City at such a violent time. "Can't you wait until it calms down?" they ask frantically. Ambika, my close, physic friend and angel author, says, "Can't delay. February 28th is the day Mary wants you to be there." My friend and I pray, meditate, and ask for guidance, we too receive confirmation that February 28th is the time to go. Mary is calling.

We left Friday the 27th for Dallas, spent the night near the airport and caught the only daily flight to Mexico City at 9:30 a.m. That day, February 28th, was, as they say, smooth sailing in the belly of the metal angel called an airplane. We landed in Mexico City at noon and my friend had arranged to have a driver waiting at the airport to take us to the hotel. Many people had warned us to never, ever take a taxi for fear of kidnapping. Mexico City was bustling; we were let off in front of the hotel; the bell man took our bags and, at the front desk, we were told that our room was not ready yet, but would be in an hour or two. We asked them to hold our bags.

Mary was calling us right then and there! We went to the concierge and he arranged for a bilingual driver to take us to the Basilica. The driver was only a block away so was waiting after we secured our bags and walked out the front lobby. He was also a tour guide and knew the Basilica very well.

We got into his car; only an hour in Mexico City and we were off to see Mary. I suddenly began to cry. After 15 years of dreaming about this, I could not believe that we would be with Our Lady within the hour. I told the driver that this was truly a dream come true. He nodded, understanding the tears of joy and anticipation to finally see the Mother in her original form on the tilma. No doubt he made this trip many, many times hauling the tearful devoted to her Basilica.

He parked in the parking lot underneath the Santa Maria Basilica and I asked if there was something we needed to take to her; he said most people bring flowers. There were open markets with Virgin Mary trinkets, posters, cold drinks, and finally, a flower shop. I bought pink roses with white baby breath. She likes pink and white. I would only go visit her with her beloved roses. I was still wearing my pink sweater from the airline flight, which happened to match the roses. Pink, pink, and more pink.

We walked up from the street to the Basilica block, across the large plaza, to the Super Dome size Santa Maria Basilica, where she is housed. We entered . . . and there she was on the golden back wall, behind the sanctuary. It stopped us in our tracks. The tilma was in a large, bulletproof plexi-glass, gold framed enclosure. Majestic was the word for it. I began to sob again. Through the tears I stared at her, wiping and sniffling and the guide led us on.

Mass was being said and thousands of people were attending the worship service. We followed a line of people moving to the left of the sanctuary where a ramp and stairs led down to the half floor below and beneath the raised sanctuary. We looked up and saw we were as close as one can be to her framed image. Oh, my Sweet Mother of God!

Four conveyor belts were in constant motion, three going left to right and one going right to left, exactly as I imagined. We stepped on the slowly moving conveyor belt, creeping along in front of the beautiful tilma, looking up into the frame and her image. We went around again... and again... and again.

In our rush, we had forgotten our cameras but the guide used his camera for a small price. We took pictures; just Mary, me with Mary, my friend with Mary, in front of, to the side of . . . all with Mary. We were dazed by the vision in front of us. Crying, praying, and watching her as we moved by.

There were many visitors that day, all in reverence and all knowing the importance of what they were seeing and visiting. We were the only non-Mexican people present – we were all there together honoring *Her*.

After going back and forth many, many times, deeply moved and in awe, we finally left this place to go to the old Basilica and to the many buildings on the plaza. The guide told us that Juan Diego forgot the exact location where Mary appeared to him on day two of their encounter. Later, as he was showing the priest the approximate place where she met with him, a spring miraculously sprung forth to mark the spot. That spring is enclosed now in a round well, inside a lovely Mexican church.

A multitude of stairs lead to the top of Tepeyac where the miracle of the roses growing in winter happened. We entered another chapel marking the location of the miracle rosebush and encountered another mass. We had brought a candle to light at the top, so, after our prayers, we lit the candle, adding our own light to the mix. We knelt with others at the altar and said more prayers.

Juan Diego was a native peasant, an Indian. As I looked at the crowds, I saw a few native peoples, mostly women, silently praying to Mary. These were the same blood line as the one chosen to carry her message. I looked into the eyes of those who would glance toward me and bowed my head to honor them. They seemed surprised to see me paying them reverent attention, but prayerfully nodded back. It was as if we prayed for each other as we remembered Her.

Our time with the guide was running out. We returned to the main Basilica and took a few more conveyor belt rides in front of the tilma, saying good-by and thank you. As we walked out to the plaza, I asked the guide if we had time to do some shopping.(!) There were so many Mary items to be had. He said, yes, we had half an hour before we needed to leave.

On our way to the Mary market, we passed an official Basilican priest who was soaking everyone, anointing them with holy water as they stopped in front of him on their way out of the plaza. He looked somewhat bored as he said the blessing, for the umpteenth time, as this pack of beloved moved on. Holy water sprinkled upon us like soft rain, blessing us as we left for our travels home.

We went to the market next to the parking lot and bought Our Lady of Guadalupe pictures, pendants, pins, rose water, Eucharist holder, holy cards, and a rose scented rosary. We left, satisfied with our brief, but poignant time with Our Lady. We were in an altered state, changed forever by Mary's holy presence. Returning to our hotel, we felt complete. We had seen the tilma, had absorbed all we could hold, and so we decided it was time to return home. We left on the next morning's flight.

It took some time for the experience to settle. We didn't even open our bags and sort all the trinkets we had purchased for a few days. Five days later, Mary told me that it was the day to write. My writing notebook had not been used on the trip; it had to be recorded later, when my head was clearer, I suppose.

My friend and I had to integrate such high holy energy, finding ourselves needing more sleep, and drinking much more water than usual. We realized it was all part of assimilating Mary's energy into our bodies. But it was done; the new began. It was glorious to be there and so much fun to ask Mary to go shopping with us at her Santa Maria Basilica in Mexico City. And, of course, we got smoking deals.

In Closing

For several months now, as I have been drawing closer to the end of this book, I have been wondering what story Mary wanted to end with. Then it came in a most unexpected way. I attended a non-denominational, spiritual gathering where an older woman, who looked as if she had been a hippy at one time, began to talk. She had tattoos, a granny dress, deep wrinkles, short grey hair, and identified as a Lesbian. She looked as if she had been in the sun, growing organic vegetables most of her life.

This eclectic woman began to talk about an important sacred saying that had brought her great comfort throughout her life. We were on the edge of our chairs wondering what Goddess, Shaman, Pagan, or Buddhist saying she might have to share with us. This elderly, hippy crone opened her mouth and began to speak: "I love to remember what Our Lady of Guadalupe said to Juan Diego on that December day so long ago when she appeared to him in Mexico. I hear it in my heart and am comforted by it so often. 'Be not troubled, nor afraid. Am I not here, I, your mother? Are you not beneath my protection? Am I not your shield?'"

Thank you, Mary, for *all* your believers who, out of their mouths and into our hearts, remind us of your truth, hope, and love. In the most unexpected ways you *always* appear and we feel your presence again.

Mary, please pray for us now and forever. Amen.

Feast Days of Mary

January 1 – Mary, Mother of God
January 21 – Our Lady of Altagracia
January 23 – Espousal of the Virgin Mary
January 24 – Madonna del Pianto (Our Lady of Tears)

February 2 – Purification of Mary
February 11 – Our Lady of Lourdes

March 25 – The Annunciation

April 25 – Our Lady of Good Counsel
April 26 – Our Lady of Good Counsel

May 13 – Our Lady of Fatima
May 13 – Our Lady of the Most Blessed Sacrament
May 24 – Mary, Help of Christians
May 31 – Mary, Mediatrix of All Graces
May 31 – The Visitation

June 9 – Mary, Virgin Mother of Grace
June 27 – Our Lady of Perpetual Help

July 2 – Mary, Virgin Mother of Grace
June 27 – Our Lady of Perpetual Help

July 2 – Visitation by Mary to Saint Elizabeth
July 16 – Our Lady of Mount Carmel
July 17 – Humility of the Blessed Virgin Mary

August 2 – Our Lady of the Angels
August 5 – Our Lady of the Copacabana
August 13 – Our Lady, Refuge of Sinners
August 15 – The Assumption into Heaven
August 21 – Our Lady of Knock
August 22 – Immaculate Heart of Mary
August 22 - Queenship of Mary

September 8 – Nativity of Mary
September 8 – Our Lady of Charity
September 12 – Most Holy Name Mary
September 15 – Our Lady of Sorrow
September 24 – Our Lady of Mercy
September 24 – Our Lady of Walsingham

October 1 – Holy Protection of the Mother of God
October 7 – Our Lady of the Most Holy Rosary
October 11 – Maternity of the Blessed Virgin
October 16 – Maternity of the Blessed Virgin Mary

November 21 – Presentation of Mary at the Temple

December 8 – The Immaculate Conception
December 12 – Our Lady of Guadalupe
December 18 – Expectation of the Blessed Virgin Mary

Feasts to Mary that are not fixed by date

Saturday after Ascension – Our Lady, Queen of the Apostles

Saturday before the last Sunday in August – Our Lady, Health
    of the Sick

Saturday after the Feast of Saint Augustine (August 28)
    Our Lady of Consolation

Saturday before third Sunday of November – Mary, Mother
    of Divine Providence

Blessing

May Mary bless you in all ways and make Herself known in your life. May Her love and healing fill you to the brim and overflowing.

With great Love and Light always,

Rev. Dr. Kermie Wohlenhaus

Acknowledgements

Thank you –

- Deanna Leah, my agent, who brings my books to the world.
- Glenna Sheperd for the great cover design and your support and encouragement during the early stages of this book.
- Kay Stitzel, for your labor of love in sharing your skill, opinions, laughter, and tears as you proofread and edited this book with painstaking precision. All writing errors within these pages do not reflect her ability, but on the fact that I still draw outside the lines.
- Jo Ann Deck and Ja-lene Clark of Gather Insight for re-creating my website and offering your knowledge and support.
- Mike White at Ghost River Images for again taking a marked-up manuscript and molding it into a beautiful book.
- Pat Schweiber and the community at Peace House for opening your doors in my time of need. May your work be forever blessed by Our Lady, the angels, and the Divine.
- My chosen Catholic manuscript readers, for your feedback and valuable perspective.
- Frances Bale for your constant enthusiasm, loving support, and sharing your love for the Virgin Mary.
-To all the people who listened to these stories in the constant rewriting of this book. You have laughed, cried, and even dozed off as I read. But I noticed that when you went to sleep, as my dying friend Cheryl did – sleep was more peaceful. The pain of cancer was relieved for just that moment and a loving smile was on your face and in your heart as you remembered a long forgotten love for the Virgin Mary.

And Thank You, Virgin Mary, Beloved Lady, wife of Joseph, mother of Jesus and Mother of us all. Your joy, fun, and touch have been never ending as I have been guided through life in these stories and ultimately the production of this book. I am in awe of your power and grace. I love you so very much.

About the Author

Kermie Wohlenhaus, Ph.D. is an author, angelologist, and clairvoyant. She teaches classes, workshops, and offers presentations nationally. Dr. Wohlenhaus is regularly being interviewed on TV, radio, podcasts, for newspapers and magazines throughout the United States. She is popular in live performance, with radio and TV audiences for her humor and accurate intuitive messages and knowledge. Dr. Wohlenhaus is the Founder and Director of the School of Angel Studies and hosted/produced the TV show *Kermie & the Angels.*

Kermie Wohlenhaus has also authored:

How to Talk and Actually Listen to Your Guardian Angel which is available in Spanish, French, German and Dutch.

Dr. Wohlenhaus has annotated foundation texts for the field of Angelology,

Angels in Sacred Texts series which includes:
The Complete Reference to Angels in The Bible
A Quick Reference Guide to Angels in The Bible
The Complete Reference to Angels in The Book of Mormon
The Complete Reference to Angels in The Koran (Qu'ran)

She is currently living in Tucson, Arizona.

For further information: www.KermieWohlenhaus.com

CPSIA information can be obtained
at www.ICGtesting.com
Printed in the USA
BVOW11s1236200316

440721BV00003B/1/P